DISCIPLINE FOR SELF-CONTROL

Tom V. Savage
California State University, Fullerton

Prentice Hall, Englewood Cliffs, New Jersey 07632

Library of Congress Cataloging-in-Publication Data

Savage, Tom V.
   Discipline for self-control / by Tom V. Savage.
      p.   cm.
   Includes bibliographical references (p.) and index.
   ISBN 0-13-217431-6
   1. Classroom management--United States.   2. School discipline-
-United States.   I. Title.
LB3012.2.S38   1990
371.1'024--dc20   90-38815
                                                            CIP

Editorial/production supervision
              and interior design: Elaine Lynch
Cover design: Ben Santora
Manufacturing buyer: Debra Kesar

PHOTO CREDITS
Page 4, Ulrike Welsch/Photo Researchers; p. 21, Roberta Hershenson/Photo Researchers; p. 24, Sybil Shelton; p. 35, Ken Karp; p. 40, Ken Karp; p. 61, Daniel Cleary; p. 69, Children's Bureau, Department of Health and Human Services; p. 77, Ken Karp; p. 87, Ken Karp; p. 93, Bruce Roberts/Photo Researchers; p. 103, Ken Karp; p. 109, Ken Karp; p. 128, James Carroll; p. 138, Ken Karp; p. 148, Hakim Raquib; p. 158, Elaine Rebman/Photo Researchers; p. 169, Ken Karp; p. 186, Erika Stone/Photo Reaearchers; p. 208, James Carroll; p. 224, Ulrike Welsch/Photo Researchers.

 © 1991 by Prentice-Hall, Inc.
A Division of Simon & Schuster
Englewood Cliffs, New Jersey 07632

Printed in the United States of America

10 9 8 7 6 5 4 3 2

ISBN 0-13-217431-6

Prentice-Hall International (UK) Limited, *London*
Prentice-Hall of Australia Pty. Limited, *Sydney*
Prentice-Hall Canada Inc., *Toronto*
Prentice-Hall Hispanoamericana, S.A., *Mexico*
Prentice-Hall of India Private Limited, *New Delhi*
Prentice-Hall of Japan, Inc., *Tokyo*
Simon & Schuster Asia Pte. Ltd., *Singapore*
Editora Prentice-Hall do Brasil, Ltda., *Rio de Janeiro*

CONTENTS

PREFACE   ix

1   DISCIPLINE IN THE CLASSROOM   1

Objectives   1
Introduction   2
How Serious Is the Problem of Discipline?   3
What Is the Cause of Discipline Problems?   6
What Is the Goal of Discipline?   7
The Management and Discipline Domain   9
Summary   13
Suggested Activities   13
Bibliography   14

**2   ESTABLISHING TEACHER AUTHORITY
     AND LEADERSHIP**   15

Objectives   15
Introduction   16
Values and Beliefs of the Teacher   16
Leadership Styles and Social Power   19
Establishing Classroom Rules   25
Teacher Consistency   30
Sharing Responsibility   30
Summary   31
Suggested Activities   32
Bibliography   33

3 MOTIVATION AND DISCIPLINE   34

Objectives   34
Introduction   35
Motivational Factors   37
Learner Needs and Interests   39
Perception of Effort Required   49
Probability of Success   50
Summary   53
Suggested Activities   53
Bibliography   54

4 ARRANGING THE PHYSICAL ENVIRONMENT   56

Objectives   56
Introduction   57
Goals to Be Considered When Planning the Environment   58
Dimensions of the Physical Environment   60
The Classroom Ambiance   66
Classroom Density   69
Summary   70
Suggested Activities   70
Bibliography   71

5 ESTABLISHING CONTROL THROUGH TIME MANAGEMENT   72

Objectives   72
Introduction   73
Understanding Different Types of Time   74
Establishing Classroom Routines   79
Pacing Classroom Activities   83
Providing Clear Directions   84
Managing Transitions   85
Monitoring Student Work   86
Summary   89
Suggested Activities   90
Bibliography   91

6 LESSON MANAGEMENT   92

Objectives   92
Introduction   93
The Dimensions of Lesson Management   95
Group Focus   102
Summary   105
Suggested Activities   106
Bibliography   107

7 GROUP DYNAMICS 108

Objectives 108
Introduction 109
Individual Needs and Group Influence 110
Roles of Individuals within Groups 114
Utilizing Group Dynamics through Cooperative Learning 117
Summary 122
Suggested Activities 122
Bibliography 123

8 SELECTING A RESPONSE TO INAPPROPRIATE BEHAVIOR 124

Objectives 124
Introduction 125
The Purpose of Discipline 125
Basic Principles of Discipline 128
Responses to Misbehavior 131
Assertive Discipline 135
A Range of Alternative Responses 137
Summary 140
Suggested Activities 140
Bibliography 141

9 S UPPORTING SELF-CONTROL 142

Objectives 142
Introduction 143
Modeling Self-Control 143
Gaining Cooperation through Communication 146
Identifying Why Problems Occur and How They Are Resolved 153
Logical and Natural Consequences 156
Low Profile Responses to Minor Problems 157
Teaching Students to Monitor Their Own Behavior 161
Summary 162
Suggested Activities 163
Bibliography 164

10 RESTRUCTURING THE LEARNING ENVIRONMENT 165

Objectives 165
Introduction 166
Modifying the Environment 166
Applying Behavior Modification 171
Summary 181
Suggested Activities 182
Bibliography 183

11 DEALING WITH PERSISTENT MISBEHAVIOR   184

Objectives   184
Introduction   185
Teacher Assertiveness   185
Identifying Mistaken Goals   186
Glasser's Steps toward Effective Discipline   194
Identifying Alternative Consequences   201
Summary   204
Suggested Activities   204
Bibliography   205

12 DEALING WITH SERIOUS BEHAVIOR PROBLEMS   206

Objectives   206
Introduction   207
Attendance Problems   207
Cheating   211
Stealing   212
Vandalism   213
Violence against Other Students   214
Violence against Teachers   216
Drug and Alcohol Abuse   218
Working with Parents   220
Some Final Thoughts   224
Summary   224
Suggested Activities   225
Bibliography   225

INDEX   227

PREFACE

In the age of educational reform, discipline continues to emerge as an area needing immediate attention. The economic, social, and educational costs related to discipline are enormous, and parents, educators, and policymakers continue to search for solutions. The sobering fact is that the discipline problem in the schools is a complex one and will not be solved with simple solutions.

There is no shortage of solutions. For decades individuals proposed suggestions and theories. Many of these have been tried and have been found to be effective for some teachers and some students and ineffective for others. Since the approach does not solve all problems, it is soon discarded only to be replaced by yet another proposal. Most of the solutions have merit. The problem is that most of them address only one part of the domain and thus are inadequate to meet the complexities of the modern classroom.

It is the purpose of this book to approach classroom management and discipline in a systematic manner and to identify those several dimensions of management and practice that combine to make a teacher an effective manager and disciplinarian. Throughout the book the basic theme is that teacher decisions about appropriate management and discipline should be directed toward helping students develop self-control, one of the most important educational goals.

The book has been divided into two major areas. The first area deals with the management and prevention aspects of the topic. Research indicates that management and prevention are more effective than merely responding to misbehavior. This, first section includes a focus on motivation, establishing authority, managing the physical environment, managing time, managing lessons, and using group dynamics to gain cooperation.

The second section outlines some basic principles to keep in mind when responding to misbehavior. A range of alternative responses is discussed, beginning with measures that support self-control, moving to the more serious response of altering the learning environment, and concluding with measures for dealing with persistent misbehavior. The book ends with a chapter on some of the serious behavioral problems and how teachers might work with parents.

This book is written for those who deal with students on a daily basis: future teachers, teachers, and administrators. It is hoped that this volume will help them secure the personal and professional rewards that education has to offer.

This book is the result of a career-long quest for understanding, and numerous individuals have made valuable contributions. The one person, however, who has contributed most is my wife, Marsha. She has been a valuable critic, colleague, proofreader, and editor. Without her assistance, this project could not have been completed.

T.V.S.

For providing reviews and advice during the preparation of this volume, thanks also go to :

Dr. Luther M. Kindall
Department of Educational and Counseling Psychology
University of Tennessee
Knoxville, Tennessee

Dr. Marian Simmons
University of Missouri
School of Education
Kansas City, Missouri

Chapter 1

DISCIPLINE IN THE CLASSROOM

OBJECTIVES

This chapter provides information to help the reader to

1. Identify the relationship between classroom management and instruction

2. Cite evidence of the seriousness of discipline problems in the schools

3. Identify the costs associated with poor discipline

4. State the relationship between discipline problems and teacher burnout

5. Define the basic goal of discipline

6. Define self-control

7. List aspects of classroom management

8. State reasons for developing a range of teacher responses to discipline problems

INTRODUCTION

The term *discipline* often carries a negative connotation equated with punishment administered by teachers in response to misbehavior. In fact, some teacher workshops on discipline focus on the types of punishment that can be administered to learners who misbehave. This negative definition is a narrow and restrictive way of viewing the topic and limits the search for productive solutions to misbehavior.

Discipline is also defined as the development of self-control, character, orderliness, and efficiency (*Webster's New World Dictionary*). This definition reflects a philosophy that discipline is much more than a response to misbehavior. It involves the following important outcomes: the development of self-control, the development of character, and the development of orderly and productive ways of living. These positive outcomes result in a satisfying and productive life, not fear and blind conformity to arbitrary rules. They are consistent with accepting the responsibility of living in a democratic society as well as with the highest and noblest goals of education. When viewed in this more positive light, discipline for self-control becomes an important goal of education. This more positive view is the focus of this book. It is hoped that readers will begin to view misbehaviors as opportunities to attain some of the highest and most important goals of education, the development of self-control and character leading to a positive and productive life.

Box 1-1
MY CONCERNS ABOUT MANAGING A CLASSROOM

Concern about the ability to manage a classroom is common among preservice and practicing teachers alike. As you begin to investigate this important topic, take a couple of minutes to identify the concerns that you have about management and discipline. Think about your values and your personality. Which aspects of your personality and which values do you think will help you become a good classroom manager? Which ones might interfere?

My major concerns about managing the classroom:

Personality characteristics and values that will be helpful in my becoming a good manager:

Personality characteristics and values that may interfere with my ability to become a good manager:

HOW SERIOUS IS THE PROBLEM OF DISCIPLINE?

I was in my first weeks of teaching when I was hit by some frightening realities. I'm spending hours trying to keep up with my work and I can't seem to manage it. I'm so tired but I must try and keep control. The students don't respect me and aren't interested in school. They are bored. The parents don't seem to care and are unresponsive. I don't have enough material or enough time in the day to meet all of their needs. Some of the students hate me and I feel terrible about myself. I'm failing and I'm afraid.

Finally, I refused to accept the challenge and I got out. (quote from a teacher who quit)

This is not an isolated case. In a 1983 Michigan study, two out of three teachers reported that unmotivated and undisciplined students were a serious problem in their classrooms (Baker 1985, 485). In a *National Education Association* study, only 10 percent of the teachers reported that discipline problems had little or no deleterious effects on their teaching. In Boston, 28 percent of the teachers identified discipline as a very severe or extremely severe problem in their schools (Baker 1985, 486).

These data suggest that problems related to misbehavior and the lack of discipline are indeed serious and have a serious impact on the instructional effectiveness of teachers. Energy that could more productively be devoted to planning and implementing quality teaching is being spent dealing with misbehavior. Efforts to improve the quality of education in the public and private schools of the United States must include ways to reduce the frequency and severity of misbehavior.

Few problems influence teacher job satisfaction more than the management of misbehavior. Those teachers who fail to establish positive and productive ways of solving discipline problems suffer the personal tragedy of the teacher quoted earlier. Those who experience numerous and persistent student misbehavior are not having their personal and professional needs met. They see their dreams and aspirations fade only to be replaced with stress, anxiety, and even fear. The lack of personal and professional satisfaction, coupled with increased stress and anxiety, leads to teacher burnout.

Teachers experiencing burnout lose the joy in teaching. Going to school each day is unpleasant. They have feelings of apathy, anger, and frustration, along with such physical symptoms as loss of energy, headaches, insomnia, and frequent illness. These individuals have difficulty facing daily problems and relating to students in positive ways. Consequently, both they and their students are seriously affected by burnout.

The contributions of poor discipline to teacher stress and burnout are well documented. In one study, 58 percent of the teachers cited student misbehavior as the primary cause of job-related stress (Baker 1985). Mendler and Curwin (1983) have identified a pattern that illustrates the relationship between misbehavior and burnout. When learners misbehave, the teacher makes an ineffective response. The result is little or no improvement in the behavior. The teacher then experiences tension and frustration and may either give up or demonstrate anger and hostility. This reaction leads to an increase in student misbehavior and, ultimately, to burnout.

Associated with teacher burnout are some very real economic costs. One example is the high cost of replacing teachers who leave the profession. School districts are finding it difficult to replace those who leave, and a shortage of teachers is a reality in many urban school districts.

The economic losses extend beyond those associated with teachers. The costs associated with the loss of student attendance directly attributed to poor discipline are enormous. In one study, 800,000 secondary students, or 8 percent of the students surveyed, reported that they stayed away from school at least one day a month simply because they were afraid to go to school (Baker 1985, 483). Their concern has been validated in other studies. A survey of California schools covering a five-month period identified 100,000 acts of violence with an average of 24 teachers and 215 learners being assaulted every day. A Boston study reported that 38 percent of all Boston high school students had been victims of robbery, assault, or larceny during the previous year (Baker 1985, 486). A 1982 Gallup poll revealed that these problems extend across all types of learners and schools. It reported that 68 percent of the white students and 81 percent of the nonwhite students responding to the poll rated discipline problems in their schools as fairly serious or very serious (Gallup 1982). Vandalism in the schools is another major problem that uses scarce resources better devoted to instructional programs. It is estimated that the annual cost of vandalism to U.S. school districts is in excess of $600 million.

In summary, it is apparent that discipline in the schools is a serious problem affecting learners, teachers, and taxpayers. All of those interested in the improvement of education and the well-being of individuals in our society need to be concerned with the problems of misbehavior and poor discipline.

It is important, however, to realize that not all teachers experience serious discipline problems. The data reported here could lead to the conclusion that all classrooms and all schools are out of control. This is simply not the case. Many teachers and many schools have positive learning environments relatively free from major discipline problems. This leads to several questions. Why do some teachers have few problems while others spend a considerable portion of their school day dealing with management and discipline matters? What teacher behaviors and attitudes contribute to the problems? Which teacher behaviors and attitudes promote respect and learning? What are the goals and purposes that guide decisions of effective teachers? These questions can be used by the reader as a guiding framework in the search for solutions for handling inappropriate discipline.

Box 1-2
CHARACTERISTICS OF EFFECTIVE MANAGERS

Reflect on your experiences in elementary school and/or high school. Identify those teachers whom you considered to be effective managers and those who were ineffective. What common characteristics can you identify in each of the categories that might account for their effectiveness or ineffectiveness?

Characteristics of effective managers:

Characteristics of ineffective managers:

WHAT IS THE CAUSE OF DISCIPLINE PROBLEMS?

The organization of a school and the classroom environment established by the teacher have an important impact on the behavior of learners. Many students do not find the school environment attractive. Rather, they view schools as largely irrelevant places where individual needs are not met (Glasser 1986). The students are developing neither a positive self- concept nor a success identity. In fact, schools are actually failure oriented rather than success oriented, and those students who have trouble succeeding face the daily humiliation of failure.

One contributing factor is a curriculum determined by someone outside the school, with students rarely given an opportunity to question the relevance of the curriculum or to search for ways of applying what they learn in school to their life outside school. Basically, they are told what to learn and how to learn it. Individual interests and abilities are given second priority to covering material and passing tests. In addition, many learners believe that they have little say in determining important issues affecting their lives in school. The democratic principle of the involvement of people in the determination of rules and laws does not apply to them (Glasser 1969).

Learners, like all other individuals, have needs that must be met—needs for belonging, affection, achievement, power, and fun. If these needs cannot be satisfied through productive and positive channels, students will seek to satisfy them in ways that may be counter to the goals of the school and destructive to themselves. Students want to attend schools where their needs are being met and where they receive respect. They need teachers who are concerned about the welfare of students and who emphasize success, not failure. They also need teachers who allow them some power and voice in decision making. Finally, they need teachers who are concerned with helping them discover the relevance of their studies and who are interested in helping them develop their unique abilities and interests.

It is important to note that the problems of discipline are not entirely those of the teacher or the school. School mirrors society, and those problems that occur in society will manifest themselves in the classroom. Mendler and Curwin (1983) identify four factors that contribute to discipline problems in the schools: the presence of violence in society, the influence of the media, the values of the "me" generation, and the lack of a secure family environment.

The presence of the "me" generation is a reflection of the permissive society in which we live. Examples abound of individuals placing themselves first, violating rules, and resorting to violence as a means of conflict resolution. These examples and the values they express do create problems for teachers. Learners cannot be expected to leave these orientations at the classroom door. Fortunately, however, this permissive atmosphere does create some positive opportunities for teachers.

In a permissive society, individuals often lose their sense of security. They find themselves searching for purpose and meaning in life, desperately wanting to belong and achieve a sense of significance. Dreikurs (1968) points out that youngsters treated in a permissive way do not become self-confident or develop a sense of belonging. Instead, they resort to self-destruction and antisocial behavior in their attempts to belong and achieve significance. Firm and fair discipline consistently applied serves as an indicator to these students that someone does care about them (Howard 1980). Students who experience a classroom where there are both love and discipline learn to become responsible individuals who are able to make wise choices about their lives (Glasser 1965).

Teachers who establish classroom environments based on mutual respect and concern, where individuals feel safe from physical and emotional threat, where rules and regulations are logical and are fairly and consistently enforced, and where individual needs are met, will discover that school can become an attractive place where the learners want to be. These teachers find that classroom management and discipline is not an onerous task but, rather, one that contributes to the deep rewards and satisfactions that can be a part of teaching.

WHAT IS THE GOAL OF DISCIPLINE?

Discipline has a purpose that extends beyond merely controlling the classroom and responding to misbehavior. The most fundamental purpose of discipline and management in the classroom is the promotion of self-control. Hyman and D'Allesandro (1986) point out that in a democracy discipline needs to originate from within rather than from a fear of punishment. Self-control is one of the most important outcomes of education and one of the basic prerequisites for a democratic society. Academic knowledge and skill in the most advanced technologies will be of little consequence if the citizens of a society do not possess self-control and can lead to the disintegration rather than the improvement of society.

Self-control is not merely submissive acceptance of authority or standards of behavior imposed on an individual by others. In this book, self-control is defined as behaving in ways consistent with self-chosen beliefs and goals. It is a necessary prerequisite for self-direction. Consequently, individuals who lack self-control are unable to take control of their lives and choose those paths that will be self-fulfilling and satisfying. Conversely, individuals exercising self-control are demonstrating what Glasser (1965) defines as responsibility. They are able to fulfill their own needs without interfering with the attempts of others to fulfill needs. Self-control involves a consideration of individual motivations and needs as well as the impact of behavior on those in the social environment.

Self-control is not an innate characteristic; it is learned. Since experiences in the social environment influence this development, individuals of the same age may demonstrate different levels of self-control. Consequently, they need to be involved with responsible, caring individuals who will help them understand the relationship between behavior and consequences. Students who have been shielded from the consequences of their behavior by overly indulgent adults or who have not been taught to consider the needs and interests of others have trouble exercising self-control. However, heavy-handed, highly authoritarian discipline is not the answer. Students who have been subjected to these methods rather than being allowed to make some of their own decisions also experience difficulty in exercising self-control.

Challenging students to think about their goals and purposes in life and how their behavior relates to these outcomes is an important first step in which teachers play a key role. We must remember, though, that individuals at different levels of self-control need to be approached differently in order to start them on the path toward increased self-control and self-direction. Glasser (1969) states that for most youngsters there are only two places where they can establish relationships and learn the responsibility necessary for developing a successful identity—the home and the school. The responsibility of the schools is so important that Glasser advocates the establishment of a program in every school to teach social responsibility.

Box 1-3
WHAT IS SELF-CONTROL?

The major thrust of this book is to teach self-control. The assumption is that self-control is learned and that how the teacher organizes the classroom and responds to misbehavior will help learners move toward self-control. What do you think?

1.   **How do you define self-control?**

2.   **How do you think an individual learns self-control?**

3.   **Do you think a teacher can have an impact when students are not taught self-control at home?**

4.   **If you accept the theory that modeling is an important method of teaching, what are the implications for you as a teacher attempting to help students learn self-control?**

5.   **How do you think teacher responses to misbehavior can help or hinder the development of self-control?**

Using self-control as a goal, teachers must decide how to organize the classroom and respond to specific incidents of misbehavior. The basic question that should guide teacher decision making is, "What can I do that will assist the student in developing self-control?" Merely stopping incidents of misbehavior is not enough. Unless the solutions help the student move toward self-control, the problems will only recur and an important educational opportunity will be lost. Quick fixes directed only at stopping the immediate behavior with little thought of the underlying causes of the behavior must be rejected. The educational and personal losses related to discipline can only be overcome if learners decide that it is in their own best interest to behave. In short, discipline problems can only be overcome when individuals, learners and teachers alike, demonstrate self-control and social responsibility.

This emphasis on self-control provides criteria for evaluating the effectiveness of a discipline plan. Students should be demonstrating more self-control as the year unfolds. If they are not, the discipline methods should be re-evaluated and alternatives considered. A growing body of knowledge is available to help the classroom teacher consider these alternatives. Unfortunately, much of this knowledge has been presented in a fragmented manner so that the teacher does not understand the relationships between different behaviors and alternative responses. What is needed is an organization of the management and discipline domain so that teachers can systematically and professionally approach the problems they experience in the classroom.

THE MANAGEMENT AND DISCIPLINE DOMAIN

The management and discipline domain can be divided into two main components. The first component deals with managing the environment so that discipline problems are prevented. Success in this area is often what distinguishes a successful teacher from an unsuccessful one. The second component encompasses the variety of teacher responses to incidents of misvehavior. Although the management component is critical, all problems will not be eliminated. There will always be some misbehavior in all classes, so teachers must develop a range of acceptable responses so that they can choose the most appropriate response for a given situation. The incident of misbehavior can then become a learning experience leading to self-control and self-esteem rather than to anger and hostility and a breakdown in the learning process.

The management component can be subdivided into the following topics. Systematic attention to these topics will not only help teachers avoid many problems but will also help them create a professionally satisfying work environment for themselves as well as their students.

Leadership and Authority

The teacher is the leader of the classroom, and the style of leadership established has an impact on the attitudes of learners and their willingness to cooperate with the teacher. Teacher leadership includes the establishment of the rules, the assertiveness of the teacher, the sharing of power, the respect shown to learners, and the level of consistency in the treatment of students.

Box 1-4
"ALL YOU HAVE TO DO IS LOVE THE STUDENTS"

One prospective teacher stated, "I know others have problems, but that is because they either do not like the students they are teaching or they are too far removed from their world. I know that I will not have any problems because I plan to make friends with all of the students. I am near their age and when they realize that I am their friend and that I understand them the class will become meaningful and fun and there will not be any discipline problems. Students do not create problems for friends." What do you think?

1. **Do you agree with this individual's statement?**

2. **What assumptions does this individual make that may not be true?**

Motivation

Motivation and discipline are nearly always linked because students who are motivated seldom create problems. It is not in a student's self-interest to interfere with an activity that is motivating or meeting a personal need. Consequently, an understanding of the principles of motivation as well as an ability to apply them is one key to preventing serious behavior problems.

Physical Environment

The fields of psychology and architecture have developed the concept of a "behavioral setting," examining the ways that the physical environment influences the inhabitants of the setting. Since schools and classrooms are places where individuals spend a considerable portion of their waking hours, it seems critical to consider the environment's physical properties and how those properties influence the behavior of the teachers and learners. The use of color and light, the arrangement of the desks, the amount of noise, and the physical attractiveness of the space are all attributes that influence behavior. These must be considered as a teacher attempts to create a behavioral setting that facilitates the learning process and minimizes discipline problems.

Time Management

The efficient and productive use of time is another key element in preventing discipline problems. Many experienced and successful teachers state that they keep learners so busy that they don't have time to misbehave. There is much wisdom in such a philosophy. Individuals who are busy, preferably on tasks they perceive to be interesting and important, seldom cause trouble. A goal of the broadcast media is to reduce or eliminate "dead air space" where nothing is being broadcast. Teachers might likewise try to reduce the "dead air space" that might be occurring in their classrooms. Studies have shown that improvement in achievement is directly related to increasing the amount of time spent on a learning task. During a day in a typical classroom substantial time is spent on noninstructional tasks. When the learners are not on-task, not only are they not learning but they are more likely to be engaged in misbehavior.

Lesson Management

Lesson management draws together some elements of motivation as well as effective use of time. In fact, the relationship between instruction and management can be seen in a direct manner in the management of the lesson. Teachers need to keep the lesson on track, moving at a rather brisk pace yet on a level so that the majority of the learners are mastering the content. They must also handle the instructional responsibilities so that learners who need assistance obtain that assistance quickly and efficiently. Many attempts to manage the class will fail unless the teacher is performing this key task and providing for a high degree of success and sense of achievement.

Group Dynamics

Individuals respond differently in groups than they do in a one-to-one situation. Any teacher can testify to the importance of the peer group on behavior. Individuals who usually are well behaved and exercise good judgment and control will often act differently when in a group setting. It is essential that a teacher understand some of the influences of the group and learn to use the group to develop support for behavioral and educational goals. Unfortunately, too many teachers find themselves caught in a power struggle with a classroom group. The classroom then becomes a battlefield between adversaries rather than a supportive environment with individuals working toward common and important goals.

Unfortunately, attention to these six subtopics will not completely eliminate discipline problems. To prepare for these inevitable problems, teachers must also address the response component of the management and discipline domain. Two criteria serve as guidelines for selecting the elements of this component—the ability of the learner to exercise self-control and the seriousness of the student misbehavior. A range of teacher responses, based on these two criteria, allows the teacher the flexibility of choosing the response most consistent with the situation.

Responses Promoting Self-Control

These are relatively unobtrusive responses that provide learners with an opportunity to self-correct their own behavior. The responsibility for the behavior and the correction is placed on the learner. As students learn to self-correct, they become more and more responsible and self-controlled. Responses in this category also preserve respect for the dignity of the individual. These responses are generally very effective for minor behavior problems and for those learners who already have some measure of self- control.

Responses That Restructure the Learning Environment

These more intrusive responses involve restructuring the environment so that it becomes easier for the learner to exercise self-control. Attempts to promote self-control through less intrusive means may not have worked, and the learner may need more direct teacher intervention in order to move toward self-control. Restructuring the learning environment may involve relatively simple responses such as moving a seat or exercising proximity control to much more complex and systematic procedures such as developing a behavior modification plan.

Dealing with Persistent Misbehavior

If altering the learning environment does not work, and the misbehavior persists, the teacher then needs to move to an even more teacher-directed and intrusive approach. This might involve enforcing the consequences for misbehavior, such as isolation from the classroom, time-out, or loss of privileges. Choosing an appropriate response for these more serious incidents involves identifying the goals of the misbehaving student. These goals include seeking attention, demonstrating power, attempting to get revenge, or to withdrawing. Understanding the goal will enable the teacher to choose a response that is most likely to correct the behavior rather than reinforce it.

Dealing with Serious Misbehavior

The majority of the problems that occur in the classroom are relatively minor and can usually be handled by the responses discussed. However, the serious problems of chronic truancy or tardiness, cheating, stealing, vandalism, violence, and drug and alcohol abuse require more persistent and serious responses. These serious misbehaviors are the ones that cause teachers a great deal of stress and worry and their solutions are not easy. Because they often involve factors that go beyond the classroom, attempts to correct these problems may require the involvement of administrators, counselors, psychologists, parents, and outside agencies.

Attention to this range of alternative responses allows teachers to develop a discipline plan uniquely suited to their needs as well as the needs of learners. This helps the teacher to become a skilled problem solver and attain a professionally rewarding and personally satisfying career. The following chapters discuss each of these topics in greater depth.

SUMMARY

Teaching involves two complementary and interrelated tasks, instructing the learners and maintaining an environment where learning can occur. Unfortunately, too many new teachers are ill prepared to deal with the management and discipline domain. Evidence suggests that the failure to maintain order in classrooms results in personal as well as economic costs: It is one of the major reasons for teacher burnout; it takes time away from the instructional program and creates an atmosphere of fear in the school; and it costs taxpayers a considerable amount of money just to repair the damage caused by vandalism.

Serious considerations of school improvement need to take into account the discipline domain. It should be approached in a systematic manner so that problematic areas can be identified and corrective action taken. The domain is a complex one that can be divided into two major areas: managing the classroom and responding to incidents of misbehavior. Each of these domains can be further divided into subcomponents.

The basic purpose of discipline—to move learners toward self- control—should be used when choosing classroom organizational procedures and when responding to problems. Each discipline program should then be evaluated with this goal in mind. The promotion of self-control is not only a goal of education but is also a prerequisite for a democratic society. It is also the basic theme of this book.

SUGGESTED ACTIVITIES

1. Interview a new teacher or a student teacher. Ask that person his or her impression of the seriousness of discipline problems in the schools. Have the person identify those things that worry him or her most and those things that were most surprising about student behavior.

2. In order to gain a perspective on recommendations on how to deal with discipline in the schools, review educational journals that were published in the past three years and develop an annotated bibliography of articles that deal with discipline.

3. Interview three or four elementary or secondary students. Ask them to state whether they think discipline is a serious problem, what they think causes the problems, and what they think are the characteristics and behaviors of teachers who have serious problems in their classrooms and those who do not.

4. Begin keeping a journal of your thoughts and ideas as you read through the book or complete the class you are taking. Reflect on yourself and your confidence in managing a class. Think about the ideas and the proposals that are presented and state why you agree or disagree with them. Include personal experiences that might be related to the ideas that are presented. Items from your journal could be shared with others in the class.

5. The development of advance organizers is an important aid to learning. In preparation for your study of the management domain, list the major categories of topics that will be covered. Take a few minutes to write down what you already know about the topic. Add to the outline under each topic and modify your previous understandings as you complete the book or the course.

BIBLIOGRAPHY

BAKER, K. 1985. Research evidence of a school discipline problem. *Phi Delta Kappan* 66, 482–488.

DOYLE, W. 1986. *Classroom organization and management*. In *Handbook of Research on Teaching*, 3rd ed., ed. M. C. Wittrock. New York: Macmillan.

DREIKURS, R. 1968. *Psychology in the Classroom*. New York: Harper & Row.

GALLUP, GEORGE. 1982. The 14th annual Gallup poll of the public's attitude toward the public schools. *Phi Delta Kappan*. 64, 1, 37–50.

GLASSER, W. 1965. *Reality Therapy*: A New Approach to Psychiatry. New York: Harper & Row.
——— 1969. *Schools Without Failure*. New York: Harper & Row.
——— 1986. *Control Theory in the Classroom*. New York: Harper & Row.

HOWARD, A. W. 1980. Discipline is caring. In *Discipline in the Classroom*, 2nd ed., ed. E. H. Weiner. Washington, D. C.: National Education Association.

HYMAN, I., and J. D'ALLESANDRO. 1986. Good, old-fashioned discipline: The politics of punitiveness. In *Education 86/87*, ed. F. Schultz. Guilford, Conn.: Dushkin.

MENDLER, A. N., and R. CURWIN. 1983. *Taking Charge in the Classroom*. Reston, Va.: Reston.

TANNER, L. N. 1978. *Classroom Discipline for Effective Teaching and Learning*. New York: Holt, Rinehart & Winston.

Chapter 2

ESTABLISHING TEACHER AUTHORITY AND LEADERSHIP

OBJECTIVES

This chapter provides information to help the reader to

1. State the importance of identifying personal values and beliefs in establishing a leadership style

2. List and define different types of social power

3. Define the types of power that are most effective in establishing positive leadership

4. Compare the advantages and disadvantages of authoritarian and democratic methods for establishing rules

5. Identify a process for establishing classroom rules

6. List the steps to be followed in implementing rules

7. State the importance of teacher consistency

INTRODUCTION

Understanding why some classrooms are relatively problem free begins with a consideration of the teacher. The teacher's values, understanding of learners, beliefs about the learning process, and leadership style all have an impact on the social and physical environment of the classroom.

Leadership is an essential component if any group is to be productive and attain satisfaction of needs. Teacher leadership is the elusive ingredient that often spells the difference between success and failure in classroom management. Cronbach (1977) points out that it is the responsibility of the teacher to establish an enthusiastic and purposeful work atmosphere. Although learners do have some influence on the style of teacher leadership, studies have shown that patterns of leadership remain relatively stable over time, leading to the conclusion that teachers establish the patterns of behavior in the classroom rather than just respond to the learners (Soar and Soar 1987).

Boles and Davenport (1975) emphasize that leadership exists only when the leader-follower relationship is such that the followers accept a particular person as the leader. In a classroom context, it is important that learners accept the teacher as the leader. When they do, problems are minimized and teacher authority is accepted. When this acceptance of the teacher as a leader is not present, a perpetual power struggle ensues. This chapter addresses some ways that the teacher can establish a productive learning climate through leadership and authority.

VALUES AND BELIEFS OF THE TEACHER

Assume that you have just been notified that you have been selected as the leader of a group that is to undertake a very important task. Further, those chosen to be a part of the group have been handpicked and are the most skilled and compatible individuals who that can be found in the nation. How would you feel about this group? What would be your expectations? How would you go about conceptualizing your style of leadership, and how would you organize the group? Suppose, now, that you are given the same assignment, but the group members have no special skills. In fact, they were selected for group membership because they lack motivation and need a challenge. They did not volunteer for the group but were drafted or assigned to the group. How would you approach the task of organizing this group? How would your expectations and your leadership style change from your response to the first group?

As you compare your responses and styles of leadership in these two situations, you will probably find some very significant differences. Many of the differences in the way teachers exercise leadership and authority in the classroom are rooted in the way they view their learners. Those who see learners as capable, trustworthy, and able will be more enthusiastic, will give students more responsibility, and will view teacher power differently.

Another variable influencing leadership style and the authority of the teacher is the view the teacher has about self. In our scenario, secure, confident individuals would have a different outlook than those who are insecure. They would approach the task with enthusiasm and optimism, expecting shared responsibility and decision making. Such leaders would not be intimidated by highly skilled individuals or discouraged by of those who lack motivation. The confidence and security of the group leader would allow for the expression and demonstration of individual strengths and needs. In this atmosphere, the group would be able to best overcome frustration and achieve success. Insecure leaders, on the other hand, could easily be threatened by highly talented individuals and discouraged by unmotivated ones. The result could well be an ineffective leadership style that would lead to group dissatisfaction and frustration. Ultimately, the productivity of the group would be hindered and the satisfaction of the leader diminished.

Similar situations exist in classrooms. Teachers often become so intimidated by the power of learners that they react by trying to retain all the power and authority or by giving up and abdicating their responsibility as a leader. This often occurs in two common situations: in the gifted and talented classroom and in the classroom containing students perceived by the class as popular and powerful. Conflict and lack of group cohesiveness and satisfaction are usually the result.

The poised and confident individual will also approach the second situation, the recalcitrant group, somewhat differently. Although specific approaches might differ, the confident leader will believe that the group does have potential and that he or she can successfully motivate and organize the group so that success will be possible. In fact, the confident leader will see such a group as a challenge and an opportunity rather than as a threat. This type of leadership will help the group members overcome obstacles and keep on working when they might otherwise quit. Insecure leaders will approach the group with a great deal of anxiety and fear. They will not be optimistic about the group's achieving success. Once again, the insecure leader may resort to excessive control and power. Group members will be assigned menial tasks to keep them busy, and failure is accepted because of the perceived lack of talent in the group.

This example also has classroom parallels. Some teachers believe that their students are incapable of learning and that they are incapable of teaching them. Teachers with these views merely go through the motions of teaching in an attempt to survive each day. They demonstrate little enthusiasm or commitment to teaching. Students are reluctant to follow the leadership or submit to the authority of a teacher who exhibits such behaviors.

Beliefs about the abilities of students exert a powerful influence on teacher behavior (Clark and Peterson 1986). Those who believe that learners are lazy, rebellious, and untrustworthy will demonstrate teaching behaviors and classroom control techniques quite different from those of the teacher who believes that students are cooperative and interested in learning. The lack of respect communicated by the first teacher will not be likely to capture the respect of the students and allow him or her to exercise positive leadership. Therefore, an important step in establishing a positive leadership style in the classroom involves a self-analysis of the beliefs the teacher holds about his or her ability to teach, the students' ability to learn, the nature of learners, and the nature of the learning process. Those who lack confidence in themselves or who believe that learners are incapable of learning need to seek ways of changing these negative attitudes and beliefs.

Box 2-1
PAT EVANS

Pat had always been somewhat insecure. He rarely shared ideas in his group because he was afraid that they were not as good as the ideas of others. Pat had a strong desire to be accepted and was careful not to do or say anything that might make others angry. Pat was attracted to teaching because it gave an individual a certain amount of power and authority. Teaching would allow him to fulfill his need for power. He was sure that working with students who were younger would allow him to be assertive and his insecurity would be overcome.

What do you think?

1. What is your reaction to Pat's reasons for becoming a teacher?

2. What is valid or invalid about the assumptions that Pat is making?

3. What problems would you predict for Pat?

4. What recommendations do you have for him?

LEADERSHIP STYLES AND SOCIAL POWER

Teacher leadership and the use of power are at the heart of classroom management. The ways a teacher chooses to exercise power and authority establish his or her leadership style. This leadership style, in turn, affects student behavior and cooperation. Many incidents of misbehavior are student reactions to teacher use of power and authority. Students have needs that must be met, including the need for power. If they believe that their ability to meet these needs is being threatened by the teacher, they may choose to challenge the authority of the teacher. Teachers cannot demand that students give them respect and submit to their power and authority. Effective teachers are those who earn this respect.

BOX 2-2
SHOW THEM YOU'RE THE BOSS!

The following words of advice were provided to a new teacher by a veteran:

You have to establish your authority as a teacher early in the year. Don't go in and try to be friends with the students; they will never respect you. Begin the year by being tough. Establish your rules, and the first time someone misbehaves, come down hard and make an example of the student. This will let the other class members know that you will not tolerate misbehavior and you will prevent future problems.

What do you think?

  1. What are the valid points in this statement?

  2. What are the invalid points in this statement?

  3. Do you think this tactic works? Why or why not?

  4. What might be some undesirable outcomes of this approach?

The need for teachers to earn the respect of the students is emphasized by Boles and Davenport (1975). They contend that admiration, affection, liking, and respect for the moral integrity of the teacher form the psychological basis on which student acceptance of teacher power is built. The notion that power and respect must be earned is related to a framework of social power developed by French and Raven (1959). This framework is helpful as teachers develop classroom leadership. The French and Raven framework defines five different types of leadership or power: expert power, referent power, legitimate power, reward power, and coercive power.

Expert Power

When an individual is perceived by a group to be an expert or to have superior knowledge about a subject, the group will give that person some authority or power. This is what is called "expert" power. Since this type of power is earned and is based on respect, the individual possessing such power is in a good position to exercise effective leadership. Teachers who are effective classroom leaders begin by obtaining expert power. Students perceive the teacher as someone who is knowledgeable about the material being presented, possesses good teaching skills, and understands the needs of individuals. Surveys of student attitudes toward teachers highlight the importance of expert power. For example, the ability to explain and clarify content is high on the list of attributes that learners identify about teachers they like (Tanner 1978).

Those who are experts often demonstrate several recognizable characteristics. They have confidence and poise when confronting an issue or problem, and their confidence gives confidence to others. In addition, the expert usually has enthusiasm for the topic or task. Because of their enthusiasm and confidence, experts demonstrate a high degree of task persistence and do not give up easily.

New teachers often have difficulty exercising expert power because they are uncertain about their skills and thus do not exhibit confidence and poise. They may have an initial enthusiasm, but it quickly diminishes if things do not go well. Their lack of confidence is also revealed in their hesitant behavior when confronting an unexpected event. Students note these behaviors and begin to lose confidence in the teacher. As a result, they are quick to question teacher decisions and authority.

How does one obtain expert power? A beginning point is the completion of a sound, well-balanced teacher preparation program. Teachers need to know their subject as well as the characteristics of learners and how to teach them. Being well prepared is also important. Teachers report that planning gives them immediate psychological rewards in terms of the reduction of uncertainty and an increase in their confidence level (Clark and Peterson 1986). These feelings are then communicated to learners through the confidence and the certainty of the teacher. It is not surprising, therefore, that there does seem to be a direct connection between the quality of teacher planning and student achievement.

Referent Power

Individuals who are liked and respected are also given some power and authority. People are willing to follow someone who is perceived to be trustworthy, ethical, and concerned for the welfare of others. This type of power is what is termed "referent" power. Like expert power, referent power is earned rather than demanded and is essential for those who aspire to leadership roles. Even the attempts of experts to lead will be ignored if they are not perceived as ethical and trustworthy.

Referent power emphasizes the importance of teachers who like students and are interested in their welfare. Glasser (1969, 1986) emphasizes the need for caring teachers who create a warm and personal classroom where youngsters feel they belong and can have their needs met. Teachers who have negative feelings about learners will not act in ways that will give them referent power. Their students will be less likely to trust them and to follow classroom rules and procedures. Referent power is especially important at the secondary level. A common reason cited by high school students for misbehavior is that they did not perceive the teacher as respectful or caring.

A teacher can work toward referent power in several ways. Simple things like learning the names of the youngsters, providing genuine encouragement and praise, and avoiding sarcasm are examples. Fairness in testing and grading is an important consideration. Many teachers lose the respect of a class because they design tests to trick students rather than measure worthwhile objectives. In addition, their standards are viewed as arbitrary and subjective.

Box 2-3
TEACHERS NEED MORE AUTHORITY

Some teachers claim that the seriousness of discipline problems in the schools is related to the erosion of teacher authority. They believe that schools need to return to the days when the teacher was the authority. Teachers laid down the law and students were expected to obey simply because it was the teachers' right to do so. Those who did not like the rules or the punishments could simply go elsewhere or drop out. Teachers cannot be expected to teach if parents, administrators, and the general public are always questioning authority. In those countries with quality education, teachers are the authority and their right to punish is unquestioned.

What do you think?

   1. Do you agree with this statement?

   2. Has teacher authority been lost in recent years?

   3. What do you see as the weakness in this proposal?

   4. What recommendations would you have for increasing teacher authority?

Legitimate Power

Some roles carry with them power or authority, regardless of who fills that role. That is, interest in the role is the "legitimate" right to make certain decisions. For example, the president of the United States always has authority to make certain decisions, regardless of who is the president. This type of power is what is termed "legitimate" power.

The role of teacher carries a certain amount of legitimate power. There are decisions and leadership roles expected of a person acting in the teacher role. The problem with legitimate power is that it is not conferred by the students and they may be unwilling to accept the authority of the teacher. That legitimate power has severe limitations is not always understood by teachers. Some teachers expect to be obeyed simply because they are the teacher and are supposed to have authority. Perhaps there was a time when the legitimate power of the teacher was so strong that this was the only type of power needed. However, such is not the case today. Unquestioned obedience is not something that is taught or valued, and even the authority of those in highest office is challenged. In fact, an important goal of education should be to teach students to resist blindly following the leadership of others (Render, Padilla, and Krank 1988). Tauber (1985, 138) clearly states the issue in his contention that it can no longer be taken for granted that learners will come to school with an automatic respect for teachers' legitimate power.

Legitimate power can be most helpful at the beginning of the school year, before the teacher has had an opportunity to develop expert or referent power. The majority of learners understand that the teacher does have some authority and will usually begin the school year by following reasonable teacher requests. During this beginning phase, when students are often on their best behavior, legitimate power can be used to establish a positive classroom environment so that expert and referent power can emerge. In fact, when expert and referent power are developed, the legitimate power of the teacher is increased. A person perceived by the group as an expert, as an ethical and fair-minded individual, and as one who has legitimate power can create such a respect that students do not even consider disobeying or challenging the authority of that person.

Reward Power

Individuals in positions of authority and leadership can give rewards and benefits to the group member. This capability is the fourth type of power, "reward" power. Teachers have many rewards that can be dispensed. There are the tangible awards—grades, special responsibilities, or privileges—and the social rewards—attention, praise, status, or prestige. Everyone enjoys getting a reward, and the person who possesses the ability to give rewards has power.

However, reward power does have limitations. One serious limitation is that the power to give rewards is not an earned power based on respect for the individual. In addition, the effectiveness of reward power depends on the ability to give rewards desired by the group. Consider grades, for example. Grades that are not valued or desired are not rewards, and the person awarding them has no power. Some new teachers have a difficult time understanding this phenomenon. They were always interested in good grades and would follow teacher and school directives in order to obtain them. However, not all students care about grades. In fact, some students ridicule those who work for them. In this situation a teacher who attempts to exercise authority and power through the reward of a grade will be quickly frustrated.

Another limitation of reward power is that individuals may find alternative sources of rewards. For example, prestige and status might be more easily obtained from peers by challenging teacher authority. In addition, the social rewards of talking with friends or of having fun are usually more desirable than the rewards obtained by attending to school tasks.

Coercive Power

Individuals in positions of leadership and authority also have the power to administer punishments, that is, "coercive" power. Some individuals believe that the only way they can obtain respect and power is through intimidation or coercion. They are quick to remind students that failure to follow their demands will result in swift and sure punishment. Some teachers argue that this is the only type of power and authority respected by students. In their attempts to establish more effective discipline, they spend their time seeking more powerful and effective punishments.

Coercive power can have some short-term benefits. It often puts an immediate stop to a behavior. This immediate benefit causes some teachers to conclude that coercive power is the best method for establishing authority in the classroom. However, coercive power has limited potential and undesirable side effects detrimental to the creation of a positive learning climate and the development of self-control. One

such side effect is that a reliance on coercive power usually leads to power struggles between the teacher and students. Students counter teacher power by trying to prove that they cannot be intimidated. Some students will resort to passive resistance and others find subtle ways of getting revenge. Vandalism, assaults, anger, and truancy are frequently the long-term consequences of the use of coercive power. The coercion might temporarily stop a behavior in the classroom, but the resulting anger and hostility are expressed in other, more destructive, patterns.

It should not be concluded that coercive power should never be used. However, it should be used only as a last resort, when a learner is out of control. Even in this extreme situation, it is likely to be ineffective unless the teacher has referent power. Punishment has maximum impact on behavior when it is administered by someone who is respected and when the individual believes the punishment is just and fair. If the punishment is viewed as excessively harsh or arbitrary, a negative reaction will occur and the relationship between learner and teacher will be harmed.

In summary, the beginning point for developing authority and power in the classroom for the teacher to is demonstrate expertise and concern for the needs of students. Treating students with respect and demonstrating fairness and consistency are important components. On this foundation of expert and referent power, a teacher can then enhance leadership through judicious use of legitimate, reward, and coercive power.

ESTABLISHING CLASSROOM RULES

Reasonable rules are an important part of any social situation. Whenever two or more people come together they must reach some agreement about appropriate behavior. The rules might be in the form of unwritten expectations assumed by both parties, or they may take a more concrete verbal or written form. Unwritten expectations, however, can lead to disagreement and conflict. This is especially true in classroom situations where there are many individuals with different expectations and understandings. Therefore, it is especially important for the teacher to spend considerable time at the beginning of the year establishing classroom rules and expectations. The way the teacher does this is an important component in developing a leadership style.

One of the first choices a teacher faces at the beginning of a school year is how to establish the rules. Some individuals advocate an authoritarian style (Canter and Canter 1976). This style is based on an exercise of legitimate, reward, and coercive power. The teacher sets the rules, communicates them to learners, and tells them what will happen if they follow the rules and what will happen if they do not. In essence, this style says to the class: "I am the boss. I expect you to follow rules, and if you do not, you will be punished. If you conform to my expectations, you will be rewarded.

This approach has some appeal because it does provide teachers with a sense of security and control. They can take time before entering the classroom to reflect on the rules that they need and to plan how they will clearly and forcefully communicate them to learners. In addition, the approach does not take much class time to accomplish and teacher authority can be communicated from the very beginning."

Box 2-4
THE GOLDEN RULE

When discussing rules in the classroom one teacher had this response:

Rules are not a problem in my classroom. I don't waste a lot of time establishing rules and I have only one rule. That one rule is basically the "Golden Rule": Treat others as you want to be treated.

What do you think?

1. What potential problems do you see in this approach?

2. What would need to be done in order to make this approach work?

3. What would your response be to this teacher?

Studies have shown that this approach does seem to increase the amount of work produced by learners (Mendler and Curwin 1983). Those who are successful in communicating to learners in a firm but positive manner that they mean business and will not tolerate disturbances find this approach useful in prompting task behavior. A potential problem is noted, however, in that the authoritarian approach also seems to prompt student aggression toward the teacher (Mendler and Curwin 1983).

Another option in establishing classroom rules is the democratic approach. This method involves shared decision making. It allows learners a voice in establishing rules. Based more on the exercise of referent, expert, and legitimate power, the democratic approach has the advantage of giving students some ownership of the rules and develops a commitment on their part to follow the rules. It also communicates to learners a respect for their needs and their ideas. The democratic approach to rule setting is preferred over the authoritarian because it does have greater potential for helping students learn self-control.

Research seems to indicate that learners in democratic-oriented classrooms also exhibit high academic output. Further, students have a more positive attitude toward the teacher and continue to behave in a manner more consistent with the rules when the teacher is out of the classroom.

The democratic approach does have some disadvantages. It is time consuming and may cause teacher anxiety. What if the class does not establish appropriate rules? The teacher must have confidence in students and skill in facilitating the formulation of rules. Inexperienced teachers sometimes lack confidence and are hesitant about using the democratic style. The advantages, though, outweigh the problems. Implementing this approach does not mean that teachers abdicate responsibility. If there are some rules the teacher must have, they should be identified at the outset and the class told that they are not negotiable. There should be no more than three or four rules of this type, and the reasons for the rules should be given. Students will accept these very basic rules and the right of the teacher to establish them.

Several elementary steps should be followed when establishing classroom rules, regardless of leadership style: rule specification, rule clarification, rule practice, and rule monitoring. Including these four steps can help ensure that behavioral expectations are clear and understood by all learners. Not only does this help prevent problems but it communicates to learners that the teacher takes the rules very seriously and so should they.

Rule Specification

Rule specification is the process of deciding on classroom rules. For the authoritarian teacher, rule specification is the responsibility of the teacher. Rules are determined by the teacher and then communicated to the learners. In contrast, the democratic teacher shares rule specification with students. Mendler and Curwin (1983) recommend the social contract approach as a democratic rule specification method. A social contract is an agreement on a set of rules reached by group consensus. Three types of rules are included in the development of the social contract. Teachers include the rules they must have and learners decide on the rules they must have for each other and those rules they want for the teacher. The social contract method of rule specification includes the following steps:

1. The teacher states the rules that must be included and that are nonnegotiable.

2. Small groups of class members discuss and propose rules that they think are needed in order to work together productively.

3. All proposed rules are discussed and voted on by the entire class. At least two thirds of the class should agree on the rule before it is adopted, but group consensus is preferred.

4. Small groups discuss and propose rules for the teacher.

5.   Rules for the teacher are discussed. If a rule is inappropriate or is inconsistent with the responsibility of the teacher to conduct the classroom, the teacher can exercise veto power.

6.   Possible consequences for all rules are then discussed. Either the teacher or the students may propose consequences for rule violation. The teacher must approve the consequences and has the right to veto any consequences that are dangerous or illegal.

Some teachers are uncomfortable with the idea of allowing students to set rules for them, concerned that students will establish unreasonable rules. However, experience with the procedure indicates that students usually take the process seriously and propose reasonable rules for the teacher. This procedure has the advantage of providing the teacher with insight into learner views of fairness and justice. Some of the behaviors they consider offensive may not have occurred to the teacher. Identifying these behaviors at the beginning of the school year helps the teacher avoid behaviors that are likely to create student hostility. In addition, allowing students to specify rules for the teacher communicates to the students that the teacher recognizes the value of rules and allows the teacher an opportunity to model the process of exercising self-control and accepting consequences when they are broken.

Rule Clarification

The purpose of rule clarification is to make sure that all learners understand what a rule means and what constitutes appropriate and inappropriate behavior. An important component of rule clarification is to ensure that each rule is stated in a clear and concise manner. When possible, a rule should state what learners should do rather than what they should not do. For example, it is more productive to state that "we raise our hand before talking," rather than "we do not talk out of turn."

Each rule then should be then discussed and ambiguous terms removed or defined. The class should identify acceptable and unacceptable behavior for each rule. Taking time for rule clarification helps eliminate the common excuse for misbehavior that the student "didn't understand."

Rule Practice

Rules, like anything else, require a certain amount of practice. Time should be taken to practice the rules so that acceptable and unacceptable behaviors are identified. Rule practice is generally more important for young learners and for rules that might be vague or unfamiliar. A concluding step in rule practice might be for the students to take a short test on the rules. One junior high science teacher identifies, clarifies and practices rules on the first day of school and gives a quiz on the rules on the second day. The quiz is kept short and simple so that all learners will pass all items. These papers are then kept by the teacher. Students who profess ignorance of the rules are then shown their test.

Box 2-5
RULES FOR THE TEACHER?

Allowing students to establish rules for the teacher is not very common. Many teachers do not consider it either necessary or desirable. They believe that the role of the teacher as a leader and the authority of the teacher will be undermined if students are allowed to establish rules for teachers.

What do you think?

1. Would you feel comfortable allowing students to set rules for you? Why or why not?

2. What is your biggest fear about allowing students to establish rules for the teacher?

3. What could be done to address this fear?

4. Do you think that allowing students to establish rules for the teacher will increase or diminish teacher authority?

5. What types of rules would be appropriate for students to make for the teacher?

Rule Monitoring

Monitoring is an important component in making sure that the rules become meaningful and are followed. Sometimes teachers do not monitor rules very closely or follow up rule violation with consequences. As a result, youngsters begin to violate rules because the probability of the teacher taking action is slight. The rules then become meaningless and the respect for the teacher and the rules is lost. Teacher monitoring of the rules is especially critical during the first few weeks of the school year (Emmer et al. 1982). It is important that the teacher provide positive reinforcement and rewards when the rules are followed, as well as follow through with appropriate consequences when rules are violated.

TEACHER CONSISTENCY

Rule monitoring leads to the issue of teacher consistency, a critical variable in developing positive teacher leadership and authority. There are several aspects to teacher consistency. One is the consistent application of the rules on a day-to-day basis. Day-to-day consistency means that if a behavior is unacceptable one day, it is unacceptable on other days. Rule enforcement is based on the rules established rather than on the mood of the teacher on a given day. Teachers who complain that the class is constantly testing their authority are often guilty of inconsistent enforcement of rules. As a result, learners test everyday to see how far they can go.

Application of consequences to all students in the classroom is another dimension of teacher consistency. A rule for one student is a rule for all students. A common complaint of students with persistent behavior problems is that they are not treated the same as other students. Because they have a reputation as problem students, teachers are quick to enforce even their slightest rule violation. High achievers or usually well-behaved students, however, are just as quickly excused for rule violations. This selective enforcement creates hostility not only between teacher and student but also among students. Students resent those who seem to be accorded special favors. Selective enforcement of rules interferes with teacher attempts to develop referent power and undermines teacher leadership.

Teacher consistency also includes consistent application of rewards when students do follow rules, as well as consistent application of consequences when they do not. Consistency in applying rewards creates a positive environment that emphasizes productive behavior, and it is an essential ingredient in helping students develop self-control. It lets them know that their productive behavior has a payoff.

SHARING RESPONSIBILITY

A willingness to share responsibility is another important aspect of teacher leadership. Research indicates that effective schools provide many opportunities for learners to assume responsibility and to participate in making decisions regarding school. Increased student participation has been found to be associated with higher levels of academic achievement and less disruptive behavior (Rutter 1983). Assigning responsibility to learners gives them a sense of power and belonging. They feel that they are important and that the school also belongs to them and not just to the school authorities. Allowing students the opportunity to participate in the operation of the classroom and in decision making gives them an opportunity to exercise power in constructive ways. They are then less inclined to try and show their power and importance by challenging the authority of the teacher. Assigning responsibilities to students not only demonstrates to the learners that the teacher has enough confidence to share responsibility and respects their views, but it also makes good sense.

Many tasks are involved in operating a classroom, and quite a few are routine and repetitive. Delegating these tasks to learners allows the teacher more time to focus on important tasks related to teaching. Additionally, many students enjoy doing them and get much satisfaction out of helping the teacher. The specific tasks that can be delegated to learners vary according to age level. Younger children enjoy doing tasks such as helping clean up the room that might not be appealing to older students. However, older students can assist in operating audiovisual equipment and in taking attendance. As a general rule, elementary teachers have more opportunities for allocating tasks to learners than do secondary teachers.

It is important that all youngsters are given the opportunity to share in classroom responsibilities. One useful way to perform this function is to list all of those areas in which learners can assist the teacher. This list can then be passed out to the youngsters and they can apply to perform a particular task. Some teachers integrate this into a lesson by developing a formal application procedure and having the students apply just as if they were applying for a job. The skills of reading an application form and filling one out correctly can then be taught. Another choice is to have the students list their first three choices and give them to the teacher. The teacher can then review the choices designated by the learners and assign them responsibilities. Care should be taken to ensure fairness in assigning the responsibilities and that the best jobs are not given to just the teacher's favorites. Responsibilities can be changed every few weeks so that different students have the opportunity to have some of the favored responsibilities.

SUMMARY

Establishing teacher leadership is one of the most important aspects of developing a classroom where problems are prevented and, when they do arise, learners are willing to follow the directives of the teacher. The approaches suggested by various authorities for dealing with discipline problems in the classroom are of limited usefulness if the teacher has not established a positive leadership style.

An important component for developing positive leadership is the way the teacher uses power and establishes authority. A teacher who approaches the classroom with confidence and enthusiasm and is well prepared develops expert power. Behaving as a fair and trustworthy individual develops referent power. Referent power and expert power form a powerful combination that multiplies the legitimate power of the teacher.

The style the teacher adopts in establishing classroom rules also contributes to his or her authority and leadership. It is recommended that the teacher use a democratic approach. This allows student needs to be heard and gives students a sense of ownership in the classroom. The social contract approach is another effective method. Once rules have been specified, rule clarification, rule practice, and rule monitoring ensure that the rules will become meaningful and contribute to a positive classroom environment. Teachers must be consistent in enforcing rules. Teacher consistency involves enforcing the rules on a daily basis, enforcing rules for all students, and providing rewards for productive behavior and consequences for inappropriate behavior.

Many time-consuming tasks must be performed in the classroom. Allowing students to perform these tasks accomplishes two important functions. First, it allows learners a sense of power and continues to build positive feelings about the teacher as a leader. Second, it relieves the teacher of many duties so that energy can be devoted to the larger items that need attention.

SUGGESTED ACTIVITIES

1. An understanding of your own beliefs and attitudes is an important step in becoming an effective classroom manager. Take a few minutes to perform a self-analysis. Are you confident in your ability to control a classroom? Are you confident in your ability to teach students? What type of students? What is your view of students and what they can be allowed to do in the classroom? What do you fear most about handling misbehavior?

2. Reflect on your experience as a student. Identify teachers who you have had that fit each type of power and authority described in this chapter. What specific indicators or behaviors led you to place them in the particular category? How effective were they as teachers and classroom managers?

3. Identify four or five rules that you think you will need as a teacher. State your rationale for each of the rules and describe how you would clarify them and have students practice them.

4. Visit a number of classrooms and write down the classroom rules. What common rules seem to appear in most classrooms? Why do you think these rules are needed? Can you define acceptable and unacceptable behavior that would be consistent with these rule statements?

5. Brainstorm responsibilities or tasks that might be performed by students in your classroom. Share your list with others and add new ideas that are suggested in your group discussion.

BIBLIOGRAPHY

BOLES, H. W., and J. A. DAVENPORT. 1975. *Introduction to Educational Leadership*. New York: Harper & Row.

CANTER, L., and M. CANTER. 1976. *Assertive Discipline: A Take Charge Approach for Today's Educator*. Santa Monica, Calif.: Canter and Associates.

CLARK, C. M., and P. L. PETERSON. 1986. Teachers' thought processes. In *Handbook of Research on Teaching*, 3rd ed., ed. M. C. Wittrock. New York: Macmillan.

CRONBACH, L. J. 1977. *Educational Psychology*, 3rd ed. New York: Harcourt Brace Jovanovich.

DOYLE, W. 1986. Classroom organization and management. In *Handbook of Research on Teaching*, 3rd ed., ed. M. C. Wittrock. New York: Macmillan.

EMMER, E., C. EVERTSON, J. SANFORD, B. CLEMENTS, and W. WORSHAM. 1982. *Organizing and Managing the Junior High Classroom*. Austin: Research and Development Center for Teacher Education, University of Texas.

FRENCH, J. R. P., and B. H. RAVEN. 1959. The bases of social power. In *Studies in Social Power*, ed. D. Cartwright. Ann Arbor: University of Michigan Press.

GLASSER, W. 1969. *Schools Without Failure*. New York: Harper & Row.

———. 1986. *Control Theory in the Classroom*. New York: Harper & Row.

MENDLER, A. N. and R. L. CURWIN. 1983. *Taking Charge in the Classroom: A Practical Guide to Effective Discipline*. Reston, Va.: Reston.

RENDER, G. F., J. M. PADILLA, and H. M. KRANK, 1988. Self-esteem and assertive discipline: What educators need to know. Paper presented at the annual meeting of the Association for Humanistic Education, Paducah, Ky.

RUTTER, M. 1983. School effects on pupil progress: Research findings and policy implications. In *Handbook of Teaching and Policy*, ed. L. Shulman and G. Sykes. New York: Longman.

SOAR, R. S., and R. M. SOAR. 1987. Classroom climate. In *The International Encyclopedia of Teaching and Teacher Education*, ed. M. J. Dunkin. New York: Pergamon Press.

TANNER, L. N. 1978. *Discipline for Effective Teaching and Learning*. New York: Holt, Rinehart & Winston.

TAUBER, R. T. 1985. Power bases: Their application to classroom and school management. *Journal of Education for Teaching*, 11, 2, 133–144.

Chapter 3

MOTIVATION AND DISCIPLINE

OBJECTIVES

This chapter provides information to help the reader

1. Identify three important components of motivation

2. State the role of physiological needs in motivation

3. List psychological needs that must be accommodated in the classroom

4. Define how teacher expectations influence learner motivation

5. Provide examples of how the identification motive might be used to increase motivation

6. State how the perception of the difficulty of a task is related to learner motivation

7. List ways that the teacher can utilize success as a means of motivating learners

8. Define the relationship between locus of control and the use of success in motivating individuals

INTRODUCTION

Richard was not an especially troublesome student. He just sat and did not work. When assignments were given, he would daydream or play with objects on his desk. Sometimes he would put his head on his desk and close his eyes. When his work was turned in, the most the teacher could expect was to see his name scribbled at the top of the paper. No matter how hard the teacher tried, Richard just did not seem to have the least interest in learning.

It is obvious that Richard has a motivation problem. Many teachers can identify a "Richard" in their class. Passive, unmotivated youngsters are often left alone because they are quiet and do not interfere with of others. Other unmotivated learners,however, may respond in more aggressive and disruptive ways. Regardless of the pattern, lack of motivation is a serious educational problem that is certain to lead to inappropriate behavior that must be responded to by the teacher. A major way of preventing behavior problems is attending to the motivational component of teaching and learning.

A statement commonly heard from teachers is that students do not seem to be as motivated as those in the past. What they really mean is that individuals do not seem to be as motivated to perform those tasks required of them in school. In some respects, all individuals are motivated. There is really no such thing as an unmotivated individual. Everyone is motivated to do something; it just may not be the things that are required of them in school. The basic question, then, is why some individuals appear to be motivated to perform well in school and others are not. This may be an uncomfortable question because sometimes a large share of the responsibility for the problem lies with the teacher and the school. It may well be that the curriculum is irrelevant, that the teacher is not doing a good job of teaching, or that the classroom environment is not conducive to learning. The notion that the lack of motivation is just a natural by-product of schooling should be rejected. Teachers can have an impact on the motivation of youngsters toward school subjects and can influence the direction of their efforts. Motivating students may not be an easy task, but it is an essential one.

All teachers dream of that class of cooperative learners who are eager to learn. However, this is not a situation that will happen merely by wishing it were true. Achieving anything near this state requires a great deal of knowledge, effort, and planning. Unfortunately, the motivational question must be addressed anew with each group of learners. What might be motivating for one group may be met with indifference by another. The motivational problem is complex, and there are no easy answers. However, research has helped to uncover some of the variables related to motivation. Understanding those variables and applying them to specific classroom problems can help a teacher move toward making that illusive dream of a motivated and eager group of learners a reality.

Box 3-1
WHAT MOTIVATES YOU?

Before continuing on in the text, stop and think about your motivation. Answer the following questions and then see if you can identify principles of motivation that might be applies to others.

1. **What are the things that interest you?**

2. **Where did you get that interest?**

3. **Which teachers were successful in motivating you?**

4. **What did they do that was motivating?**

5. **Are there some activities that have high interest for you?**

6. **What keeps you from getting involved?**

7. **Based on the answere you have given, what conclusions can you make about motivation?**

MOTIVATIONAL FACTORS

A beginning point in understanding what motivates individuals to expend time and energy in a given direction is understanding the basic factors that influence individual motivation. The three basic forces that influence the amount of effort expended on a particular act include the interests and needs of the individual, the perceived difficulty of the task, and the expectation of success (Klinger 1977, 304). Taken together, these three forces explain a great deal of behavior.

Needs and interests are important motivational factors because they serve to attract the attention and focus the energies of an individual. Attention will be drawn to those activities that are seen as having potential for fulfilling unmet needs or those that appear interesting. This can be viewed as a sort of trade-off. People have only a limited amount of time and energy, and resources will be directed toward those things that appear to have the greatest potential for meeting needs and interests present at that point in time. The economic term *opportunity cost* accurately describes this phenomenon. When an individual chooses one option, other options are eliminated. Therefore, individuals will choose the option that they think will have the greatest personal benefit at the lowest possible cost.

A major task of the teacher is to identify learner needs and interests. Much of the advice to teachers about how to motivate learners stops at this point. The assumption is that if learners are interested in a topic or activity, they will be motivated. Interest, however, is not the whole picture. An individual may have a high level of interest in an object or an activity and still not be motivated to get involved. This phenomenon is obvious every fall when thousands of spectators fill a stadium to watch a football game. They are interested in the sport, yet less than 100 of those present in the stadium are actually involved in the game. Thus, the problem for the teacher is how to reduce the number of spectators and increase the number of participants. Clearly, interest alone is not enough.

The second factor involved in increasing the possibility of movement toward an object or activity is the perceived effort required to obtain success. Although many individuals might have an intrinsic interest in the activity or see the potential for meeting a need, if the activity is perceived to require a great deal of effort, only a few individuals will be motivated to become involved. Few of the spectators at the game are willing to spend the several hours each day in practice and in conditioning needed to become participants. This also explains why some individuals do not follow through on the advice of their physicians. Even though the prescribed treatment relates to a very basic need, that of good health, if the regimen is seen as requiring too much effort, then it may be done poorly or not at all.

This implies that the teacher needs to attend to learner perceptions of task complexity and difficulty. If learners believe that the task is very complex and difficult, they may attempt to avoid the task altogether and seek an alternative means of meeting their needs or following through on their interests.

Let us return to the stadium full of spectators. There may be a large number of people willing to expend the effort required to be a participant in the game. In fact, many would go to great lengths for the opportunity to play in the game. Then why are they still in the stands? This can be explained by looking at the third major factor in motivation, an estimation of the probability of success. They simply do not believe that the expenditure of effort would have the desired result of participation in the game. An individual may have a keen interest in a topic or an activity, may be willing to expend a great deal of energy pursuing the activity, and still not be motivated to try because he or she believes that there is little chance of success. Those individuals who have chosen to try out for the team believe that they have some opportunity for success. For some, it may be an unrealistic assessment of their opportunities, but as long as that hope exists a great deal of effort will be expended.

Thus, teachers must make sure that each learner has an opportunity for success. However, just making sure that each learner has a probability for success is not enough. Some learners need to be convinced that they can succeed. This is especially true of those who have a history of failure. They are actually afraid to try because they fear failure. Their battered self-esteem simply cannot stand the threat of more failure.

Reflect the description of Richard. His lack of interest might have stemmed from a perception that the tasks were unimportant or did not meet any of his needs, he may have been overwhelmed with the complexity of the tasks, or he may have felt that no amount of effort on his part would result in success. The remaining sections of this chapter take each of the three motivational factors, discuss them in depth, and provide some classroom application suggestions.

Box 3-2
DEALING WITH RICHARD

Reread the description of Richard. Apply what you have just read concerning motivation to his case.

1. **How might you identify Richard's needs and interests?**

2. **How could you relate the school subject you plan on teaching to his interests and needs?**

3. **How would you try to help him perceive that getting involved and learning the subject would not take an inordinate amount of time and effort?**

4. **What would you do to help ensure that Richard would have success?**

LEARNER NEEDS AND INTERESTS

There is a direct link between need fulfillment and motivation. Time and energy are geared toward those activities that appear to have potential for meeting needs or that are intrinsically interesting. There is also a connection between need fulfillment and discipline problems. Learners who feel that their needs are being met in the classroom seldom cause discipline problems because interfering with something that is meeting a need is contrary to their self-interest. Glasser (1986, 15) emphasizes this point in his description of a good school: "A good school could be defined as a place where almost all students believe that if they do some work, they will be able to satisfy their needs enough so that it makes sense to keep working." His contention is that many school problems stem from the false assumption that all students want to learn what is taught and therefore the school does not take into account whether or not the experience is satisfying to the learner.

This section identifies some of the needs that should be considered in order to make school a more satisfying experience. There are many ways that needs can be categorized. Here, needs are divided into three groups: physiological, psychological, and social. Although they are discussed separately, in reality needs are interrelated.

Physiological Needs

Physiological needs are fundamental needs that must be accommodated before any other needs can be addressed. If their physiological needs are not met, it is almost impossible for individuals to be motivated toward any activity other than the fulfillment of the unmet physiological needs. The teacher should consider the physiological needs of food, rest, comfort, freedom from illness, movement, and stimulation of the senses. Although some of these needs may be beyond the teacher's control, understanding that these factors may cause discipline problems can aid him or her in a search for causes of motivational problems.

It is unfortunate that many youngsters come to school with inadequate nutrition. The popularity of junk food has contributed greatly to this problem—and it is not one that is confined to the impoverished. Not only is it difficult for malnourished youngsters to stay on task, but, according to research, malnutrition plays an important role in behavior disorders and violence (Schauss 1985, 21). An understanding of the crucial role of this physiological need led to the establishment of free breakfast and lunch programs in schools. Also, nutritional therapy involving the use of vitamin and mineral supplements has been found to have significant positive effects on the behavior of some youngsters. Note, though, that testing and prescribing treatment should be done only by trained and licensed health specialists.

Teachers occasionally forget that learners, especially younger students, need to move and be mobile. It is physically impossible for some youngsters to sit still for extended periods of time. Unrealistic expectations or poorly planned schedules will surely give rise to discipline problems. For example, the author observed a first-grade class in which the teacher expected learners to stay in their seats doing a worksheet for 45 minutes. When the inevitable restlessness occurred, the teacher became upset and punished the class for violating the out-of-seat rule. While the rule governing movement around the classroom was reasonable, the expectation that young children could remain at their desks working on one task for 45 minutes was not. The problem was not with the learners but with the poor planning of the teacher.

In another case, primary grade youngsters arrived by bus 30 minutes before the start of school. They were expected to sit quietly in the cafeteria until the start of school and then spend two to three hours working on academic tasks with little opportunity for physical movement or exercise. It was not surprising that many of their teachers had discipline problems during the latter part of the morning. The wise teachers provided opportunities for controlled movement and had a much more satisfying and productive teaching experience.

The comfort of learners is another aspect of the physiological dimension that needs to be considered. The advent of climate control and uniform lighting has led to the assumption that the comfort dimension has been met. However, other aspects of the classroom environment may cause discomfort and therefore interfere with learning. A typical problem involves the work area. Youngsters may be sitting in chairs that are the wrong size or working on wobbly desks. These conditions interfere with the learner's ability to work on a task for any length of time. The resulting physical discomfort will demand relief. If not met, this relief will often take the form of disruptive behavior.

All individuals have a need for sensory stimulation so that the brain has information to process. In severe cases of sensory deprivation, individuals may begin to hallucinate. Sensory deprivation is a very painful experience. For example, sitting in the waiting room of a physician's office with nothing to do can result in physical discomfort such as a headache. Sensory deprivation is boring, and there are few enemies to motivation more serious than boredom. Bored students will seek relief and that relief might be in the form of unacceptable behavior.

Psychological Needs

All individuals have emotional and psychological needs. We all want to be accepted, loved, respected, worthwhile and physically and psychologically secure. Glasser (1969) points out that the school is one of the few places where learners have an opportunity to feel significant and important. Teachers and schools that work toward helping learners feel significant and important discover that even the most difficult students can develop a commitment to school and an excitement about learning.

One of the major psychological needs is that of security, a need to feel safe. This begins by helping individuals feel safe from physical danger. In schools where learners worry about their physical safety, the schools must take steps to remove the threat of physical harm, or little learning will take place.

Box 3-3
PSYCHOLOGICAL HARM

Psychological threats to an individual's well-being can be very devastating to the classroom climate. Take a few minutes to answer the following questions.

1. **What is meant by the term** *psychological harm*?

2. **What are some of the ways that an individual can be psychologically threatened?**

3. **Have you ever felt psychologically threatened?**

4. **What was the cause of the threat?**

5. **How did you respond?**

6. **What are some of the things that teachers do that might result in psychological harm?**

7. **What can be done to create an environment that is free of psychological threat?**

A more serious problem in many classrooms is the threat of psychological harm. Learners may feel that the environment is not psychologically or emotionally safe, fearing failure and ridicule. Every mistake is turned into a major failure and so they are afraid to try or take risks. Psychological intimidation creates a level of anxiety that blocks learning. Learners need to believe that they are entering a room where they will be physically and emotionally secure and where they are accepted as worthwhile and important. The need for acceptance and respect is overlooked in some classrooms. It is sometimes difficult to accept the behavior of a given youngster, but the teacher should never communicate a lack of acceptance of the learner as an individual. Lack of respect by the teacher is often cited by learners as a reason for misbehavior.

Self-esteem needs are critical needs that the teacher must understand. Self--esteem can be thought of as the self-portrait that individuals have in their mind, a series of subjective beliefs about self. Everyone has a need for a personal sense of identity, worth, adequacy, and competence. We learn this self-portrait in the "mirror of others." That is, the way others respond to us reveals what they think of us and therefore leads to this subjective self-portrait. Since the teacher is an important "other," his or her response to each learner is critical in helping students develop a positive self-portrait.

Understanding the importance of the teacher's meeting the self-esteem needs of students underscores the importance of teacher expectations. Teachers are significant others for many youngsters and their treatment is especially important. If teacher behavior communicates to a youngster a low estimate of ability or worth, then that student is likely to have a lower self-esteem. Good and Brophy (1987) postulate that teacher expectations influence learners in the following ways:

1. The teacher forms differing expectations for learners.
2. The behavior of the teacher toward these students is influenced by these expectations.
3. This behavior communicates to the students how they are expected to perform or behave.
4. When this behavior pattern persists over some length of time and the individual does not seek to actively refute these expectations, then the self-esteem, the achievement motivation, and the classroom conduct of the students will be influenced.
5. The behavior of the individual then confirms and reinforces the original teacher expectations.

Learners are very aware of the way teachers treat different members of the class (Weinstein 1985). This emphasizes the potential for teacher expectations to influence the self-esteem of learners.

The self-esteem of individuals serves as a guide to their behavior and to their response to situations. High self-esteem individuals tend to approach a task quite differently than low self-esteem individuals. High self-esteem individuals usually have more confidence and expectation of success and are willing to take more risks. Low self-esteem individuals demonstrate more anxiety, stress, and apathy when approaching a new task.

Box 3-4
TEACHER EXPECTATIONS

The following are some of the ways that teachers communicate their expectations through their behavior.

1.   After asking a question they wait less time for an answer from the low expectation learners.

2.   The answer is given to lows or someone else is called on rather than providing cues when the low expectation learner has difficulty.

3.   Less accurate feedback is given to low expectation learners when they do respond. The teacher may respond with praise when the answer is wrong.

4.   Low expectation learners are called on less frequently.

5.   High expectation learners are given the benefit of the doubt more frequently.

6.   The teacher interacts with the high expectation learners more often and on more friendly terms.

7.   Low expectation learners are criticized more for their failures and praised less for their successes.

8.   The instructional approaches used with low expectation learners tend to be at a lower cognitive level and demand more memory and recall than application and conceptual understanding.

9.   The nonverbal behavior toward lows tends to include less eye contact, less smiling, and fewer indicators of approval or support.

10. There is less acceptance and use of lows' ideas.

11. Low expectation learners are seated farther away from the teacher.

Adapted from T. Good and J. Brophy *Looking in Classrooms*, 4th ed (New York: Harper & Row, 1987) pp. 128-129.

Success experiences are another important component in building a positive image of self. It is through success, not failure, that a sense of adequacy and competence is developed. Unfortunately, some teachers seem to have the notion that failure is somehow "good" because it prepares learners for life. The best way to prepare individuals for the difficulties that are experienced in life is through a great deal of success and a strong self-image. The occasional failure can then be tolerated. The teacher should be concerned with providing as many success experiences as possible. It should be noted that all individuals, even those who are not successful in school, have self-esteem needs. If an individual is not able to develop a sense of adequacy, competence, and power in school, other means of meeting this need will be pursued. And some of those means might involve behavior that is disruptive or antisocial.

Social Needs

The classroom is a social setting, and much of what happens in that setting is part of an effort to be accepted and belong to a significant group. An understanding of the social needs of students helps the teacher to understand the importance of the peer group. Peer group norms and sanctions counter to those held by the teacher can frustrate the best of intentions. Accommodating social needs in the classroom can prevent many problems.

Dreikurs (1968) considers the need to belong one of the most basic of human needs. This need becomes especially acute during adolescence. Adolescents spend a considerable amount of time worrying about acceptance and striving to become a part of the in group. When youngsters are frustrated in their attempts to belong through positive and constructive ways, they may develop what Dreikurs calls "mistaken goals"—attention getting, power, revenge, and withdrawal. Youngsters who are pursuing these goals cause many of the serious problems that teachers encounter.

Love and affection are powerful social needs that influence all individuals. Everyone needs to feel that someone cares. Unfortunately, changes in contemporary society often make it difficult for a child to feel loved. The mobility of society often separates youngsters from an extended family that can communicate a sense of love. The increase in one-parent families removes another source of love. The employment of both parents may leave them little energy to show the affection and love desired by an individual. These circumstances do not always result in a youngster feeling a need for love, but they can contribute to this need in many students.

It is very difficult for a teacher to meet the needs of youngsters for love and affection. The teacher cannot become a surrogate parent. However, this does not remove the need for the teacher to become aware of this powerful force and to try and accommodate it in the classroom. Communicating a sense of caring and affection for youngsters can pay tremendous dividends in fewer discipline problems and increased achievement.

It is important to note that firm and fair discipline is interpreted by youngsters as a sign of caring. Our goal is for it to be interpreted as a sign that someone cares enough to take an interest in their welfare. Dreikurs (1968) asks the question—who do we discipline? He answers that we discipline those we love; the others we leave alone. It is because we care about someone and his or her ability to achieve a satisfying and productive life that we discipline. This echoes once again the major purpose of discipline: We are disciplining youngsters so that they can move toward self-control. Remember, however, that it is firm and fair discipline that keeps concern for the learner at the forefront, not arbitrary and harsh discipline administered in order to meet the needs of the teacher.

Student Interests

All individuals have certain interests apart from those that might be seen as meeting personal needs. If these interests can be identified and classroom tasks structured so that the content is related to these interests, more than likely learners will be motivated. For example, the author once had great success increasing the reading ability of a group of young boys by tying reading to the preparation for taking a driver's license test and in finding out about cars.

Understanding individuals' interests can be enhanced by considering what is called the "identification motive." People attempt to increase their similarity, or identification, with those they perceive to be important individuals in command of desirable resources, such as attractiveness, popularity, money, status, and power. The identification motive helps explain why youngsters may seek to dress, talk, and act like popular musicians or athletes. These individuals are seen as having command of resources desired by students. Unfortunately, they are not always those who have gained that status through intellectual achievement.

Interest can also be stimulated by things that are novel or different. The unusual or unexpected will attract interest for at least a short time. Remember, though, that the value of novelty in motivation is rather short-lived. The novelty will soon fade unless other interests and needs are included in the learning task.

Accommodating Needs and Interests in the Classroom

Accommodating the needs and interests of learners demands considerable time and effort on the part of the teacher. However, the rewards of doing so far outweigh the costs. Not only will discipline problems be prevented, but the classroom will be a more rewarding and exciting place to work. One of the advantages of teaching is that teachers can structure their own work environment to include excitement and novelty. Teachers who take advantage of this opportunity find themselves more satisfied with their job.

The teacher should take several factors into account when accommodating the physiological needs of the learners. First of all, the environment needs to be safe and comfortable. It is a reality that many youngsters start the school day with fear of physical assault. Incidents of assault against students have risen in the last several years. Students who fear assault either in school or on their way to and from school will have difficulty approaching school tasks. Completing schoolwork is relatively unimportant when compared to the need to survive.

Creating a safe school generally requires the cooperation of the entire community as well as the entire school. It sometimes takes a great deal of effort and extra work on the part of the school staff to identify and correct problem areas. The community may need to be made aware of problems that occur off school grounds and assistance requested.

Box 3-5
SCHOOL VIOLENCE

School safety has become a serious concern for educators during the past decade. A number of articles have appeared in the news media concerning crime and violence in the schools.

1. **How serious do you think the problem really is?**

2. **Why do you think there is a problem of violence in the schools?**

3. **What can be done to prevent violence in the schools?**

4. **Does the issue of violence in the schools frighten you as a future teacher?**

5. **What can you do to prepare yourself for a potentially violent confrontation?**

The class schedule should be examined to make sure that there is an appropriate mix of passive and active components so that the need for movement can be met. The environment might be checked to make sure that temperature and light are satisfactory in all parts of the classroom. Work spaces should be inspected to ensure that students are able to sit comfortably, work on a stable surface, and see the teaching stations.

Design the classroom environment so that there is some sensory stimulation and plan lessons with the need for sensory stimulation in mind. Bulletin boards can be used to stimulate the senses through pictures and artifacts and by posing unanswered questions. Thought-provoking displays or "centers" where individuals can touch and manipulate objects or conduct experiments also provide stimulation. Changing from listening to responding or questioning and changing the configuration of the group from large to small are simple ways to meet the need for sensory stimulation during a lesson.

After the physiological needs are accommodated, the teacher then needs to consider how to meet the psychological needs. A major ingredient in creating a safe and productive psychological climate is the attitude of the teacher. Does the teacher accept all of the youngsters in the class? Does she or he show respect for all learners, even those who are problems? Does the teacher believe that all of the learners are capable of learning and hold high expectations for them? Does the teacher respond to discipline problems with a respect for the dignity of the learners and their need for acceptance, or through displays of power and intimidation and fear? It is imperative that the teacher seek to create an environment that is psychologically safe and supportive in which learners feel free to make mistakes and to experiment.

The need for love and affection can be accommodated in the classroom by listening nonjudgmentally to youngsters, by being aware of their accomplishments both in and out of the classroom, by remembering personal events such as birth dates, and by letting a disciplined youngster know that while you cannot accept inappropriate behavior, you are not rejecting him or her as a person.

Some students do not understand how to become a part of the group. They may not see that their behavior actually interferes with their goal of gaining acceptance. In these cases the teacher has a special responsibility to help students begin to see the link between what they do and how others view them. Some individualized instruction and personal counseling might be needed in order for the learner to begin to understand how to behave in ways that will gain acceptance from others. Role-playing situations can be developed to help the class understand how it feels to be left out and to help them learn how to include others and make them feel that they belong.

Interests of the students need to be identified so that they can be integrated into the classroom curriculum. Administering an interest inventory and becoming personally interested in each learner are important ways of finding out what is of interest for each individual.

The identification motive can be taken into account in a variety of ways. First of all, the school should seek to accept, as much as possible, the different dress and grooming styles of youngsters. Standards of dress should be related to those things that interfere with the learning process. School authorities that ignore the identification motive when seeking to enforce dress standards are unknowingly casting the school as a place out of touch with contemporary reality. Capricious and arbitrary standards of dress and grooming communicate to youngsters that the authorities are more concerned with the exercise of power than with the needs of learners. Some individuals will challenge standards just for the sake of proving independence. It is unfortunate that so many schools waste a considerable amount of time trying to control individual behavior in ways that do not relate to improved learning.

Initial attention of learners can be captured by relating the content of the lesson to student interests, by beginning with something that is novel or unique, by using humor, or by being unpredictable in the way a lesson is introduced. The problem with these techniques is that learners may focus more on the introductory event than on the lesson. Novelty and humor are useful in gaining attention: however, unless something soon follows that is perceived of value, attention will quickly fade.

The use of discrepant events or puzzling situations to challenge existing concepts or ideas is yet another way of capturing attention. Learners are then motivated to look for a way to include the event or situation in their conceptual framework. Such a technique can have long-lasting effects. The author once received a letter from a former student who enclosed a newspaper article containing information about a discrepant event a full three years after the event had been presented in class.

Box 3-6
USING NOVELTY AND HUMOR TO MOTIVATE

Novelty and humor can be used to stimulate interest. Take some time to reflect on a topic you plan to teach and then answer the following questions.

1. **How might this subject have a direct relationship to some personal needs or interests of learners?**

2. **What are some novel facts or examples that might be appealing?**

3. **List some ways that you might use humor to capture attention.**

4. **Identify a discrepant event or puzzling situation that could be used to stimulate interest.**

PERCEPTION OF EFFORT REQUIRED

Dealing with this component of motivation may be one of the most difficult tasks faced by a teacher. The teacher needs to view the task as the learner views it and this is often very hard. The teacher may have found the subject interesting and easy or may assume that all individuals view it in the same positive light. Remember that it is the perception of reality held by the learner that is important, not that held by the teacher. If the learner believes that the task requires an effort not in line with the expected benefits, then there is little likelihood that he or she will be motivated.

Perceptions of task difficulty are related to several factors—an understanding of what the task requires, an understanding of prerequisites, views of task complexity, and estimates of task length. If the nature of the task is unclear, those learners with a history of low achievement and low self-esteem will usually assume that the task requires too much effort. Even when the nature of the task is understood, individuals who do not believe they possess the necessary prerequisites may also be unwilling to become involved. In addition, if the task is perceived as very complex or one that requires a long time to complete, individuals will be less likely to attempt the task.

Understanding these variables can help the teacher structure the learning environment so that students are not overwhelmed by their perception of the effort required. This does not mean that the task should be perceived as not being difficult. Some effort and difficulty are required in order to offer a challenge to the student. The degree of perceived difficulty needs to be related to the educational background of learners. Those with a history of educational success will tolerate, and even welcome, tasks that appear to require a great deal of effort. Those with a history of failure must be presented with tasks that appear to require minimal effort.

Altering Perceptions of Required Effort

Several things can be done to help learners understand how much effort is required in a given task. A first step is to perform an informal task analysis. Break the task down into all of the subtasks and steps that are required for success. The basic question to be answered is "What does a person need to know or be able to do in order to perform this task?" After brainstorming these subtasks, arrange them in a logical order. This provides a "map" of the route to successful completion. This map is very useful in communicating task complexity to learners.

The second step involves using the task analysis to diagnose the extent to which students have the necessary prerequisites or can already perform some parts of the task. This diagnosis need not be very complicated and can be based on the teacher's knowledge of learners' performance on previous assignments. This diagnosis helps match the learner and the task at a correct level of difficulty.

At this point, the teacher should have a clear understanding of the requirements for successful task completion and the match of the learners' abilities to the task. This sets the stage for the third step, presenting the task to the class.

Perception of task difficulty is strongly influenced by the way the task is presented. Most college students can relate to this principle. Even though professors take the first day of class to spell out the course requirements for the semester, this is often done quickly with a minimum of directions as to how each assignment is going to be accomplished. The immediate reaction of the students is usually fear. They are fearful that they will not be able to complete what is demanded of them. After they have gone through this routine for all of their classes, they feel completely over-whelmed. A few even drop out. However, since most of them have been successful learners, they will persevere and try to meet the challenge.

This approach will not work for learners who have a history of school difficulty and already doubt their ability to succeed. The teacher needs to reduce task complexity and task length. This can be done by presenting learners with only one part of the task at a time. This is where the task analysis becomes invaluable. The class can be presented with a series of subtasks, each of which is perceived as being within the ability of learners and of a relatively short duration. In some instances it is worthwhile mentioning the long-term goal so that class members understand the relevance of each subtask to the whole.

Presenting students with very clear and precise objectives is another means of reducing the perceived difficulty of a task. Stating the objectives in clear terms helps lessen the uncertainty and ambiguity so that learners can make a more accurate assessment of the effort required. If the teacher has already performed an informal diagnosis and a task analysis, then a clear objective stated at an appropriate level is likely to be an encouragement and lead to a perception that learners can complete the task without an inordinate amount of effort.

A clear outline of the task and demonstrating or modeling is yet another helpful technique. When learners see another perform the task and are presented with a clear outline of the procedure to be followed, they are more likely to arrive at a realistic assessment of the effort required.

Once the task has been presented and learners have started working, they then need to be provided with encouragement and feedback. This feedback should be concrete and specific, including both affirmation of what is being done correctly and correction of those aspects that are being performed incorrectly. This informs learners that their effort is paying off and that progress is being made toward the objective.

PROBABILITY OF SUCCESS

Few factors are more powerful in motivating individuals than success. All individuals have a need for achievement and a feeling of competence. Learners who feel that they are in a situation where their competence is stunted will not be motivated to continue working. Such is the case of many adults who believe that they are stuck in a job where there is no increase in skill or chance for advancement. These individuals, when possible, seek a better job, or if stuck in their current job, exert only a minimum amount of effort. Unfortunately, many youngsters arrive at school each morning with the attitude that they cannot be successful and that failure is inevitable.

Fear of Failure

Few people will attempt to perform a task for which they believe that they have little opportunity for success. One of our greatest fears is the fear of failure. Some anxiety about failure, if kept in perspective, can be a tool for motivating individuals. However, when this anxiety turns into an overpowering fear, learning is blocked.

Most of us seek to avoid situations where the probability of failure is high. And this is what occurs in many school settings. Students perceive little or no opportunity for success, so they emotionally and psychologically drop out. They see the situation as threatening and seek to avoid it. This avoidance may be accompanied by rationalizations that discredit the value and relevance of school or the learning task. If the teacher is perceived to be the cause of the threat, efforts may be made to discredit the teacher and cause him or her to feel like a failure. The anger and bitterness that accompany a situation where a youngster perceives little opportunity for success often result in aggressive and destructive behavior.

Competition as a Motivator

The importance of high expectations of success in motivating individuals prompts a reconsideration of the role of competition in the classroom. Many view competition as a major motivational tool. Competition does have value as a motivator, but only for those who think they can win. Contests where only one winner emerges are not likely to motivate a large number of learners. Only a very few will believe that they have an opportunity to win and thus expend the time and energy that the teacher desires. The rest of the class may make a token effort and then sit back and watch the others.

This principle helps explain the success of cooperative learning approaches. In cooperative learning approaches many individuals, not just one, can emerge as winners. Therefore, the estimation of the probability of success is significantly higher. In addition, the individual is encouraged because several individuals are working together toward the goal.

The Need for Achievement

Individuals must believe that they are achieving a higher level of competence in something that is important or relevant. Becoming more skilled in an area that is of no importance has no appeal for most people. Relevance or importance might be defined as something that is valued by society, something that is of importance to a significant other, or something that is related to a goal of the individual. If society places high status and respect on the acquisition of certain skills and an individual feels that it is emotionally safe to try and there is a possibility of success, then he or she will be motivated. If the skill is something that a significant other has (the identification motive), or if a significant other may reward the individual for acquiring the skill, motivation is increased.

Locus of Control

Understanding what has been termed the locus of control is important when using success as a motivator. Of central concern are the factors to which an individual attributes success or failure. People with an internal locus of control attribute success to their own effort or ability. Those with an external locus of control attribute success to luck or chance factors beyond their control. The basic question is "Why did I succeed or fail?"

Individuals with an internal locus of control tend to have higher task persistence and set higher levels of expected achievement, traits that the teacher desires (Fanelli 1977). Success is reinforcing for this type of individual because it confirms that his or her ability or effort paid off. On the other hand, individuals with an external locus of control do not believe that effort has any relationship to success, so there is no reason to exert much effort. Success has less impact on the motivation of such people because it is attributed to chance rather than effort. In sum, in order for success to have the desired impact on behavior, individuals need to believe success is a product of their effort and ability, not luck.

Increasing the Probability of Success

The classroom is an excellent setting for helping individuals meet the need for achievement and success. However, schools are typically based on competitive goal structures that minimize opportunities to identify and celebrate success. In addition, the typical reward, the report card, is administered too seldom to really help the youngster see progress and achievement. It is also very typical for the youngster then to view grades received as something "the teacher gave me" rather than something earned.

The teacher needs to find ways of visibly indicating short-term growth in achievement. One way of doing this is to establish reference points where achievement will be identified. Plotting or charting growth in achievement at these frequent reference points can help learners see the progress they has been made. The more failure that an individual has experienced in the past, the greater the need to have visible and concrete displays of success.

Making a realistic assessment of the probability of success can be facilitated by providing the learner with the criteria that will be used in evaluating the learning. Learners who have a clear understanding of what they will need to do to in order to be successful will be more prone to try than those who are uncertain of what is required. Teachers can inform learners of the criteria for success by clearly delineating them in the objectives for the lesson or by providing examples of the finished product.

Teachers may need to adjust the objective for those learners who have a history of failure. Even when the criteria for success are clear and successful models are provided, they may still believe that the task is impossible. For example, one elementary teacher was experiencing difficulty with a group of boys who never seemed to learn the spelling words for the week. After several weeks of failure, the teacher asked the group how many words a week they thought they could learn how to spell. After a short discussion the boys agreed that they could easily learn three words. The teacher then gave this group a three-word spelling list rather than the usual twenty. At the end of the week nearly all of the boys had learned the three words. After a couple of weeks of success, the teacher then asked if they thought they could learn five words. When they replied that they thought they could, he provided them with five-word spelling lists. Over the course of the year the teacher began to add more words as the group continued to experience success.

One important component in emphasizing success in the classroom is the attitude of the teacher. The attitude that is desirable is one that emphasizes success rather than failure. The teacher should stress the positive rather than the negative. One device that can be effective is marking and highlighting what a learner gets right on a paper rather than what is wrong. Taking a couple of minutes at the conclusion of a lesson to summarize, or have the class summarize, the important points of the lesson is yet another way of using success as a motivator. This summation reemphasizes to learners that they have learned something and are making progress.

It is important that the teacher constantly relate success to effort. Learners need to believe that success does not result by chance factor but is a product of their own effort. Through their testing procedures teachers often enforce the notion that success is merely the product of chance. Tests that include trick questions or those that are unrelated to important objectives communicate to the learner that effort is not as important as is trying to guess what the teacher might ask. The test needs to be viewed as an assessment of what an individual has learned, not as a device to spread students out on a grading curve. Testing, when done properly, can be an important tool for helping individuals feel successful and therefore be motivated to work even harder.

SUMMARY

Motivation is an essential component in preventing discipline problems. Human beings are complex and have a variety of needs and interests. This obvious fact makes motivation something that requires a great deal of knowledge, thought, and action. The successful teacher understands motivation and how it can be used to further the goals of the classroom. Three factors of motivation can be helpful as a teacher seeks to apply motivation theory in the classroom: the needs and interests of the individual, the perception of the difficulty of the task, and the probability of success. If the teacher can relate school tasks to the interests and the needs of the youngsters, reduce the perception of effort required to an acceptable level, and increase the probability of success, the resultant increased attention to school tasks and decrease of discipline problems will help make teaching a very rewarding career.

SUGGESTED ACTIVITIES

1. Interview several students and ask them the following questions:
   a . What are the things you like to do when given an opportunity?
   b.   What are the things you do in school that you find interesting? Why?

    c.   What are the things you do not like to do in school? Why?

    d.   Do you think that your teacher believes you are a good learner? Why do you have this feeling?

    e.   What could be done to make school a better place?

2. Choose a grade level that interests you and identify a figure from popular culture that the class might try to emulate. Develop a lesson plan that uses this person to motivate students to learn some academic content.

3. Identify content in your teaching area and perform a task analysis by doing the following:

    a.   Identify prerequisites that an individual should possess before starting the task.

    b.   State how you identify whether or not learners possess the prerequisites.

    c.   Brainstorm what a person would need to know or be able to do in order to be successful.

    d.   Order tasks and skills in a manner that they might logically be taught.

    e.   Develop an objective for each subtask or skill that could be communicated to the learners.

4. Observe a classroom and look for instances where physiological, psychological, and social needs are being accommodated and instances where you believe that they are not. State how you would attempt to meet those unmet needs.

BIBLIOGRAPHY

AMES, C., and R. AMES, eds. 1985. *Research on Motivation in Education, Vol. II: The classroom milieu.* Orlando, Fla.: Academic Press.

AMES, R., and C. AMES, eds. 1985. *Research on Motivation in Education, Vol. I: Student motivation.* Orlando, Fla.: Academic Press.

BALL, S. 1977. *Motivation in Education.* New York: Academic Press.

BROPHY, J. 1987. Synthesis of research on strategies for motivating students to learn. *Educational Leadership* 45, 40–48.

DREIKURS, R. 1968. *Psychology in the Classroom,* 2nd ed. New York: Harper & Row.
FANELLI, G. 1977. Locus of control. In S. Ball, ed. *Motivation in Education.* New York: Academic Press.

FEATHER, N., ed. 1982. *Expectations and Actions.* Hillsdale, N.J.: Erlbaum.

GLASSER, W. 1969. *Schools Without Failure.* New York: Harper & Row.

———. 1986. *Control Theory in the Classroom.* New York: Harper & Row.

GOOD, T., and J. BROPHY. 1987. *Looking in Classrooms,* 4th ed. New York: Harper & Row.

KLINGER, E. 1977. *Meaning and Void: Inner Experiences and the Incentives in People's Lives.* Minneapolis: University of Minnesota Press.

SCHAUSS, A. 1985. Research links nutrition to behavior disorders. *School Safety* (Winter), 20–28.

STIPEK, D. 1988. *Motivation to Learn*. Englewood Cliffs, N.J.: Prentice Hall.

WEINER, B. 1980. *Human Motivations*. New York: Holt, Rinehart, & Winston.

WEINSTEIN, D. 1985. Student mediation of classroom expectancy effects. In *Teacher Expectancies*, ed. J. Dusek. Hillsdale, N.J.: Erlbaum.

WHITE, M. N. 1977. Effects of nutrition on educational development. In *Motivation in Education*, ed. S. Ball. New York: Academic Press.

Chapter 4

ARRANGING THE PHYSICAL ENVIRONMENT

OBJECTIVES

This chapter provides information to help the reader to

1. State ways that the physical environment impacts behavior

2. List goals that a teacher should have when planning the classroom environment

3. Define the "action zone" in the classroom and state how it might be used to solve educational and behavioral problems

4. State the advantages and disadvantages of different types of seating arrangements commonly used in schools

5. List elements of the spatial dimension of the classroom that need to be considered in planning the environment

6. Define what is meant by the ambiance of a classroom and state the factors involved in creating the ambiance

7. Define the term *behavioral setting* and identify how to create a behavioral setting in the classroom

8. Discuss the impact of classroom density on student and teacher behavior

INTRODUCTION

The impact of the environment on behavior has been studied by scholars in several disciplines. Psychologists, sociologists, and architects are among those who have systematically studied the relationship between people and their physical surroundings. Their findings provide the basis for environments that are supportive of selected human activities. For example, shopping centers and stores are designed to support and encourage the buying behavior of customers. Similarly, workplaces in business and industry are designed to increase the productivity of employees.

Box 4-1
WHAT MAKES A PLACE COMFORTABLE?

All of us know places where we feel comfortable and places where we feel uncomfortable. Take a couple of minutes to reflect on a comfortable place and an uncomfortable place. Identify features of the physical environment that help create those feelings. Compare your conclusions with those of others in the class to see if common elements seem to make people comfortable or uncomfortable.

A place where I feel comfortable is _____.

A place where I feel uncomfortable is _____.

Elements of the environment that contribute to feelings of comfort:

Elements of the environment that create feelings of discomfort:

The physical setting does more than just enhance or inhibit certain activities. The very design of the space sends a silent message to all who enter. Weinstein and David (1987) point out that created environments in schools have both direct and symbolic impacts on learners. The direct impact of the built environment is the manner in which certain activities are facilitated and others are inhibited. For example, a certain arrangement of furniture and equipment may enhance large-group instruction and inhibit small-group approaches. The symbolic impact is the manner in which the values and intentions of the teacher are communicated, the excitement toward learning generated, the status or respect given to different individuals and activities, and the sense of comfort or threat that is present (Weinstein and David 1987).

The impact of the environment on behavior was also studied by Becker (1981). He indicates that the proportion of behavioral variance attributable to the environment will vary according to the level of competence, health, intelligence, and ego strength of those using the space. Those individuals with high feelings of competence and success will be less affected by the physical environment than those with low feelings of success and competence. This emphasizes the importance of the physical environment when dealing with learners with persistent behavior problems. It is probable that the physical environment will be more important in dealing with these students than with those who have few problems.

The organization of the environment influences learner perceptions of their place in the classroom, the sorts of activities that will be appropriate, and how they are expected to behave. Although the impact of these perceptions may change over time, first impressions have a lasting impact. They can facilitate the establishment of a positive learning environment and help move students toward self-control, or they can interfere to make progress and learning more difficult. It is therefore important for teachers to consider the impact of the environment they create on the behavior of students and consciously create environments that facilitate desirable behavior.

GOALS TO BE CONSIDERED WHEN PLANNING THE ENVIRONMENT

The systematic development of an environment conducive to learning begins with one's goals and purposes. The goals and purposes can then be used as a framework when considering various dimensions of the environment. Weinstein and David (1987) identify a number of goals that can be used for planning an environment: help learners develop a personal identity, encourage feelings of competence, promote intellectual growth and stimulation, provide a sense of security, and allow for both privacy and social interaction.

Developing Personal Identity

The development of a personal identity is enhanced by creating a classroom where learners feel they belong and where they have a sense of ownership. Students spend hundreds of hours in a classroom during an academic year. They must feel a sense of personal identity in the classroom, and it must be a place where they feel comfortable if they are to be open to learning and change.

Feelings of ownership and feelings of personal identity are enhanced by allowing students to participate in decision making about the use of space—the grouping of desks, room decorations, the organization and placement of learning centers. Allowing them the freedom to personalize their classroom helps students to develop a sense of belonging and pride. Elementary school students, who inhabit the same classroom sitting at the same desk all day, can be allowed to decorate their desk.

Secondary school students, who only inhabit the room for one period a day, can decorate or personalize at least some part of the room and make it their own.

Enhancing Competence and Security

Individuals thrust into an unfamiliar environment generally feel threatened and insecure. The goal of teachers should be to remove the threat and insecurity by helping students master the environment and feel comfortable in it. An important part of making the classroom a place where students have a feeling of comfort and competence is to make sure that the furnishings are appropriate for the size and the development of students. Individuals of any size or stage of development cannot be expected to demonstrate much task persistence if they are sitting in an uncomfortable chair or writing on an unstable work surface. It is not uncommon to visit classrooms where some students are sitting in chairs that are an improper size and where the work surfaces are inadequate for the tasks they are assigned. Fortunately, recent attempts in school design are considering the fact that not all students are physically the same and that there is a need for flexible furnishings.

For students to develop a sense of competence and security, the environment must be free of threat. The potential for physical harm is often a problem in shop classes, where there are lots of unfamiliar equipment, or science classes, where students might be afraid of the experiments. Young children might be fearful of unfamiliar equipment or animals that are kept in cages. Overcoming this fear requires that the teacher inform students of the use of the various objects in the classroom and help students become familiar with them.

Developing feelings of competence also requires that the classroom be a place where students have success and where success is celebrated. Teachers can structure the environment to celebrate success by making sure that bulletin boards and display areas include examples of successful work. This is relatively easy to accomplish in elementary schools, where students' work is often a prominent part of the classroom environment, but it can be more difficult in secondary schools. One high school teacher accomplished this task by displaying articles cut out of newspapers, recital programs, or other publications where students in her class were named. She made a concerted effort to find something to display for every student in her homeroom. The effort paid off with student respect and affection and an almost total absence of discipline problems.

Promoting Intellectual Growth and Stimulation

Promoting the intellectual growth of learners requires a rich and varied environment. This implies that the environment needs to be dynamic and changing rather than static. A classroom that is same for the entire year or from year to year communicates stagnation and boredom—a symbolic statement inviting discipline problems. Bulletin boards and display areas can be changed and updated on a regular basis in order to promote intellectual stimulation and communicate that the classroom is a dynamic, changing, and exciting place. Although this is an aspect of the physical environment that is overlooked by many teachers, the long-term effects of an ever-changing environment are very positive.

Changing the environment in order to promote cognitive growth and stimulation must be balanced with the need to develop a sense of security. Security is enhanced by continuity and predictability in the environment. Massive change in the organization of the space and seating assignments should be done infrequently. When changes are made learners should be involved.

Stimulation can be provided by occasionally changing the classroom seating and grouping patterns. Studies show that teachers tend to spend a great deal of their time in certain areas of the classroom. Therefore, they may not monitor the work of all students or provide good feedback to them. Changing the arrangement of seats from time to time so that different students sit close to the usual teacher work area will enhance students' at-task behavior and academic growth. A seating arrangement that facilitates quick teacher assistance to students helps create an environment in which intellectual growth is encouraged.

Accommodating Privacy Needs

Classrooms are generally organized to facilitate group activities and social interactions. They seldom consider individual needs for privacy. Although the typical classroom design makes it difficult to accommodate this need for privacy, it is one that can have an important impact on learner behavior. Probansky and Fabian (1987) note that a convincing case could be made that withdrawal, fantasy, and acting-out behaviors are strategies used by students for attaining privacy and isolation not normally permitted in classroom environments.

Weinstein and David (1987) also emphasize the need to consider privacy needs of students when designing the classroom environment. There are times when individuals like to be alone, away from the scrutiny of others. One way of accommodating this need is to designate one corner of the classroom as a private work area. This area may be set off by bookcases, file cabinets, or study carrels. Students move to that area to study or simply to be alone. Providing some sort of a retreat for students communicates to them that the teacher is concerned about them and their personal needs.

DIMENSIONS OF THE PHYSICAL ENVIRONMENT

Several aspects of the physical environment should be considered. One important dimension is the spatial dimension—the size, shape, and organization of objects within the space. Another is the classroom ambiance, or the feeling that one has when entering the space. The density of students in a given classroom also has an impact on behavior. Each of these dimensions is discussed in turn.

The Spatial Dimension

The size and shape of the room, the location of doors and windows, and the circulation and traffic patterns all form the spatial dimension of the classroom.

Although windows and doors cannot be moved and the size of the classroom cannot be changed, many aspects of the spatial dimension can be altered or controlled by the teacher. Some studies indicate that teachers are not very good at recognizing alternative arrangements and do not use space very effectively. Smith (1987) found that more than 45 percent of all classroom activity took place in just one-twelfth of the classroom space. So, even though space might be limited, teachers need to consider ways of using more of the classroom space. For example, teachers may move teaching stations around the room or designate different areas of the classroom for different activities so that learners use all of the available space.

The seating arrangement deserves special attention. Evidence of its importance for student behavior was found by Weinstein (1979). In a second-grade classroom a teacher and a researcher worked together and identified a number of behavioral problems. The seating arrangements were then systematically changed in an attempt to solve the problems. The result was a statistically significant decrease in the number of behavioral problems. Studies indicate that the participation of high school and college students in classroom   discussions is influenced by seating arrangement (Becker, 1981). Weinstein (1979) also indicates that student attitudes toward the class and toward the teacher are influenced by seating position. Studies of classroom "action zones" contribute additional support concerning the importance of student seating arrangements.

Action Zone. Several researchers have identified an area of the classroom that they have labeled the "action zone." The action zone consists of the seats across the front of the classroom and down the center. Those students sitting in this action zone participate in the class more, attend to a task a greater length of time, have higher achievement, and have more positive attitudes toward the class. One possible explanation for these findings is that the better students tend to choose these spots. There is some validity to this contention. Dykman and Reis (1979) found that the students who choose to sit on the periphery of the classroom generally feel more threatened and exhibit lower self-esteem that those who sit in the action zone. They contend that students who choose to sit on the periphery want to distance themselves from the threat posed by the teacher.

However, there is some evidence that the same positive outcomes occur when students are assigned seats in the action zone. Dykman and Reis (1979) offer a partial explanation for this finding. Those learners with lower self-esteem and who feel less secure and more threatened by the teacher tend to choose seats most distant from the teacher. As a consequence they get called on less frequently, are monitored less often, and are generally less involved in the class than those in the action zone. This neglect leads to increased failure, which in turn confirms their original feelings of self-doubt and fear. Moving such individuals into the action zone gets them involved, provides them with more opportunities for interaction with the teacher, and therefore begins to remove feelings of self-doubt and fear.

This knowledge about the action zone can be used in several ways to arrange the physical environment. One application is to arrange the seating so that students with academic and behavioral difficulties are in the action zone. Moving students into this area will increase the amount of time they spend on-task, allow them to receive more constructive feedback, and result in higher feelings of competence and intellectual growth.

Since the action zone is defined in reference to the position of the teacher, the location of the action zone will depend on the position of the teacher when instructing the class. The teacher can change the action zone by changing the teaching station. Teaching from different spots in the classroom is one way of utilizing the findings of the action zone without assigning seats. Some teachers prefer to allow students the opportunity, at least at the beginning of the year, to choose their own seats. This practice does have some merit. Smith (1987) found in a study of achievement that gains were greater in classes where students were allowed to choose their own seats. The security and comfort of choosing one's location in the classroom may well create a positive climate in which students are more open to instruction. A variation of this is to allow students to initially choose their own seats. Those few students who experience difficulty might then be gradually and unobtrusively moved into the action zone.

Teacher Proximity. The presence of an action zone in the classroom indicates the importance of teacher proximity to students. Other studies also indicate the importance of the teacher remaining as close to learners as possible. For example, Weinstein (1979) found that grades decrease as a student is seated farther away from the teacher. In addition, student participation and positive student attitudes decline as the distance between the teacher and students increases (Smith 1987). This is probably the result of teacher difficulty in monitoring and making contact with students who are some distance away. Students tend to stay on-task when the teacher is physically closer and this increased learning time translates into higher achievement and grades.

It is important that teachers attempt to be as close as possible to the largest number of students for the greatest amount of time. Thus, it is preferable to arrange the physical environment so that there are more students across the front of the room where the teacher spends much time rather than in fewer, longer rows. In addition, the teacher may choose to put the teacher's desk in a location that would be near the largest number of students. The arrangement of the traffic patterns should facilitate teacher movement so that teachers can easily spend a considerable amount of time in the midst of the learners as opposed to the periphery.

Arranging Student Desks. Student desks are the most dominant feature in the classroom. The discussion of the action zone and teacher proximity highlights the importance of giving the desk arrangement considerable thought. The arrangement of the desks provides the major setting or "frame" that shapes teacher-student interaction and the behavior of students (Rosenfield, Lambert, and Black 1985). Because different arrangements influence behavior in different ways, there is no best way to arrange desks. The arrangement will depend on several factors: the teaching approach used, the interaction pattern desired, the characteristics of learners, and the ability of the teacher to maintain control of the group.

Three basic seating arrangements are most commonly used in classrooms—rows, clusters, and circular or semicircular patterns. The advantage of rows all facing in one direction is that student interaction is limited, listening is enhanced, and independent work is facilitated. In addition, many teachers find that the row arrangement is easier to monitor and helps them establish and maintain classroom control. Weinstein (1979) cites studies indicating that organizing desks so that only two or three students could interact led to higher on-task behavior, less off-task movement, and less loud talking. The advantages of the circular arrangement are cited by Rosenfield, Lambert, and Black (1985). In fifth- and sixth-grade classrooms, they found a higher percentage of on-task verbal comments and higher attending behavior in discussions when the class was arranged in a circular pattern. They also found higher incidents of out-of-turn responses by students seated in a circle. This may indicate more student spontaneity when they are arranged in this format. Students seated in cluster arrangements demonstrated more ordered turns while still maintaining a high percentage of on-task verbal behavior. When participation in a discussion was used as a criterion those seated in rows had higher incidents of withdrawal and more off-task verbal comments.

These findings imply that if the teacher is concerned with limiting student interaction, promoting independent work, and prompting at-task behavior, then the row arrangement would be the proper choice. However, if the intention is to promote a discussion climate where freedom and spontaneity are the primary goals, then a circle would be best. Those teachers who want high participation in a discussion yet want to maintain a more ordered less spontaneous environment might group the students into clusters.

Box 4-2
EVALUATING A ROOM ARRANGEMENT

The room arrangement shown here was observed in an elementary school. Look at the arrangement and answer the following questions.

1. **What activities are enhanced by this arrangement?**

2. **What activities would be difficult in this room?**

3. **What does the arrangement reflect of the philosophy and values of the teacher about teaching and learning?**

4. **What advantages, if any, do you see with this arrangement?**

5. **What problems, if any, do you see with this arrangement?**

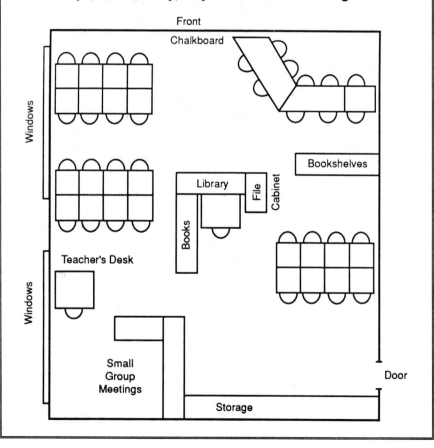

Some authorities recommend that teachers begin the school year with desks in rows facing the major instructional areas and then move to other desk arrangements after the teacher has established control of the classroom (Emmer et al. 1989). This helps prevent discipline problems during the critical beginning phases of the school year. This suggestion has a great deal of merit for teachers who are insecure or who are concerned about their ability to control the classroom. Once teacher confidence grows, the teacher may move to less traditional arrangements.

Student self-control is another factor to consider when arranging seating. Those students who have a high degree of self-control might be grouped into clusters for a large portion of the day. Such students are able to overcome the distractions of others seated near them and can resist the temptation to socialize at inappropriate times. However, those learners who lack self-control should be arranged in rows so that the possibilities of social interaction are limited. As they develop self-control and learn to participate in discussions and cooperative learning groups, then the arrangement can be gradually changed to more of a cluster arrangement.

Traffic Patterns. Attention needs to be directed to how individuals move around the classroom. High traffic areas need to have plenty of space and be kept free of desks and obstructions. Teacher movement is important in order to monitor student work and behavior. Therefore, the room arrangement should allow the teacher easy access to all learners. The best design would make it easy for the teacher to be at any student's desk within seconds. This arrangement facilitates movement around the room and helps keep the teacher in close proximity to the learners.Teacher's Desk. The traditional place for the teacher's desk has been in front of the classroom. However, this location is probably not the best. A better spot for the teacher's desk is in a less dominant and obtrusive spot, preferably in a corner or near the rear of the room (Weinstein 1979). One major reason for this recommendation is that the desk at the front of the room makes it easy for the teacher to teach from the desk. This prompts the bad habit of directing all activities from the desk and cuts down on the amount of movement of the teacher around the room. Teaching from behind the desk usually results in higher off-task behavior and lower positive student attitudes toward the teacher (Smith 1979).

Placing the teacher's desk in an unobtrusive spot also allows the teacher the opportunity to conduct conferences with students with some degree of privacy. The conference does not become a central focus of the class, and the privacy needs of the student can be accommodated. Students will feel more comfortable sharing feelings with the teacher, as the embarrassment that might accompany a conference is reduced and the temptation to save face in front of peers is eliminated.

Finally, placement near the rear of the room tends to promote higher student at-task behavior. Students tend to stay on-task if they are unaware of where the teacher is. In order to check on the location of the teacher, students must turn around. This behavior often indicates difficulty and allows the teacher to opportunity to move to the area and prevent problems from occurring.

Identifying Activity Boundaries. Identifying boundaries for different activities helps to provide students with a sense of security and assists them in maintaining self-control. Clearly delineated boundaries serve as reminders of the types of behavior appropriate in different areas of the room and for different activities. Bookcases and file cabinets are especially useful for this purpose and can be used to change the shape of the physical environment—for example, to separate small-group work areas, learning centers, and independent work areas from large-group instruction. As indicated earlier, they can be used to separate off an area to meet privacy needs of students.

In addition, changing the shape of the classroom serves to promote sensory stimulation by making the room different from others. Students tend to get bored when every classroom is the same size, the same shape, and organized in rows facing in the same direction. Care should be taken, however, that boundaries do not interfere with the ability of the teacher to monitor quickly all areas of the classroom. The placement of visual barriers so that student behavior cannot be quickly and quietly observed creates a condition that invites misbehavior.

THE CLASSROOM AMBIANCE

Ambiance refers to the feelings that an individual gets when entering a place. An environment might communicate a feeling of excitement or a sense of quiet and peace. Some environments are attractive and inviting, others ugly and forbidding. The ambiance of a place is created through orderliness, light, sound, texture, color, temperature, and odor. These elements can be combined in ways that are pleasant to create feelings of comfort, security, and warmth, or they may create a sense of insecurity, threat, and coldness.

The ambiance of the classroom and classroom decorations have been the subject of debate. Some teachers argue that their role is not that of an interior decorator and that "beautiful" environments are not important. It is true that some teachers lose their sense of perspective and place too much emphasis on order and beauty at the expense of comfort and function. The basic issue, however, is not the creation of beautiful classrooms, but how the classroom impacts those who must spend a considerable amount of time there. The classroom is a living and a work space for both teacher and learners for a significant part of the day, and the ambiance will influence the attitudes and the work of both.

The influence of the classroom ambiance on teacher and student behavior is noted by Weinstein (1979). Studies indicate that as the quality of the classroom ambiance decreases, incidents of teacher control statements increase, teacher behavior becomes less friendly and sensitive, students are involved less, and conflict among students increases. Other studies provide additional support for the importance of the classroom ambiance. These studies indicate that environments or classrooms classified as "ugly" produce greater feelings of fatigue and discontent and a desire to escape by those who inhabit them. On the other hand, environments classified as "cheerful" contribute to task persistence.

Box 4-3
I WAS HIRED TO TEACH NOT DECORATE!

A teacher made the following statement:

I was hired to teach, not to serve as an interior decorator. I think that time spent on the room environment is wasted time. It would be better spent planning lessons and developing material. Students are in school to learn, not to attend an art show. If the school district thinks it is important to have beautiful classrooms, let them hire a decorator.

What do you think?

1.   **Are there any points that this teacher makes with which you agree?**

2.   **What is the impact of the room environment on students?**

3.   **What is the purpose of room decorations?**

4.   **How can a room be made attractive with a minimum of time and effort?**

These findings indicate that the creation of a classroom ambiance is an important part in creating an environment where problems are prevented and desirable behaviors supported. The idea that the environment does exert a powerful influence on those who inhabit the space has been refined in the concept of "behavioral settings."

Behavioral Settings. Researchers in architecture and psychology who have conducted studies on the impact of the environment on behavior developed the concept of behavioral settings. The concept is widely used by architects as they design space. A behavioral setting is a place where the behaviors exhibited in the space remain relatively constant even though the occupants of the space may change (Weinstein 1979), as in churches, offices, restaurants, and schools. Some behaviors are desirable in these settings and others are not. The ambiance that is formed using combinations of light, color, temperature, and spatial organization creates a behavioral setting.

Since a classroom is a behavioral setting, it is important for teachers to ask, What types of behaviors do I want the students to exhibit? Do I want to excite students or calm them down? Do I want to encourage or discourage social interaction? Once teachers are clear about the answers to such questions they can consider how the environment needs to be changed in order to create the setting that will elicit the desired behaviors. Teachers who design very informal classrooms should not be surprised when students behave informally. Similarly, teachers who design very stiff and formal classrooms should not expect their students to demonstrate spontaneity.

Teachers who wish to create behavioral settings where creativity is promoted should use bright colors, a variety of objects to provide sensory stimulation, and bulletin boards that pose problems rather than give information. Teachers concerned with decreasing student activity should use softer colors, plan bulletin boards that are decorative rather than provocative, soften the lighting, and have a very orderly room arrangement. These dimensions are aspects of the room environment that can be manipulated to create the desired ambiance or behavioral setting.

Softening the Environment. Softer environments can be created by having flexible lighting and by adding carpeting to the floors, decorations to the walls, and live plants to the room. Studies of high school and college students revealed better attendance, more student participation, and higher student evaluations of the teacher in those rooms where the environment was classified as softer.

Classroom Lighting. Changing the lighting is difficult because many rooms have overhead lights controlled by one or two light switches. However, not everyone works best with the same type of lighting. Some individuals work better under the softer glow of desk lamps or floor lamps. If possible, teachers should try to provide spaces where students can choose to work under the type of lighting most favorable for them.

Background Music. Another feature of the ambiance of the classroom might be soft background music when learners are working independently. Charles (1983) cites research indicating that background music lowers the pulse rate and blood pressure and increases academic performance. One problem with music is that not everyone enjoys the same type of music. Music that might be stimulating to one individual might be irritating to another. However, a background of some soft music provides sensory stimulation and masks intruding sounds.

Generally, the goal of the teacher in creating a classroom ambiance and behavioral setting should be an environment that is businesslike, yet warm and stimulating. Students should get the feeling that learning is important and that the teacher is serious about teaching and learning. However, they should also get the

feeling that learning in this room is going to be stimulating and exciting. The classroom should be a pleasant place where they like to be.

CLASSROOM DENSITY

The density of individuals in the space is another aspect of the physical environment that influences behavior. Density refers to the numbers of individuals who occupy a given space. Teachers are concerned about classes that are too dense or overcrowded and report increased difficulty teaching and managing student behavior in such environments. Although the impact of increased density on student achievement is still an item of debate, some researchers have studied the impact of density on behavior. Learners in crowded classrooms demonstrate less attentive behavior and more aggression and deviant behavior (Probansky and Fabian 1987). Withdrawal is another common behavior exhibited by students in crowded classrooms (Weinstein 1979).

How much density is too much is influenced by cultural norms. Individuals from certain cultures are able to tolerate a large number of people in a given space without classifying it as crowded, whereas individuals with a different cultural background would find the same density excessively crowded. The important concern is not the actual number of learners but, rather, their perceptions of whether or not they are crowded. One study found that those students who performed poorly in a classroom with relatively high density were those who classified the room as crowded (Weinstein 1979).

Several factors help to explain the impact of density on student and teacher behavior. High-density classrooms decrease the amount of privacy for students and increase opportunities for social interaction. These two factors may then result in anxiety and interpersonal conflict. High-density classrooms also create competition for the attention of the teacher. Students who have high attention needs may feel forced to misbehave in order to attract attention. The loss of opportunities to interact with the teacher may also be a factor influencing student achievement in high-density classrooms.

Lowering the density of individuals in a given space may not always be desirable. Placing more individuals into a smaller space will increase the interaction among individuals. Therefore, higher densities are desirable when the task to be completed requires communication and cooperation among students. Activities such as cooperative learning and small-group work are then enhanced.

SUMMARY

The physical environment of a classroom does influence student behavior. The design of the classroom makes some activities possible and eliminates others. In addition, the environment sends symbolic messages to all who enter about the values and the intentions of the teacher. Teachers who wish to minimize problems are well advised to consider the messages their classroom environment is sending to students and how it is facilitating the outcomes they desire.

In order to design productive environments, teachers should plan environments that help students develop personal identity, encourage feelings of competence and security, promote intellectual stimulation and growth, and allow for privacy when it is desired. Attending to the spatial dimension of the classroom, which includes the way seats are arranged, the proximity of the teacher to the students, the movement of the teacher around the space, and the ambiance of the room, helps teachers accomplish these goals. The concept of behavioral settings is useful when teachers begin consideration of the classroom plan. Creating a behavioral setting that is consistent with teacher expectations requires that teachers consider the goals and expectations they have for the classroom. Clearly delineating these goals and expectations can then be used to plan an environment where desired behaviors can occur.

SUGGESTED ACTIVITIES

1. Analyze a classroom in your school. What is the ambiance of the room? What is there about the classroom that creates the ambiance? How does the arrangement of the room facilitate the attainment of educational objectives? How does it interfere with the attainment of educational objectives?

2. Visit several classrooms and note the extent to which the rooms are organized to meet the goals of developing a personal identity, encouraging competence and security, providing for intellectual stimulation and growth, and allowing for

privacy. Identify changes that might help create an environment more supportive of these goals.

3 . Observe two or more teachers as they conduct class. Map their movement patterns in the classroom. Which parts of the classroom are visited most frequently? Which students are in closest proximity to the teacher more of the time? What recommendations would you make regarding teacher movement in the classroom?.

4. Observe a classroom and note the location of the students who are called on most frequently. Where are these students seated in the classroom? Is the interaction pattern consistent with the action zone?

5. Draw a plan for your ideal classroom. Write a statement explaining your plan and giving your reasons for the arrangement.

BIBLIOGRAPHY

BECKER, F. 1981. *Workspace: Creating Environments in Organizations.* New York: Praeger.

CASTALDI, B. 1987. *Educational Facilities.* Boston: Allyn & Bacon.

CHARLES, C. 1983. *Elementary Classroom Management.* New York: Longman.

DYKMAN, B., and H. REIS. 1979. Personality correlates of classroom seating position. *Journal of Educational Psychology,* 71, 3, 346–354.

EMMER, E., C. EVERTSON, J. SANFORD, B. CLEMENTS, and M. WORSHAM. 1989. *Classroom Management for Secondary Teachers,* 2nd ed. Englewood Cliffs, N.J.: Prentice Hall.

PROBANSKY, H., and A. FABIAN. 1987. Development of place identity in the child. In *Spaces for Children,* ed. C. Weinstein and T. David. New York: Plenum.

SMITH, H. 1987. Nonverbal communication. In *The International Encyclopedia of Teaching and Teacher Education,* ed. M. Dunkin, pp. 466–477. New York: Pergamon.

ROSENFIELD, P., N. LAMBERT, and A. BLACK. 1985. Desk arrangement effects on pupil classroom behavior. *Journal of Educational Psychology,* 77, 1, 101–108.

WEINSTEIN, C. 1979. The physical environment of the school: A review of the research. *Review of Educational Research,* 49, 4, 577–610.

———, and T. DAVID, eds. 1987. *Spaces for Children.* New York: Plenum.

WIATROWSKI, M., G. GOTTFREDSON, and M. ROBERTS. 1983. Understanding school behavior disruption: Classifying school environments. *Environment and Behavior,* 15, 1, 53–76.

Chapter 5

ESTABLISHING CONTROL THROUGH TIME MANAGEMENT

OBJECTIVES

This chapter provides information to help the reader to

1. Identify three different concepts of classroom time and state their importance in teaching

2. List those factors that influence time-allocation decisions

3. State the importance of maximizing time spent focusing on the lesson objective

4. List tasksand activities for which classroom routines are needed

5. Identify how teachers can use a reference group in making pacing decisions

6. State the importance of providing clear directions

7. Identify problems associated with transition time

8. List ways teachers can improve the monitoring of student work

INTRODUCTION

Members of the class were noisily filing into the room as the bell rang. Most seemed unconcerned about the bell and continued socializing with friends. The teacher asked the students to be seated so that she could take attendance. Several students complied while continuing to talk. The teacher began taking attendance and occasionally inquired about the presence of a particular student. Once attendance was completed, the required form was completed and posted near the door to be picked up by the attendance monitor and taken to the main office. At this point, the teacher announced the return of homework papers and began calling out names and moving about the room to return the papers. Afterward, the teacher began asking for silence. Initial calls were unheard because of the conversation level. Gradually the class began to quiet down. At this point the teacher began to admonish class members for the high noise level. The students were then told to open their books to page 100. This was greeted by several groans and two inquiries concerning forgotten books. A third youngster wanted to know if a pencil would be required. A general undercurrent of murmuring and discussion began to swell up in the room. Ten minutes of the class period had now elapsed, and the frustration and anger of the teacher were beginning to show.

This scenario illustrates the importance of time management in preventing discipline problems. The youngsters in the class were having trouble getting started because they had been allowed to sit with nothing to do. This prompted a considerable amount of socialization and made it difficult for the teacher to establish a positive climate for learning. In addition, the teacher's frustration prompted a lecture about poor behavior, which started the class on a negative tone. It is likely that this frustration will continue to build, and the day will not be a good one for the teacher or the students.

What is regrettable about this incident is that it could have been prevented. Careful planning and some attention to basic time management could have completely changed the climate of the classroom and started it off on a positive direction. The fact that students showed no concern about being on time is indicative of a classroom where the teacher does not communicate the importance of being on time. A rule about students being in their seats when the bell rings would help eliminate one problem. The inefficient procedures for taking attendance and returning corrected work wasted more valuable time. Correcting these management errors and establishing a routine for all students to follow at the beginning of class would eliminate many problems and help this teacher find much more satisfaction in teaching.

Is this a realistic example? The answer to that is yes! A large portion of every class day and instructional period is spent on tasks unrelated to learning. In the usual classroom a number of minutes each day are wasted because of inefficient time management. Capturing these wasted minutes has great potential not only for preventing discipline problems but for enhancing student achievement. For example, if teachers were able to claim only 5 more minutes a day for instruction, they would add 15 hours of instructional time for the year, the equivalent of adding 18 more class periods to a secondary class that meets for 50 minutes a day. It is a relatively safe prediction that those students receiving the equivalent of 18 more class periods will learn more than those who do not.

This chapter outlines some of the methods a teacher can use for managing class time and promoting on-task behavior. The discussion covers using time productively, giving directions, pacing classroom activities, establishing classroom procedures and routines, monitoring student work, managing transitions, and responding to inappropriate behavior.

Box 5-1
WHAT WOULD YOU DO?

Reread the scenario at the beginning of the chapter. See if you can identify the management errors that the teacher made. Write your suggestions for helping the teacher start the class promptly.

Management Errors Made by the Teacher:

Recommendations for the Teacher:

UNDERSTANDING DIFFERENT TYPES OF TIME

Effective time management that keeps students on-task is a key element in preventing problems and in stimulating student achievement. Individuals with nothing to do become bored and search for some sort of sensory stimulation. Unfortunately, the stimulation they seek will probably be something that will create problems for the teacher.

Decisions about time management begin during the planning stage and continue through the conclusion of the lesson. Three different types of time can be used by the teacher to plan and implement a lesson that will minimize discipline problems and maximize student achievement.

Time Allocation Decision Making

One type of time that needs to be considered in improving time management in the classroom is "allocated time." This refers to the actual time that the teacher allocates for teaching a skill or a concept. Considerable evidence indicates that the time allocated for a given subject in the curriculum or for a given concept varies greatly among teachers (Berliner 1984). For example, one elementary school teacher may allocate 30 minutes a day for reading instruction, whereas another teacher at the same grade level in the same school may allocate 90 minutes to reading instruction. Secondary school teachers also show great variation in the amount of time they allocate their content area. Science teachers vary considerably in the amount of time they spend in the lab and the amount they spend in direct instruction, English teachers differ in the amount of time they spend on writing and literature or on different types of literature, social studies teachers differ in the amount of time they spend on different topics, and math teachers vary in the amount of time they spend on different concepts.

Although one would expect some variation among teachers in the allocation of time because of the ability level of the students, the skill of the teacher, and the interests of the students, the wide variation observed in many classes is extensive. In fact, time-allocation decisions are more often made according to teacher interest and preference than student needs and abilities. Teachers who like reading teach more reading; teachers who dislike science or social studies allocate little time to those subjects. An English teacher who feels comfortable with and likes a particular work by Shakespeare will allocate more time to that work than to others. A social studies teacher who is fascinated with one historical era will spend considerable time on that era and may skip some periods altogether.

It is natural for an individual to spend more time on something that is enjoyable, and teachers are certainly no exception to this rule. However, teachers must remember that school is for the learner, not the teacher. They have a professional and ethical obligation to teach those subjects and concepts that are important for the future well-being of learners. Many adults end up ill-prepared for a future class or assignment because of teachers who had ignored important segments of the curriculum. To ignore a subject, such as science in an elementary classroom or significant lab experiences in a secondary classroom, may well hinder the performance of students on future tasks. In addition, omitting some aspects of the curriculum in the classroom may actually deprive some students of the opportunity for success. Because some students might be interested in or skilled in the subject, including the topic could help them achieve success as well as enhance motivation in other topics.

Teachers faced with decisions about how to allocate time can obtain guidance by asking several questions:

First, *What do learners need to know?* The decision about how much time to spend on different topics should be related to educational needs and objectives rather than the personal interests of the teacher. If a given group of learners is deficient in some necessary skill, time should be allocated to teaching that skill. The future needs of the youngsters should also be considered so that their development in a given subject is not hindered.

Second, *How much time will be required for this group of students to achieve success and a sense of competence?* Covering topics too quickly creates a sense of frustration and will lower future motivation. Students need to develop a growing sense of competence and mastery, and the amount of time needed to meet these needs will vary from student to student.

A third question is, *Am I allocating so much time to this subject that students will become bored and lose interest in the topic altogether?* Too much time can be just as deadly as too little. While students need to master the subject, they should not be drilled to the point where they lose interest.

Finally, *Am I providing a balanced curriculum?* Time should be allocated to all of those areas that the students will be expected to learn. This question addresses the ethical and professional concerns of whether teachers are meeting district and state requirements and are doing so in a fair and responsible manner. Providing a balance will also increase the probability that all learners can find some place to achieve success.

Box 5-2
KEEP THEM BUSY AT ALL TIMES

Mrs. Tao believes that students should be kept busy the entire time they are in class regardless of what they are doing. She prepares a number of tasks and assignments for students to complete when they finish daily assignments. This work is of a general nature and often includes practice of previously learned material. For the most part, this procedure works very well. However, Mrs. Tao does have a couple of concerns. It seems that fewer and fewer students are completing their assigned work. In addition, she states that she must constantly patrol the classroom in order to keep students on-task. She attributes this poor work pattern to short attention spans and the need for students to be constantly entertained. "Students can't seem to stay on-task for more than a couple of minutes at a time. I think it is because they are used to watching television. and being entertained all the time."

What do you think?

1.   **Do you agree with Mrs. Tao's analysis?**

2.   **What parts of her plan have merit?**

3.   **What alternative hypothesis might explain the behavior of the students?**

4.   **What would you recommend that Mrs. Tao try to get more students to complete their work and yet prevent misbehavior at the end of the class time ?**

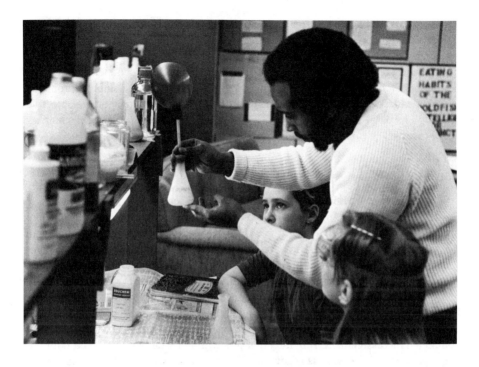

Time Spent Focused on the Lesson Objective

Once the time-allocation decisions are made, the focus should then shift to how time is actually spent in the classroom. One guiding principle is to spend a maximum amount of classroom time focused on the instructional objective. This concept is sometimes referred to as "engaged time." Engaged time is often used to indicate the amount of time students actually spend working. However, time related to the objective is a little more precise and useful than just engaged time. Some teachers, in an effort to increase engaged time, require students to work on a large number of tasks and assignments so that they will be kept busy or engaged. Unfortunately, some of these assignments are merely busywork and serve no useful function in helping the students further their understanding of the lesson's objective. So it is not merely the engaged time that is important but the amount of time that is spent working on the objective.

The amount of time related to the objective is determined by subtracting from the allocated time the amount of classroom time that is spent doing tasks unrelated to the objective for the lesson, such as the routine duties of taking attendance, returning papers, distributing materials, or handling discipline problems. For example, a teacher may have allocated 45 minutes for teaching a given concept. However, if 5 minutes are spent taking attendance, 2 minutes for announcements, 3 minutes to return papers, 3 minutes to distribute materials, 3 minutes to handle discipline problems, and 4 minutes to clean up at the end of the period, 20 minutes have been spent on tasks unrelated to the objective so that the actual time spent on the objective was only 25 minutes.

A teacher can begin to maximize the amount of time spent focusing on the objective by considering all those places where time might be spent performing tasks that are not directly related to the lesson objective. Interruptions, discipline problems, taking attendance, and making announcements take away time spent on the objective. Although some of these are necessary and can be dealt with in an efficient manner, the unessential ones should be eliminated.

Maximizing Academic Learning Time

A third aspect of time usage is maximizing the academic learning time of each learner. Academic learning time is a step beyond the amount of time spent focusing on the objective and is the most important aspect of time management. Academic learning time is the amount of time the learner is focusing on the objective and being successful. For example, Johnny may spend 30 minutes of the allocated time actually working on tasks that are related to the objective. However, at the conclusion of the lesson, he has no success because he has done the assignment incorrectly. Johnny has had 0 minutes of academic learning time. On the other hand, Jose spent only 15 minutes of the allocated time actually focusing on the objective. However, he successfully completed the assignment. Provided that this was an assignment he could not do at the beginning of the class, his academic learning time would total 15 minutes.

Academic learning time is time that translates into success and achievement gains for students. It provides them with a growing sense of competence and a realization that time spent working will have a payoff. This translates into increased motivation. Therefore, it is not just allocating more time or keeping the students busy that is key to successful time management. It is keeping them working with a high level of success.

Increasing the academic learning time for all students is an important part of the link between good teaching and the prevention of discipline problems. Teachers interested in maximizing academic learning time need to ask the basic question, What is preventing students from achieving success on this lesson? Those barriers directly related to teacher behavior need to be eliminated. These include teaching at a level that is too difficult or too easy for the academic level of the students, providing unclear instruction and confused directions, not identifying and correcting student misunderstanding and learning difficulties, or maintaining an inappropriate lesson pace. To overcome these potential problems, teachers must stay active and alert during the entire lesson. They must also keep students alert and constantly check for student understanding. When students are working independently, the teacher needs to actively monitor student work in order to provide individual assistance and give corrective feedback quickly.

Consideration of these three aspects of time is the beginning point for making good time management decisions. Teachers who consider how they are allocating the time, spend most of the time focusing on activities relevant to the objectives, and try to ensure maximum learner success will eliminate the boredom and frustration that are at the root of many discipline problems. The following section focuses on those areas related to the productive use of time in the classroom.

ESTABLISHING CLASSROOM ROUTINES

Much time is lost in handling routine chores. Such tasks as taking attendance, distributing materials, making announcements, and collecting work are central to the role of the teacher. Other problems, such as students who come to class without proper materials, with broken pencils, and requests for special privileges, occur less frequently but are just as predictable. Success in handling these interruptions is basic to effective time management. These concerns should be considered before the school year begins and appropriate procedures developed for handling them in a quick and efficient manner.

Identifying Predictable and Recurring Events

The first step in eliminating wasted time is to identify those events that occur in the normal course of a day and develop a routine to handle each one. This is a basic management principle regardless of the setting. A good manager, whether in the classroom or the business office, will anticipate routine events and know on how to handle them. This is important for the well-being of the manager/teacher. If he or she must stop and respond to each routine event, not only is time lost but the teacher/manager will soon become mentally and physically fatigued. Energy needs to be conserved and directed toward the exceptions or unpredictable events.

Teachers need to develop classroom routines that are simple, easily understood, quickly performed, and as unobtrusive as possible. These routines should then be taught to the students as they are needed. The first few weeks of the school year should include time to teach these routines and to reinforce them. This time spent at the beginning will save a great amount of time during the school year.

Areas Where Routines Are Needed

The areas where routines will be needed, as well as the types of routines, vary according to grade level and learning environment. Kindergarten youngsters demand a different set of routines than do upper elementary. Secondary school classrooms require different routines than self-contained elementary school classrooms. However, in general, some tasks and events are predictable for all classes. Discussion of some basic areas where routines might be needed follows.

Beginning the Class Period or the School Day. It is important that the class period or the school day begin quickly and efficiently. Several routines may need to be done during this time: attendance taken, homework collected, absences from the previous day checked, lunch count taken, announcements made. Other tasks include handling tardy students and making sure that each student has the required books and materials.

Box 5-3
GIVE THE STUDENTS RESPONSIBILITY

Ms. Epstein believes in giving students responsibility. In addition, she likes to reinforce those students who have been following the rules. She does not assign certain students tasks but chooses students to pass out materials, collect papers, and perform other classroom tasks based on their behavior at that time. By the time she chooses students and they do what is required, several minutes of class time have elapsed. In addition, those students not chosen get upset and complain that they never get a chance. Handling their complaints also wastes additional time and sometimes creates a discipline problem.

What do you think?

1.   **What is positive about Ms. Epstein's approach?**

2.   **Why do you think she has these problems?**

3.   **What do you suggest as a solution to her problems?**

Whenever possible, students should perform these routine tasks. This allows the teacher time to make sure that everyone is starting to work. One efficient way of handling the opening routines is to have an activity on the board or on the overhead projector for students to begin as soon as they are seated—perhaps, review questions, an outline or advance organizer for the day's lesson, the answer sheet for homework, or some fun activity such as a puzzle or riddle. This helps engage student attention at the beginning and helps eliminate the excessive socialization that often delays the start of class. While students are working on the activity, the teacher and student helpers finish the administrative tasks.

Use of Classroom Space and School Facilities. Teachers must establish procedures so that students understand what is expected of them while in the classroom, as well as in other parts of the school. This includes procedures for entering and leaving the room, moving from one group or activity to another, going to learning centers, using the computers, using the pencil sharpener, using the drinking fountain, working with other students, or leaving the classroom to go to the restroom, the library, the cafeteria, the nurse, the counselor, or the main office.

Also consider procedures for handling student and teacher possessions. If possible, student possessions should be kept in an unobtrusive place such as under the student desk or in a designated area of the room. This helps eliminate unnecessary distractions during classroom presentations. The teacher should also have clear procedures for borrowing or using teacher-owned materials and the teacher's desk. Most teachers inform students that they are not to take anything from the teacher's desk without permission, and they are not to go through the desk or personal possessions of the teacher. The teacher should also respect the privacy of students and not borrow any student-owned possession or look through their possessions without being invited to do so.

Managing Student Work. Managing student work involves developing procedures for collecting completed work, returning papers, making up missed assignments, turning in late assignments, and correcting or redoing poorly executed assignments. Developing routines for how papers are to be headed, the writing instrument to be used, and how to handle mistakes can also result in time savings and more efficient handling of student work.

In managing student work, the teacher needs to consider how assignments will be made. Many teachers write assignments on an overhead projector or on the chalkboard before the beginning of class. Others place written assignments in student folders or notebooks. It is helpful to post long-term assignments on a designated bulletin board so that students are constantly reminded of due dates. Do not rely on oral explanations of assignments. Oral assignments are easily, and conveniently, forgotten. When making an assignment for seat work, the teacher should provide the instructions along with an example of what is to be done. This can be included on the paper or on the overhead projector so that it is visible for all students. This simple procedure saves an amazing amount of time by eliminating the several minutes of delay caused by numerous students claiming that they don't know what to do. It is especially important that homework assignments include clear directions. This helps parents to understand the assignment, assist their children, and hold them accountable for doing the work. Few things are more frustrating for a parent than trying to help a child with schoolwork and not being able to understand the assignment. Such a situation can seriously erode the credibility of the teacher in the eyes of the parent.

Another important part of managing student work is establishing a procedure for students to follow when they have completed the assignment. Teachers often instruct them to read a book, complete unfinished work, move to a learning center, or engage in acceptable free-time activities. The type of routine will vary with the type of the class and the preferences of the teacher. The important point is to make sure that when students finish their assignments, they do not become bored or begin bothering other students.

Managing Materials. Classrooms are generally materials-rich environments. Books, papers, reference works, audiovisual equipment, art supplies, lab equipment, and special machines are found in most classrooms. The constant use and distribution of supplies can be a source of wasted time. Materials and equipment should be ready before the students begin a lesson. They should be stored in a location that is easily accessible so that they can be returned efficiently. Procedures are also necessary for passing out needed materials quickly with a minimum of movement and disruption. Students should know when they are free to obtain needed material and how they are to behave when doing so.

Those teachers who have special equipment in their classrooms should remember that careful instruction is needed before allowing students to use the equipment. Not doing so is to invite legal charges of negligence should a student become injured. Careful supervision of objects such as paper cutters and audiovisual equipment is an absolute must. Not only does the teacher need to ensure that students have been instructed in their use, but the equipment also needs to be inspected to make sure it is in proper working order and that all safety guards are in place.

Ending the Class Period. Youngsters are keenly aware of the time when the class is over. Some students begin preparing for their exit several minutes before the bell rings. Even college professors do not need a bell to remind them of the end of the class. The behavior of the students sends them a very clear signal that the end is near. In order to avoid the wasted time caused by class members preparing for their departure before the allocated time, teachers should develop a procedure to cue students when it is appropriate for them to begin their end-of-class activities. It is important for the teacher to insist that students continue working until they are told to finish.

One practical procedure might be to set aside a minute or two to review what was accomplished during the period and then to verbally dismiss the students. This helps the teacher make sure that the students leave with the important points and helps avoid the chaos that can occur when youngsters jump up to leave the second the bell rings. In order to make this procedure work, the teacher needs to follow it on a daily basis, insist on compliance, and make sure that class activities are terminated on time. Teachers who are often late in dismissing their students create anxiety and invite disobedience. Instead, they should develop the following agreement with the class: "If you work until I tell you to stop, I will dismiss you on time." Consistently following this informal agreement will prompt a sense of trust and will have the effect of keeping the students on-task rather than constantly watching the clock.

Routines for Emergencies. Each school has a set of procedures to be used during fire and emergency drills. It is imperative for teachers to identify these before school starts, teach them to their students, and practice them early in the school year. In fact, most schools hold emergency drills some time near the beginning of the year so that the school is prepared for any emergency that might arise.

Developing and Teaching Routines

Teachers should develop routines that can be performed quickly, are easily learned and remembered, and involve minimum amounts of movement, noise, and disruptions. Once the routines are developed, they need to be taught to class members as they are needed. It is unnecessary to teach all of the routines during the first week of the class. Only the most important should be taught at the beginning. New routines can be added as new situations arise.

Routines are learned like anything else, through explanation, modeling, practice, and reinforcement. When introducing the routines to the class, the teacher should identify the problem, state the rationale for the procedure, teach it step by step, have some students demonstrate the procedure, and then have the class practice it. The practice should continue until the teacher is certain that everyone understands how it is to be performed.

It is unrealistic to expect to teach a procedure during the first day or two of the class and have it followed perfectly for the rest of the year. Those who do follow the routines should be given occasional reinforcement; if the class begins to ignore the routine or become lax in its application, the teacher may need to remind students of the routine and have them practice it again. These two actions signal that the routines are important and that students are expected to follow them. Establishing routines for recurring and predictable events, insisting on compliance, and monitoring them during the school year can result in more learning time, more positive relations between class members and the teacher, more teacher energy for dealing with the exceptions or the serious problems, and fewer behavioral problems.

PACING CLASSROOM ACTIVITIES

One of the most important elements of time management is the pace of activities during the lesson. The obvious result of any activity that proceeds too slowly is boredom. However, deciding on an appropriate pace for classroom activities is difficult. Since classrooms are composed of individuals with diverse backgrounds and abilities, some students may grasp a concept or master a skill very quickly while others struggle. Many teachers find themselves in a bit of an ethical dilemma. They want to make sure that all learners have an opportunity to learn and are reluctant to move too quickly out of a fear that some will become lost. However, to move at a pace so that all youngsters succeed runs the risk of losing the attention of those who have mastered the material.

Another problem in making pacing decisions is that many teachers are unaware of the pace of the classroom. Some teachers seem to have an intuitive feel for moving at a rate appropriate for their learners, whereas others are nearly always moving too rapidly or too slowly. It is probable that those teachers who do seem to make appropriate pacing decisions do so with the aid of something more than mere intuition. Teachers tend to form "reference groups" that provide them with cues on the pace of classroom activities. Although many teachers are unable to consciously identify particular students whom they observe for cues, this reference group may still exist.

The influence of the reference group in pacing works something like this. Mrs. Garcia is teaching a difficult concept. As the concept is being taught, she is also attending to the nonverbal behaviors of the class. She observes the puzzled expression on the face of one of the high achieving students and interprets this expression to mean that the student is lost. Since this is a high achieving student, she infers that the difficulty must be in the pace of the instruction and not with the concentration of the student. Her action is to slow the pace and reteach the earlier portion of her lesson. Later on, Mrs. Garcia notes an expression of boredom on the face of another student. This student in also an academically able student, so she interprets this to mean that the pace is too slow and needs to be accelerated. Later, during another lesson, Mrs. Garcia sees a puzzled expression of the face of another student. This time the student is one who often has difficulty. She interprets this to be due to the lack of attending behavior on the part of the student and not something that is symptomatic of wide-spread student misunderstanding. Therefore, she does nothing to alter the pace of the lesson.

Many nonverbal behaviors are ambiguous and open to several interpretations. Teachers who are successful in managing a classroom and in establishing an appropriate pace are those who check their inferences and become more skilled at reading and interpreting the nonverbal behavior of a reliable reference group. Unsuccessful teachers attend to the wrong students or misinterpret student behavior.

A beginning step in learning how to develop an appropriate pace is to develop a reference group and make sure that it is composed of students who are most helpful for making pacing decisions. For example, if the teacher selects those students who are usually at the top of the class as the reference group, the pace may be too fast. Most of the students will get lost and fail. However, if the teacher chooses the slowest students in the class as the reference group, the pace may be too slow for most of the class. Boredom and behavior problems may then result. A better solution is to choose students at about the twenty-fifth percentile for the reference group. This means that the pace will be appropriate for 75 percent of the class. Although this pace may still be a bit slow for the more able learners, it will keep the lesson moving at a moderately fast pace while providing for the success of the majority of the students. Establishing a reference group at the twenty-fifth percentile does not mean that the teacher ignores the bottom quarter of the class. If these students are having difficulty, they can be retaught as a group. The point is that neither the slowest student nor the fastest should be the indicators for pacing decisions.

PROVIDING CLEAR DIRECTIONS

Much time is lost in getting students to work after a task is assigned. A major contributor to lost time at this point is unclear or poor teacher directions. Students who do not understand the directions will ask for clarification or begin doing the task incorrectly. In both cases, the teacher has to stop the flow of classroom activity to repeat directions or to assist a large number of students.

The teacher can implement several measures to increase the clarity of directions. One basic step is to write the directions and have another teacher read them and suggest clarifications. Written directions also prompt teachers to be more concise in their direction-giving behavior. Another method is to give give oral directions and then randomly choose a couple of students to explain in their own words what they are to do. The students may be able to state the task in a manner that is easier to understand, thus allowing the teacher the opportunity to identify any missing points or misunderstandings.

MANAGING TRANSITIONS

Transitions between lessons or between activities are another major source of wasted time. There are approximately 30 major transitions each day in a typical elementary classroom (Doyle 1986, 406). Although secondary school teachers may have fewer transitions, the average number, counting the transitions between classes, is still in the range of 12 to 15.

Transition times provide students with opportunities to talk, move about the room, and engage in other nontask behaviors. Therefore, it is not surprising that many discipline problems occur during transition times. Once students become off-task, they are likely to stay off-task for some time. Getting them back on-task can then lead to confrontations and power struggles between the teacher and the students. It is important that these transitions be handled quickly and smoothly with a minimum of disruption.

Teachers can minimize wasted time and the problems that occur during transitions through planning in much the same way as lessons are planned. The teacher should outline the steps of the transition carefully, give clear directions to the students, and make sure that all students understand where they are to go and what they are expected to do. Transitions that occur frequently should be developed into routines and practiced.

Another part of the teacher responsibility in providing for smooth transitions is to make sure that all material is ready and at hand before the lesson begins. Trouble will almost certainly occur if the teacher has to make the class wait until the material is located or prepared for distribution. Posting daily schedules and notifications of any changes in the daily routine is also useful in preparing students for transitions. When they understand what is going to be happening and when time limits are established for activities, students develop a sense of security. Transitions then tend to be smoother and less disruptive. Students do get accustomed to a schedule, and when an unusual break occurs, they may waste considerable time complaining that it is not yet time to change.

Box 5-4
MANAGING TRANSITIONS

Mr. Rashad likes teaching and is a good teacher. It is obvious that he knows American history and is able to make it meaningful and exciting for his students. He has always believed that a key to good teaching is interesting and relevant lessons. He still believes that this is true, but his classes do not accomplish as much as he believes they should. A particular problem seems to occur when he stops teaching and asks the students to move to another activity such as independent work, cooperative learning groups, or simply reading the text. When he stops to give a direction to change activities, the class erupts into talk. It always seems to take at least 5 minutes for the class to change activities and do something else. In addition, they have trouble completing the tasks that are assigned. He is tempted to spend the entire period lecturing because that seems to be when the class is most on-task and is on their best behavior.

What do you think?

1. Why do you think Mr. Rashad is having difficulty?

2. Do you think his idea to spend the entire class lecturing would solve the problem?

3. What would you suggest he do to try and solve the problems he experiences in getting students to work?

MONITORING STUDENT WORK

Research has shown that elementary school students spend nearly half their time working independently on seat work activities (Jones and Jones 1986). Although the amount of independent work in secondary schools may be somewhat less, it is still a significant portion of the school day. In order to facilitate success during this time,

and therefore increase the academic learning time of each student, the teacher should actively monitor the progress of each learner.

Monitoring should be done continuously and systematically so that all parts of the room and all learners are included. Some teachers stay in one spot, often at the teacher's desk, or check only one part of the room. These habits are discouraged, for several reasons: Having students who need assistance come to the teacher's desk creates problems. First of all, many students who need assistance will not actively seek it. Second, when students get out of their seats, the potential for mischief increases, and those students lined up at the teacher's desk cannot be doing any work. Also, students gathered around the teacher's desk prevent the teacher from actively monitoring the classroom for any behavior problems or off-task behavior. Because student misbehavior decreases with an increased physical proximity of the teacher, the teacher should try to stay close to learners. This cannot be done if the teacher is seated at the teacher's desk. These points suggest a general principle successful teachers have found very effective: The teacher should go to the student rather than having the students come to the teacher.

Two basic components need to be considered when systematically monitoring student work: teacher movement around the class and provision of assistance to those who need help.

Teacher Movement

The teacher needs to move around the classroom. Many teachers develop the poor habits of checking only certain parts of the classroom and of interacting with only a few learners. Since it is important to monitor all learners, it is helpful to develop a systematic plan for moving around the room.

One principle that should be considered is checking the work of every student within the first 5 minutes of assigning independent work. Once the assignment is given and directions reviewed, the teacher should immediately start moving around the classroom, checking to make sure that all students are working. At this point the teacher should not stop to provide in-depth assistance to those who request it. A reminder, a quick hint, or a promise to return in a minute or two is all that should be done at this point. If many students seem confused, the teacher might need to stop the class and review the assignment with them. Positive reinforcement should be given to those who have promptly started to work on the task.

After making this initial pass through the room, the teacher should then return to those who need more assistance, making sure also to check the work of those who do not require assistance. Some students may think they are doing the work correctly when they are not; others may be reluctant or embarrassed to request assistance. Checking student work and providing positive comments as well as corrective feedback are important parts of monitoring. If no students require assistance, the teacher may move around the room in a more leisurely manner. However, the teacher should have a movement plan in mind that will place him or her next to every student in the room a minimum of one or two times during the independent study portion of the lesson. A simple checklist of groups of students might be needed to remind the teacher of the spots that have been monitored and those that have been overlooked. When more constructive habits of movement have been established, the teacher may eliminate the checklist.

It is often very productive to have someone observe in the room and plot the movement patterns of the teacher. This can be very revealing and can help the teacher target some specific areas that are being neglected.

Providing Assistance

One of the most important components of effective monitoring is providing effective assistance to those who need help. Those students who need help, yet must wait an extended period of time before receiving assistance, are wasting their time waiting for the teacher. Therefore, an effective technique for providing fast and efficient help needs to be developed.

It is important for the teacher to have interactions with as many students as possible. The more feedback the teacher can give, both positive and corrective, to the most number of students the better. Therefore, spending an extended period of time interacting with a few youngsters decreases the impact of effective monitoring. For example, suppose that a classroom has been assigned a 20-minute independent study task. If the teacher spends an average of 4 minutes with each student who requests assistance, no more than five students can receive teacher feedback.

Jones (1979) studied this aspect of the classroom and discovered that teachers did spend an average of about 4 minutes per student when providing assistance. He concluded that effective assistance could be provided more quickly, so he developed and tested some procedures that have been effective in helping teachers provide assistance. Those procedures, with some modification, are as follows:

1. Arrange the seating so that the teacher can easily and quickly get to the desk of every student. The teacher should not have to waste time hurrying from one end of the room to the other.

2. Provide models, charts, or displays of the directions and of the assignment so that students can consult them independently.

3. Provide a signal system for the students to use when they need help. Rather than waving their arms in the air, students placing a colored card on the desk or leaving a book open is more useful to signal their need for assistance. Students can be instructed to attempt the next problem or to work on some part of the task they can do while waiting for assistance.

4. When the teacher arrives at the student's desk, the following procedure should be used. Quickly identify and comment on something the student has done correctly. Then give a very brief and concrete hint or direction, by reminding the student about something that was forgotten, hinting about what to do next, referring the student to the appropriate model or step, or simply telling the student what to do next. Then quickly move away to assist someone else. In a minute or two, return to make sure that the student is now on the right track. If not, another concrete hint or suggestion should be made. This whole process should take place in less than a minute.

Some teachers have difficulty with the suggestion to move on quickly. Moving quickly from student to student, however, not only maximizes contact with the students but continues to make them independent learners. Some students have learned the benefits of playing dumb. If the teacher can be convinced that the student needs extensive help, the teacher will end up doing most of the work. Other students are simply insecure and demand teacher assistance even when it is not needed, and some just want teacher attention. Moving away quickly can help eliminate these problems by removing the reinforcement of gaining teacher attention when it is not needed. Attention is provided to more students, and the teacher can provide reinforcement for those who are doing their work without assistance.

SUMMARY

Time management is one of the more important aspects of classroom management. Not only does proper time management prevent discipline problems but it also facilitates student achievement. An inordinate amount of time is spent on nonacademic tasks during the typical school day. Capturing this time and using it to teach the content can actually add several days to the academic calendar. One dimension of classroom time of special importantance is the academic learning time. Academic learning time is the amount of time that students spend working on the lesson objective with success.

It is not enough for students to be busy; they must also be encountering success, or the time is the same as wasted.

Another important component of managing time is to plan procedures and routines for predictable, recurring events. If time has to be taken to deal with each of these events, a considerable number of minutes can be lost. Planning routines for these events, teaching them to students, and monitoring the application of these routines during the year make the task of teaching considerably easier. Time is also lost in inappropriate pacing of lessons. Lessons paced too rapidly will result in confusion and lost time reteaching; lessons paced too slowly will cause boredom and misbehavior. Establishing a reference group of students to monitor during the lesson is a useful way to make pacing decisions.

Much misbehavior occurs during the transition time between lessons or activities. It is important that teachers plan for transitions so that they are done quickly and efficiently. Keeping students focused on learning and not allowing them an opportunity to misbehave are important aspects of problem prevention. Managing transitions requires well-planned routines and constant attention. Many teachers spend more time providing assistance to students than is necessary. As a result, they are unable to monitor and provide assistance to the maximum number of students. Some students learn quickly that by playing dumb they can get the teacher to do a significant amount of work for them. Learning how to provide assistance quickly and then move away from the students helps teachers solve this perplexing problem.

SUGGESTED ACTIVITIES

1. Observe in a classroom and use a second hand or a stopwatch to keep track of the time spent on tasks that are not related to the objective. Compare this time to the total class time allocated for the lesson. Identify those places where time could be saved.

2. Visit two or more classrooms where the same content is being taught. Compare the amount of time allocated for the different topics and activities in the class. Ask the teachers to provide you with their rationale for their time-allocation decisions. Note differences between allocations and the actual time spent focused on the objectives during the class.

3. List those areas where you think classroom procedures and routines are needed. For each of these areas develop a routine. Share your list with others, and from your work together, compile a master list of routines.

4. List instances when directions are given. Try to write these directions verbatim. After writing them, read them back and see if they are clear. Rewrite unclear directions to increase their clarity.

5. Plot the movements of a teacher around the classroom. Identify those places where the teacher spends the most time and the least time. Which students are closest to the teacher more often? Which students receive the most help? Do you notice any patterns to the teacher movement? How might the movement patterns be changed to provide more efficient monitoring?

BIBLIOGRAPHY

BERLINER, D. 1984. The half-full glass: A review of research on teaching. In *Using What We Know About Teaching,* ed. P. Hosford, pp. 51–78. Alexandria, Va.: Association for Supervision and Curriculum Development.

CHARLES, C. 1983. *Elementary Classroom Management.* New York: Longman

DOYLE, W. 1986. Classroom organization and management. In *Handbook of Research on Teaching,* ed. M. Wittrock. New York: Macmillan.

EMMER, E., C. EVERTSON, J. SANFORD, B. CLEMENTS, and M. WORSHAM. 1989. *Classroom Management for Secondary Teachers,* 2nd ed. Englewood Cliffs, N.J.: Prentice Hall.

EVERTSON, C., E. EMMER, B. CLEMENTS, J. SANFORD, and M. WORSHAM. 1989. *Classroom Management for Elementary Teachers,* 2nd ed. Englewood Cliffs, N.J.: Prentice Hall.

JONES, F. 1979. The gentle art of classroom discipline. *National Elementary Principal* 58 (June), 26–32.

JONES, V., and L. JONES. 1986. *Comprehensive Classroom Management,* 2nd ed. Boston: Allyn & Bacon.

KOUNIN, J. 1970. *Discipline and Group Management in the Classrooms.* New York: Holt, Rinehart & Winston.

Chapter 6

LESSON MANAGEMENT

OBJECTIVES

This chapter provides information to help the reader to

1. State the relationship between good lesson management and the prevention of misbehavior

2. Define aspects of teacher clarity that interfere with effective lesson presentation

3. Give examples of "withitness" and overlapping in lesson presentation

4. Identify those teacher behaviors that impede lesson momentum

5. Describe lesson smoothness and how it can be accomplished

6. Give examples of how student attention can be gained at the beginning of a lesson, maintained during a lesson, and reinforced at the lesson's conclusion

7. State how task variety and keeping students alert and accountable increase student work involvement and participation

8. State the principle to use in responding to misbehavior during a lesson

INTRODUCTION

Teachers are responsible for two major tasks in the classroom: instruction and maintenance of discipline. Beginning teachers are often told to plan and deliver exciting lessons as a means of preventing misbehavior. There is much wisdom in this advice. Well-planned and well-executed lessons not only help students achieve a sense of satisfaction from their work but also promote prompt cooperation. Planning and delivering effective lessons, however, are a complex task. Several basic and generic components must be considered regardless of the philosophy of the teacher, the content of the lesson, or the teaching strategy. These components include gaining student attention, presenting content, distributing materials, keeping students involved, monitoring student progress, and concluding the lesson.

Doyle (1986) identifies several characteristics of classrooms that make managing them more difficult than might be assumed. He points out that classrooms are multidimensional, simultaneous, unpredictable environments that have a sense of immediacy and are very public.

The multidimensional aspect takes into account the fact that classrooms have a large number of participants, events, and tasks. In addition, any one event can have multiple consequences. The behavior of any one student can affect not only that student but the motivation and interest of others, as well as the behavior of the teacher. Classrooms are reciprocal places where the behavior of the teacher influences learners and the behavior of learners influences the teacher. Therefore, understanding and managing the dynamics of this multidimensional environment can be a complex task.

Classrooms also have the characteristics of simultaneity and unpredictability. Many things happen at once in a classroom. Teachers must not only try to deliver the content but also keep track of time, monitor student understanding, decide if additional instruction is required, attend to the pace of the lesson, and scan the class for

misbehavior. Distractions and disruptions are frequent, making it difficult to predict how learners will react to a given activity.

Immediacy is yet another dimension that makes classroom management difficult. The rapid pace of activities does not allow the teacher much time for reflection. He or she simply does not have the opportunity to put an individual student concern on hold until an appropriate solution can be found. It must be dealt with immediately. The problem is that teachers must deal with a great number of these immediate concerns during a given day. Gump (1967) and Jackson (1968) estimate that an elementary school teacher has more than 500 exchanges with individual students during a single day.

Box 6-1
CLASSROOM COMPLEXITY

Janis Lam has always believed that exciting lessons prevent discipline problems. However, she has changed her mind. During the first weeks of her first teaching experience she worked hard every night to plan interesting lessons that required a lot of student involvement. However, it seemed as if that was the wrong thing to do. The students got too noisy and spent their time talking and joking around. Finally the class gradually became totally out of control. They were not accomplishing anything, Mrs. Lam was spending most of her time trying to keep them under control, and she finished every day totally exhausted. "Boring, lock-step lessons where all students are doing the same thing at the same time and where all stay in their own seat and quietly follow directions seem to be the only way students know how to behave. I now understand why so many teachers use this approach."

What do you think?

1. **Do you agree with Mrs. Lam's analysis of the problem?**

2. **What do you think could have been causing her difficulties?**

3. **How would you try to prevent this problem from occurring in your classroom?**

Classrooms are public places where the actions of the teacher are observed by a large number of students. The management skills and perceptiveness of the teacher are known by all students. In addition, the presence of many individuals in a classroom provides a ready audience for those students who desire attention and decide that misbehavior is the easiest way to obtain it. Taken in combination, the factors of multidimensionality, simultaneity, unpredictability, immediacy, and publicness make the management task a considerable one.The research of Minnick (1983) clearly identified the relationship between lesson management and discipline problems. In a study of an inner-city junior high school with serious discipline problems, Minnick found that teachers with a high incidence of discipline problems did a poor job of planning activities, had little variety in their lessons, infrequently communicated to students the importance of the lesson, rarely had students discuss or evaluate what they had learned, and did a poor job of monitoring student work.

Kounin (1970) and his associates conducted impressive studies on the relationship between discipline and management two decades ago. They began their research by focusing on discipline problems. They were interested in how teachers responded to incidents of deviant behavior and how those reactions created a ripple effect on the subsequent behavior of the student disciplined and the others in the classroom. After some time, Kounin became convinced that management issues were more important. As a result, he developed a number of management concepts that are especially helpful in presenting lessons so that incidents of misbehavior are minimized. In recent years new concepts of lesson management have emerged from research on teaching effectiveness. This chapter focuses on these concepts.

THE DIMENSIONS OF LESSON MANAGEMENT

Attending to the several generic skills or concepts that are necessary when managing a lesson can enhance teacher success regardless of the teacher's philosophy or method of instruction. A general conclusion that emerges from numerous studies indicates that teachers need to be active while engaged in lesson management (Brophy and Good 1986, 361). Being active means that teachers should spend most of their time instructing students or monitoring their progress and providing feedback. A review of the characteristics of classrooms as outlined by Doyle would seem to reinforce this notion of active teaching. Managing an environment that is multidimensional, immediate, public, and unpredictable requires a teacher who is involved and active to keep a diverse group of students moving in the desired direction. The following concepts will help teachers manage lessons so that desired outcomes are attained and problems are minimized.

Clear Objectives

A beginning step to effective lesson management is the specification of clear objectives and goals for the lesson. Clarity about his or her goals helps the teacher identify those activities and approaches that are most likely to bring about student success. Further, it helps the teacher to focus on the main points of the lesson and keeps him or her from wandering off the topic and confusing students. When students are clear about the goals and objectives of the lesson, their motivation is enhanced. They are better able to understand the logic of the lesson and the reasons for the various activities.

These clear goals and objectives should reflect what students should learn or be able to do as a result of the lesson and *not* what the teacher intends to do. Some teachers tend to define goals and objectives in terms of their own behavior. For example, a teacher might have as an objective for a lesson a discussion of the similar themes in literature. The teacher then proceeds to lecture the class on literary themes. The basic question is, What should the students be able to do as a result of this particular lesson? Will they be able to identify similar themes from literature? When teachers begin to consider what they want students to know or be able to do, they often discover that the activities they have designed and the time they have allocated are inappropriate.

Clear objectives serve yet another purpose. In fast-moving and unpredictable environments, teachers must make quick decisions. Some criteria should be established to enable teachers to make such decisions. A clear sense of purpose or clear goals can assist the teacher in making management decisions that are more likely to keep the group on track and moving in the right direction. A lack of clarity often results in a lesson without cohesion and in student confusion.

Clear goals and objectives benefit students. They help students understand the purposes of the activities and the content that is being covered. Clarity of purpose enhances student motivation and helps students make time and effort choices. In addition, clear goals become a framework or advance organizer for the material that is being presented. Such a framework helps students organize and understand the material with greater comprehension and clarity. This increased understanding facilitates student achievement and creates a climate of success.

Teacher Clarity

One of the most important variables in implementing and managing successful lessons is teacher clarity. Substantial verbal communication goes on in a typical classroom. The clarity of that communication will have a profound effect on the success of the lesson. Teacher messages that are confusing, garbled, or unclear will result in learner confusion and frustration. Although it is easy to say that a message is unclear, it is much more difficult to identify specifically what makes it unclear. Clarity involves a number of teacher behaviors and is made more difficult by the fact that it is a combination of what the teacher does and says and how students interpret the message (Gephart, Strother, and Duckett 1981).

A deterrent to clarity is the use of vague and ambiguous terms. These include approximations (about, almost), ambiguous designations (somehow, somewhere, someone), bluffing (everyone knows, it's a long story), indeterminate quantification

---

Box 6-2
WHAT IS THE OBJECTIVE?

Mrs. Liang is teaching a math lesson to a group of elementary students. She begins by presenting the objective to the class. "Class, today we are going to talk about percentages and fractions." She then continues the lesson by presenting them with a problem. "What is the fraction 1/4?"

What is your recommendation?

1.   **Do you think Mrs. Liang's objective was clear?**

2.   **Write an objective that you think might be clearer.**

3.   **Was her problem stated with clarity? How could she have stated it?**

(a bunch, a lot, a few), and statements of probability (frequently, generally, often). While these terms cannot be eliminated entirely, their repeated use during a lesson signals lack of teacher knowledge and precision

Another dimension of clarity is the presence or absence of "mazes." Mazes might best be thought of as a winding path, including blind alleys, that one must traverse in order to get to the central point. When teachers are clear about their goals and careful about their communication style, they can avoid leading students into mazes out of which they may never emerge. Mazes often involve statements that lack logic or semantic sense. Teachers often create mazes when giving verbal directions to a class. Too many directions are given at once and are not given concisely. As a result the class is unsure of what to do. This confusion becomes a fertile ground for misbehavior.

"Withitness"

One of the basic concepts that Kounin developed out of his research is the concept of "withitness." The "with-it" teacher, according to Kounin, is one who is aware of what is going on in the classroom. Such teachers are the ones that might be working with a small group of students in one part of the classroom and still be aware of the behavior of individual students in some other part of the room. Their awareness of student behavior allows them to respond quickly to student problems and concerns. Teachers who exhibit this characteristic are often described by students as "having eyes in the back of their head." Withitness is related to how teachers respond to misbehavior. One aspect of the response of the with-it teacher is the ability to identify correctly the misbehaving student. Teachers who do not have withitness often respond to the wrong student or target. In addition, withitness is enhanced by correct timing. The with-it teacher identifies when misbehavior is occurring and stops the behavior quickly before it has a chance to spread to other students or become a serious problem.

Because it is one of those talents that is probably acquired with experience, withitness would seem to be difficult to teach beginning teachers. However, it is enhanced when a teacher has planned well and is confident when teaching. This confidence allows the teacher to change the focus from what he or she is doing to what the learners are doing.

Overlapping

Overlapping is another Kounin concept that is important in explaining successful classroom managers. Overlapping refers to the ability of a teacher to handle more than one task or item at a time. Once again, this concept is consistent with Doyle's description of the multidimensional and simultaneous classroom. While working with one group of students, the teacher must evaluate the relevance of answers to questions, select additional questions, decide who needs to be asked to respond, monitor the comprehension of the entire group, monitor the pace of the lesson, attend to the portion of the class not involved in the small group, provide assistance to those outside the group, and make sure that all materials are ready for the next class or topic. In addition, unpredictable intrusions such as an inquiry from the office or a request from another teacher require a response. The successful teacher must attend to all of these factors while keeping the entire class on-task and moving in the right direction. Teachers who lack the skill of overlapping simply get lost in the maze of events and lose control of the direction of the lesson. They seldom get anything accomplished and finish each day or period with a keen sense of frustration.

An element of overlapping not included in Kounin's description but that also seems important is an ability to know which events need to be handled immediately and which ones can be ignored. The mistake of many beginning teachers is to focus on the wrong events. Those that need attention are overlooked while attention is directed to minor incidents. In a comparison of successful and unsuccessful teachers, researchers noted that successful teachers make rapid judgments during teaching, group events into larger units in order to deal with them effectively, and are able to discriminate among the units in terms of their immediate and long-term significance (Clark and Peterson 1986). In summary, the successful teacher is one who is able to simplify and make sense out of the complex environment of the classroom.

Overlapping, like withitness, would seem to be a difficult skill to teach. Research studies (Clark and Peterson 1986) seem to indicate that it might be a skill acquired through experience. However, for experience to be beneficial, teachers must develop a schema, or frame of reference, related to classroom teaching and learning that helps them select cues to attend to, understand the meaning of the cues, and make an appropriate decision. It is probable that a well-developed and context-appropriate schema is what makes teaching look so easy when demonstrated by an outstanding teacher. Student teachers often become painfully aware of this phenomenon when they take over the class of just such a teacher. The act of teaching and managing suddenly becomes much more difficult than it did during observations.

Lesson Momentum

What Kounin calls lesson momentum involves keeping the lesson moving forward at a steady and appropriate pace. In a class with good lesson momentum, students move ahead at a relatively brisk pace and keep on-task and no breaks occur in the flow of the lesson. Although unpredictable events, such as an announcement over the loudspeaker, will break the lesson momentum, there are things that teachers do that slow down or break the momentum. Kounin identified two of these teacher behaviors: lesson fragmentation and overdwelling.

Fragmentation. Fragmentation, identified by Kounin as the major problem in maintaining lesson momentum, occurs in several ways. One way is breaking a lesson or directions for an activity into several unnecessary steps when the the task could be quickly accomplished in one or two steps. As a result, students spend time waiting rather than maintaining their focus on the lesson and lesson objectives. Another common example of fragmentation is the teacher asking one student to come to the front and solve a problem while the rest of the class sits and watches. This often produces boredom and provides an opportunity for students to focus their attention on something other than the lesson.

Overdwelling. Overdwelling occurs when teachers spend too much time in needless repetition and elaboration of instructions, the result of a teacher not being cognizant of the students' ability to understand. Also, teachers have a tendency to talk too much. This is particularly evident in giving directions. Teachers tend to give too many directions at once and to deliver them in a rambling discourse that would confuse the most dedicated student. When the class does not understand, the teacher must then stop and repeat the directions. Teachers need to be concise in their presentations, make a quick assessment of student comprehension, and then move on.

Another form of overdwelling occurs where the teacher spends an inordinate amount of time on a minor or insignificant part of a task rather than emphasizing the main ideas. Since students may fail to see the relevance of what is being discussed, their motivation drops. In addition, students lose sight of the lesson objectives and attend, instead, to insignificant content. They then become confused and angry when they fail to achieve success.

Lesson Smoothness

Lesson smoothness, another concept developed by Kounin, is also concerned with the flow of the lesson. Not only does a lesson need to move forward at an appropriate pace but it also needs to be thematically related so that one part of the lesson flows smoothly into the next. Two aspects of lesson management that contribute to lesson smoothness are connected discourse and creative repetition. Factors that detract from lesson smoothness are thrusts, dangles and truncations, and flip- flops.

Connected Discourse. Connected discourse refers to the logic or connectedness of teacher talk. The parts of the lesson should be thematically connected so that there is a logical flow and the lesson makes sense. Observations of teachers reveal that they frequently get off the topic into areas that are not logically or thematically connected to the objective of the lesson. This causes confusion as students try to sort out the point that the teacher is trying to make. Although connected discourse is not one of the factors of lesson smoothness identified by Kounin, it has been identified in research on teacher clarity and fits nicely with the concept.

Lesson smoothness can be increased by detailed planning. Clear objectives specified before the class begins help keep the teacher focused on the points of the lesson and help eliminate fruitless digressions. In addition, the lesson plan needs to be evaluated for the logical flow of concepts and activities. Do the pieces fit together to make a whole? Does it make sense, and is it likely that a student following that sequence would learn the material presented?

Creative Repetition. Some amount of repetition is necessary for learning to occur; telling students once is seldom enough. However, merely repeating the same thing over and over stops lesson momentum and is ineffective. Instead, creative repetition is needed at key points in the lesson so that the structure of the lesson is clear to the students. When reminded of what happened during the first part of the lesson and how that relates to subsequent parts, students can follow the flow of the lesson. Consequently, their learning and attending behaviors are enhanced. Rather than merely repeating the same idea or concept, effective teachers try to find a new application, a new problem, or a new way of illustrating the main points of the lesson. Internal summaries included at key points are one way of planning for repetition. Like connected discourse, creative repetition is not one of Kounin's concepts, but has emerged out of the research on teacher clarity.

Thrusts. One of the ways that teachers interfere with lesson smoothness is by bringing in statements or questions for which the class is not ready. These abrupt statements are called "thrusts." An example of a thrust is an order given to certain students to pass out books or papers in the midst of a discussion. Although this material

Box 6-3
CATCHING THE TEACHABLE MOMENT

Bill Brundidge believes that the key to effective teaching is finding the "teachable moment." He believes that very complete plans make the lesson too rigid and therefore the teacher misses teachable moments. He prefers to identify a topic and then let the discussion be free-flowing. As the discussion progresses, he picks up on ideas that interest the students and they become the focus of the day.

During a typical day several of his students are actually involved in the discussion. About five of them appear to be working on assignments for other classes and two or three have their heads down on their desks. Bill does not consider this inappropriate because no one is actively disturbing the discussion.

What do you think?

1. Do you agree with Bill's approach to teaching? Why or why not?

2. Does planning interfere with catching the teachable moment?

3. Would you agree with Bill's assessment that he does not have a discipline problem?

4. What recommendations would you give him?

is required for the lesson, giving the order during the discussion thrusts the interferingactivity to the forefront and effectively stifles further discussion. Thrusts are often evidence of a poor sense of timing. Teachers who are guilty of thrusts often forget to consider when it is best to ask questions or give orders or directions.

Dangles and Truncations. Dangles and truncations are breaks in the lesson flow. They occur when a teacher leaves an activity in midstream. For example, a teacher suddenly terminates an activity before the objective has been reached. If that activity is resumed, it is a dangle; if the activity is not resumed, it is a truncation.

Dangles and truncations interfere with student concentration and feelings of achievement. Lessons are not properly brought to a close and the smoothness and logic of the lesson are destroyed. Dangles often occur when teachers fail to keep an eye on the clock. Suddenly they realize that time is almost up and they panic. They abruptly stop the lesson in order to move on to the next order of business.

Flip-Flops. In some respect, flip-flops are like dangles. They occur when the teacher stops one activity, begins a second activity, and then returns to the first activity. An example might be a teacher who stops the class while they are reading a story, has them practice spelling words for a few minutes, and then returns to the story. Flip-flops indicate poor planning or poor decision making. Some beginning teachers use flip-flops when they realize that they don't have enough material to last the entire period. They then try to fill the time by bringing in some unrelated activity before continuing with the lesson. Unfortunately, though, most students never return to the original focus.

GROUP FOCUS

Maintaining a focus on the group is another area identified by Kounin as important when managing a lesson. Teaching is an activity involving groups of students rather than individuals. Although this fact seems obvious, teachers often have trouble because they focus on individuals rather than on the entire group. The ability to keep the entire group focused and on-task is an important aspect of successful teaching. There are several dimensions of group focus: gaining student attention, providing a variety of tasks and avoiding satiation, keeping individuals in the group alert and accountable, gaining the active participation of the students, and responding to misbehavior.

Gaining Student Attention

Gaining and keeping student attention throughout the lesson is a central element of effective group management. Some teachers think that if they have students' attention at the beginning the task is accomplished. A variety of alternatives are available to help gain students' attention at the beginning of the lesson; some are helpful to maintain attention, and yet others facilitate a successful lesson conclusion and build motivation for future lessons (Wlodkowski 1978).

Gaining student attention at the beginning of the lesson can be accomplished by appealing to the sense of curiosity and by starting the lesson with something novel or unique. Relating the lesson to student needs and developing a positive attitude toward the subject are also important. Maintaining student attention throughout the lesson is

enhanced by making the experience an enjoyable and challenging one. Additional sensory stimulation needs to be included when students have been engaged in one activity for some time or when they are likely to become bored. Ending the lesson with an emphasis on what the student has learned and a reinforcement of positive student effort and behavior is important. Students need to end the class or topic feeling good about the class and their efforts. Those who believe that their efforts will have a payoff and that their need for achievement is being satisfied will begin to develop an intrinsic interest in the topic and exercise more self-control.

Providing Variety and Avoiding Satiation

To provide sensory stimulation throughout the lesson have a variety of tasks. Kounin identified this as one of the crucial variables in managing a lesson. Variety helps to avoid satiation. When students are satiated, they become restless, make more errors in their work, and start seeking escape from the activity.

Several techniques can help provide for variety during a lesson. One is changing the group configuration from large to small group or to independent study. Variety can be added by using slides, pictures, or videotapes to supplement the lesson. Rotating activities that call for teacher input with activities that require student production also adds variety. One high school modern language teacher planned her lessons using the rule that students should not be asked to perform any one activity for more than 15 minutes. This meant that she had at least three different tasks during any one period. Boredom and satiation were seldom a problem in her classes.

Keeping the Group Alert and Accountable

Throughout a lesson the teacher should make sure that all students are kept alert. This can be accomplished by holding the students in suspense so that they never know when they might be called upon to respond to a teacher question or perform a task. Group alerting techniques such as having all students signify their agreement or disagreement with a statement or question by holding up hands are useful in keeping students on their toes. When students realize that a teacher has started a lecture during which there is little probability that they will need to respond, their attention will begin to wander and their involvement in the lesson will decrease.

Keeping students accountable means letting them know that they will need to use what is taught in some manner. A good example of accountability can be observed in college classrooms. Students often ask a professor, "Will it be on the test?" This is their way of determining accountability. They want to know whether or not they will be required to do something with the information. Observing students when a professor says that material will not be on a test reveals why accountability is an important variable in managing a lesson. These students will stop taking notes and no longer focus their attention on what is being covered.

Teachers should always try to have students extend the material presented in class. Extension activities include simple assignments, a reaction paper, a short quiz, or the completion of a worksheet. When students know that they will be required to demonstrate their understanding, their attending behavior shows a marked increase.

Gaining Active Participation and Involvement

As Doyle (1986) points out, for an activity to succeed, a sufficient number of students must cooperate with the teacher and participate in the lesson. Individuals who are not involved will seek some diversion. More often than not this diversion will be destructive to the progress of the lesson. Regaining the attention of those learners who have wandered off the task is a difficult task at best. It is better to keep the entire group focused throughout.

As teachers conduct lessons, they must be alert for opportunities to involve the class. Students should not be expected to sit passively for more than a few minutes at a time. The basic goal is to get a high percentage of involvement during every stage of the lesson. To do this, students might be asked to complete an outline or signal their agreement or disagreement to statements. Well-designed cooperative learning groups are an excellent way of facilitating the active involvement of a large percentage of learners.

Kounin divided work involvement or active participation into two types: work involvement during recitation or whole group instruction and work involvement while doing seat work. His research indicated that withitness, lesson smoothness, lesson momentum, group alerting, and accountability were all positively associated with maintaining high levels of active participation and involvement in lessons involving recitation or whole group instruction. Lesson variety was most strongly associated with a high level of work involvement during seat work (Dunkin and Biddle 1974). Applying these group management concepts to the various parts of the lesson can be helpful in maintaining high levels of group participation in the lesson and in delivering the types of lessons where misbehavior is prevented.

Responding to Misbehavior

Responding to misbehavior is the focus of several later chapters of this book. However, it does need to be mentioned here in relation to lesson management. Unfortunately, many teachers spend a considerable amount of their instructional time responding to discipline problems. In such situations, the lesson cannot be delivered in an effective manner: Lesson smoothness and momentum are destroyed, student attention is diverted from the lesson to the misbehavior, and participation and cooperation drop to unacceptable levels.

A major principle to use when responding to misbehavior during a lesson is to respond in such a way that the attention of the class remains on the lesson rather than diverted to the misbehavior or the teacher's response. Teachers are often guilty of responding to minor misbehavior in such an obtrusive manner that student attention needlessly focuses on the misbehavior and the misbehaving student. Therefore, teachers are often more guilty of disrupting lesson momentum and smoothness than are misbehaving students. Instead, they should respond as quietly and as unobtrusively as possible.

Teachers also must consider the likelihood that the behavior will spread and be disruptive to others. If a behavior is not attracting the attention of other learners and appears to be confined to one student, a response that might disrupt the flow of the lesson is inappropriate. However, if the behavior is attracting the attention of others, the teacher must act quickly before the problem spreads. This is one of the aspects of withitness, discussed earlier in the chapter. Even when acting quickly, the teacher should still attempt to do so in an unobtrusive manner so that attention is not focused on the behavior. Later chapters provide readers with more guidance on choosing an appropriate response.

SUMMARY

Lesson management is one of the primary tasks of teachers. Those who can manage a lesson with skill prevent problems and help students move toward the goal of self-control. Outstanding teachers often make the task seem simple. In fact, managing a classroom takes considerable skill and knowledge. Classrooms are multidimensional, simultaneous, unpredictable, public places where teacher action must be taken immediately. These aspects of the environment make classroom management difficult.

A beginning step for successful management is to develop clear goals and objectives so that teacher decisions can keep the lesson moving in the proper direction.

Teacher clarity is important in delivering instruction so that confusion is avoided and students remain focused on the task. The work of Kounin identified "withitness," overlapping, lesson momentum, and lesson smoothness as important variables in lesson management. Teachers must be aware of what is happening in the classroom at all times, be able to handle more than one task at a time, and keep the lesson moving at a good pace with a logical flow of activities and events.

Maintaining the attention of a large number of the group members is necessary if the lesson is to be successful. This can be facilitated by considering how to gain student attention at the beginning of the lesson, how to maintain it during a lesson, and how to reinforce learning at the end. Adding variety to the lesson, keeping students alert and accountable, and maximizing work involvement are also important dimensions of lesson management.

Finally, teacher response to misbehavior is yet another important consideration. Teachers may, by their responses, cause more disruption than does the misbehavior. Therefore, they should respond in ways that are unobtrusive and that keep the focus on the lesson rather than on the behavior. When the behavior appears to be one that might spread, quick action is required in order to prevent the spread and to keep the maximum number of students focused on the lesson.

SUGGESTED ACTIVITIES

1. Classrooms are multidimensional, simultaneous, unpredictable, immediate, public places. Make a chart with these dimensions as headings. Under each heading state the implications of the dimension for the classroom teacher and what a teacher needs to do to cope with this dimension.

2. "Withitness" is an important aspect of classroom management. Brainstorm with a group of individuals those things that indicate teacher withitness and what teachers can do to develop this important skill.

3. Observe a lesson from beginning to end. Identify how the teacher tries to keep momentum and smoothness in the lesson and those things that interfere with smoothness and momentum.

4. Tape-record a lesson. Listen to the tape and identify instances where there seems to be a lack of clarity. Suggest ways that clarity could be improved.

5. Meet with a group of individuals and brainstorm techniques that can be used to keep students alert and accountable during the course of a lesson.

BIBLIOGRAPHY

ARLIN, A., and I. WESTBURY. 1976. The leveling effect of teacher pacing on science content mastery. *Journal of Research in Science Teaching*, 13, 213–219.

BROPHY, J., and T. GOOD. 1986. Teacher behavior and student achievement. In *Handbook of Research on Teaching*, 3rd ed., ed. M. C. Wittrock. New York: Macmillan.

CLARK, C., and P. PETERSON. 1986. Teachers' thought processes. In *Handbook of Research on Teaching*, 3rd ed., ed. M. C. Wittrock. New York: Macmillan.

DOYLE, W. 1986. Classroom organization and management. In *Handbook of Research on Teaching*, 3rd ed., ed. M. C. Wittrock. pp. 392–431). New York: Macmillan.

DUNKIN, M., and B. BIDDLE. 1974. *The Study of Teaching*. New York: Holt, Rinehart & Winston.

ERICKSON, F. 1982. Classroom discourse as improvisation: Relationships between academic task structure and social participation structure in lessons. In *Communicating in Classrooms*, ed. L. Wilkinson. New York: Academic Press.

EMMER, E., C. EVERTSON, J. SANFORD, B. CLEMENTS, B. and M. WORSHAM. 1989. *Classroom Management for Secondary Teachers*. 2nd ed. Englewood Cliffs, N.J.: Prentice Hall.

EVERTSON, C., E. EMMER, B. CLEMENTS, J. SANFORD, and M. WORSHAM. 1989. *Classroom Management for Elementary Teachers*, 2nd ed. Englewood Cliffs, N.J.: Prentice Hall.

FROYEN, L. 1988. *Classroom Management: Empowering Teacher-Leaders*. Columbus, Ohio: Chas. E. Merrill.

GEPHART, W., D. STROTHER, and W. DUCKETT. 1981. Practical applications of research. *Phi Delta Kappa*, 3, 3.

GUMP, P. 1967. The classroom behavior setting: Its nature and relation to student behavior. Final Report. ERIC Document Reproduction Service No. ED 015 515. Washington, D.C.: U.S. Office of Education, Bureau of Research.

JACKSON, P. 1968. *Life in Classrooms*. New York: Holt, Rinehart & Winston.

KOUNIN, J. 1970. *Discipline and Group Management in Classrooms*. New York: Holt, Rinehart & Winston.

MINNICK, B. ed. 1983. Student disruption: Classroom chaos linked to teacher practices. *R&DCTE Review*, 1, 2–3.

RINNE, C. 1984. *Attention: The Fundamental of Classroom Control*. Columbus, Ohio: Chas. E. Merrill.

WLODKOWSKI, R. 1978. *Discipline and Motivation: A Genuine Partnership*. Washington, D.C.: National Education Association.

Chapter 7

GROUP DYNAMICS

OBJECTIVES

This chapter provides information to help the reader to

1. Identify individual needs that are met in groups

2. Define three different types of goal structures commonly used in the classroom

3. State the functions of leader and followers in a group

4. Define roles that different students might play in the group and state how the teacher should deal with individuals who play those roles

5. Identify the roles that the teacher plays in the classroom and state which roles the teacher should try to avoid and which the teacher should try to develop

6. State the ways that cooperative learning uses group dynamics to make the classroom a more satisfying place for learners

7. Identify the basic characteristics of different cooperative learning models

8. State the advantages and disadvantages of cooperative learning approaches

INTRODUCTION

This past year was a nightmare. It seemed as if the class never really came together. They were fighting each other from the first day until the last. There was no sense of cohesiveness and everyone wanted to be the leader. They were unwilling to work with each other and were always competing. As individuals, they were a good class. Most of the youngsters were above-average achievers, and I had looked forward to teaching them. However, by the end of the year I was considering quitting. I felt that if I could be successful in teaching this type of a class, I could be successful with any class.

The teacher in this scenario discovered that groups develop a personality. Some groups seem to work well together; others do not. More importantly, individuals behave differently in groups than they do when acting alone, and many classroom discipline problems are the result of these interpersonal dynamics. The teacher who wants to be successful in preventing discipline problems must consider group dynamics. Teacher expectations of individuals in the group, the influences of the group on individual behavior, and the roles played by different individuals are important elements in understanding group personality.

Many "experts" who advise teachers about behavior problems tend to forget peer influence and group dynamics. Consequently, their advice falls short, and incidents of misbehavior continue. Actually, many of these problems are simply students' attempts to accommodate their needs in a social setting. They find themselves fulfilling certain roles and behaving in expected ways, often not understanding why they are behaving the way they do or what to do about it.

This chapter identifies some of the social needs that students bring into the classroom and some of the roles both students and teachers play. It also suggests some methods of restructuring the classroom to emphasize cooperation so that peer influence and the social needs of individuals actually contribute to the learning climate and prevent the occurrence of major discipline problems.

INDIVIDUAL NEEDS AND GROUP INFLUENCE

Students are social beings with needs that can best be met through interaction with others. These needs—love, belonging, affection, acceptance, fun, and power—are usually met in the context of groups. Glasser (1986, 68) states that these needs, especially the need for power, have become dominant for students in school today. However, because the schools have failed to recognize a change in need priorities, they still operate on the faulty assumption that youngsters understand the importance of what is being taught and will continue to put forth effort if pressured by the teacher. Glasser states that in most classes there is little sense of fun and belonging and, except for a few high achievers, little sense of power. The question is posed: "Do we have to stick with the rigid tradition that academic classes must be restricted to individual effort and individual competition, a structure that by its very nature, limits the opportunities of almost all students to gain not only the power but also the fun and belonging they all desire?"

Glasser contends that the majority of schools are failing because they cling to a rigid tradition of individual effort and accomplishments. Because the structure of the schools limits the ability of many students to satisfy their dominant needs, many students quit trying and find other ways of satisfying these needs—and these other ways frequently lead to discipline problems. He further contends that discipline problems will be largely eliminated if teachers are able to create an environment where students believe that if they make an effort they will gain some immediate satisfaction of basic social needs.

One of the most important needs for teachers to address is pupils' need for power. Individuals want to feel as if they are making a difference and have some control over their environment. However, this need for power is one that is difficult to achieve in a traditional classroom, and few students believe they have any power. Students are expected to obey. What is taught, how it is taught, and how it is evaluated are under the control of the teacher. Those teachers who do attempt to give their pupils some sense of power often do so by giving them control over insignificant matters that do little to change the classroom environment. When students feel that they have no influence on what happens in the classroom, they begin to find ways of resisting the power and the authority of the teacher. Some may do this through passive resistance and others through aggressive and acting-out behavior. They are basically sending the same message, "You cannot make me do what I do not want to do!" The teacher must find some way of allowing students to feel that they have some control over their destiny while at the same time accomplishing the educational goals of the school.

Box 7-1
STUDENT NEEDS AND DISCIPLINE PROBLEMS

Glasser contends that the priority needs of students have changed over the past two or three generations. The failure to understand this shift and to accommodate student needs in the structure of the classroom is a major source of discipline problems.

What is your opinion?

1.　　Do you agree with Glasser's assertion?

2.　　Cite specific examples of discipline problems created by denying students power.

3.　　Why do you think teachers are reluctant to give students more power and control?

4.　　What specific examples can you cite that might counter Glasser's assertion?

5.　　How did the structure of your classrooms as a student take into account your needs for belonging, affection, power, and fun?

Classrooms also tend to frustrate individual desires for affection and belonging. The classroom is a place where students compete with one another, and the successbelonging. The classroom is a place where students compete with one another, and the successbelonging. The classroom is a place where students compete with one another, and the success
of one individual means the failure for others. Competition among students makes it difficult for individuals to feel accepted and to belong. In fact, many high achievers soon learn that their success causes resentment in others in the class, and consequently they often do less than their best out of a fear of rejection.

An important goal for the teacher is to find ways of using group dynamics to promote individual effort and prevent problems associated with peer pressure and group membership. This is often accomplished when teachers help students satisfy their needs, give students some power over what is learned and how it is learned, and reduce competition among students so that the success of one individual means success, rather than failure, for others.

Goal Structures

In creating the type of learning environment where needs might be met, it is helpful to understand three types of goal structures commonly found in classrooms. Goal structures are methods of classroom organization that allow individuals within the class to attain academic and personal goals. These three goal structures are individualistic, competitive, and cooperative.

Individualistic Goal Structures. This organizational method structures the learning environment so that each student is working to attain goals with little or no relationship to others in the classroom. They are not competing against each other but rather against a set standard of performance. No relationship exists between the success of any one individual and the success of the group. Individualized learning approaches, mastery learning, and criterion-referenced grading systems all utilize individualistic goal structures. Students can achieve success if they achieve the minimum performance level required. The success of individualistic goal structures depends on students believing that they have the ability to succeed if they try. Those students who believe they do not possess ability will try only when the criterion performance level is very low. In turn, low performance standards lessen the challenge for the more able learners.

Competitive Goal Structures. Competitive goal structures are the most common ones found in classrooms. They are based on the assumption that youngsters like competition and are motivated by winning. In a competitive goal structure, individuals are competing with each other, so the success of any one individual is based on the performance of others in the group. A common example is grading individuals on the curve. Students' scores are listed from the highest to the lowest performance, with a certain percentage receiving A's, B's, C's, D's, and F's. There is a negative correlation between individual performance and group success. It is to the advantage of any one individual in the group for the other group members to do poorly. When this happens, the opportunity for an individual to succeed by keeping the average lower increases. In competitive goal structures, it is not advantageous for any one student to help others succeed. In fact, high achievers are often seen as threats to the group and have difficulty being accepted by the class members. Therefore, competitive goal structures tend to interfere with the attainment of the social goals of belonging, acceptance, and power.

Box 7-2
ARE COOPERATIVE GOAL STRUCTURES UNDEMOCRATIC?

Some individuals are critical of noncompetitive goal structures because they see them as contrary to some of the basic values of American society. They contend that the free enterprise system and innovation thrive in a competitive environment. Furthermore, they point out that the world is a competitive place and individuals must be prepared to compete.

What do you think?

1. **Do you agree or disagree with this contention?**

2. **What evidence can you cite that would tend to support this point of view?**

3. **What evidence can you cite that would refute this contention?**

4. **What are some specific places in society where competition is appropriate and where cooperation is appropriate?**

5. **How can both competition and cooperation be included in the classroom?**

Cooperative Goal Structures. Like competitive goal structures, cooperative goal structures link individual success with group success. However, the relationship is positive rather than negative. In cooperative goal structures, the success of an individual is linked to the success of the group. It is to the advantage of any one group member that all other group members do well. Cooperative goal structures emphasize teamwork and mutual support. Common examples occur in athletic events, where high performance of every team member is an important component. If any one team member does poorly, the success of the team is jeopardized. High performing team members are accepted and given respect because of the contribution they make to the entire team effort. Their success is encouraged rather than discouraged.

Cooperative goal structures also have the potential to fulfill the social needs of students. Structuring the class so that pupils are individually accountable yet interdependent with other class members can help them meet their needs of acceptance, belonging, and power. Cooperative goal structures emphasize group dynamics as a way of accomplishing academic and personal goals.

All three goal structures are appropriate in different situations. There are times when we must work individually to meet a prescribed standard, when we must compete with others, and when we must cooperate with each other for the benefit of all. However, the teacher who wants to use group dynamics in a positive way in the classroom might consider increased use of cooperative goal structures.

ROLES OF INDIVIDUALS WITHIN GROUPS

The personality of the group is a reflection of the needs and aspirations of individuals who are fulfilling different roles within the group. In general, two roles might be observed in the classroom—leader and followers. The leader assists in decision making, helps shape group expectations and direction, initiates group actions, and helps hold the group together. The followers carry out directions, persevere, and cooperate with the group leader. Groups do not achieve a high degree of success unless both leader and followers are present in the group. If everyone in a group tries to be a leader, a great deal of strife will take place and the group will lack cohesiveness. A leaderless group, on the other hand, will lack direction and purpose.

Group Leaders

The teacher must be aware that the group members, not the teacher, give individuals the status of group leader. Group leaders are key class members who exert a powerful influence on their groups. When the teacher and leaders are working cooperatively, a positive group dynamic is present (Howell and Howell 1979). On the other hand, if the teacher and class leaders are opposing each other, there will be constant conflict and power struggles, behavior problems will be numerous, and the teacher will have difficulty accomplishing worthwhile educational goals. Therefore, it is important for the teacher to identify classroom leaders and the impact they have on class members. If the teacher and the group leader do not share the same goals and purposes, or if the group leader believes that the teacher is undermining his or her role as leader, power struggles between the teacher and group members will be a constant barrier to learning and progress.

Once classroom leaders have been identified, the teacher should secure their cooperation. This can be accomplished by realizing that leaders like to lead, so they should be given responsibility in influencing the class in positive directions. However, care must be taken not to reinforce efforts at negative leadership. Such attempts should be ignored. To challenge or try to undermine a leader will only promote power struggles and develop a negative classroom climate. Howell and Howell (1979) point out that teachers' attempts to discredit leaders result in the loss of teacher power and credibility.

Group Followers

The role of follower may be subdivided into several categories. The roles that these students play are very important in shaping the dynamics of the classroom group. Understanding these roles and using them in a positive manner is important if a positive group climate is to be created.

Instigators. Instigators are those individuals who work beneath the surface to sow seeds and plant ideas. They then withdraw and observe the results of their efforts. Instigators have many ideas, but usually lack the courage or the confidence to try and become group leader. Since they lack confidence, they are afraid to take risks and prefer for other students to act out their ideas.

Instigators have a negative influence on the group when they sow seeds of discontent and suspicion. They may plant the idea that the rules and the authority of the teacher need to be challenged. They may suggest that the teacher really does not intend to follow through on consequences, and nothing will happen if someone chooses to violate classroom rules. When a teacher becomes aware of the influence of an instigator in the classroom, an effective approach is to discuss the role of an instigator and to have some role-playing exercises that focus on how students might be manipulated by others. Because an instigator lacks the courage to step forward as a leader, confronting the instigator with the fact that the teacher is aware of his or her role also serves to stop instigator behavior.

Instigators can be used to exert a positive influence by providing them with recognition and reinforcement when they do express good ideas. Enhancing their self-confidence and reducing their fear of failure allow them to be more open with their ideas and concerns so that teachers can deal with them in a direct and positive manner.

Class Clown. The class clown is the group entertainer. Often a class clown is a student with inferiority feelings and a high need for acceptance. Because of their feelings of inferiority, such students believe that the way to gain acceptance is through clowning and humor. They will often act on the unspoken feelings of the group in an effort to gain group acceptance. Their antics can provide the teacher with some clues to unspoken group feelings, such as anger and hostility.

Since the goal of the class clown is to get attention, the teacher should ignore attempts as unacceptable. This removes the audience and communicates the seriousness of the problem to the student. A clear understanding that inappropriate uses of clowning in the classroom will carry consequences is usually enough to help the class clown find other avenues for gaining acceptance. The teacher can assist by providing opportunities for the class clown to gain recognition and by providing him or her with opportunities to demonstrate humor at appropriate times and in appropriate ways. Creative use of the abilities of the class clown can be a benefit to the classroom climate by providing for some fun and a break from the routine.

Scapegoat. Scapegoats have a high need for acceptance. They are usually the students who have few friends in the class and have a very negative self-concept. They attempt to gain friends and acceptance by taking the blame for any problems. By accepting blame, they feel that they are becoming a part of the group. Unfortunately, the scapegoat orientation can lead to a maladjusted individual with a potentially destructive personality.

Teachers needs to be alert to the possibility of a scapegoat's assuming responsibility for group failure. Such efforts should be ignored, and the responsibility for the problems shared with the entire group. Instead of allowing this student to try and gain acceptance through negative means, the teacher should provide him or her with opportunities to gain group membership through constructive and positive channels. Scapegoats need friendship and success. Once they have learned that they can be productive and accepted for making worthwhile contributions, their willingness to accept blame will begin to disappear.

Teacher Roles

The teacher is a key member in the classroom, and the role assumed by the teacher will have a profound impact on the dynamics of the group. Teachers may play the role of a facilitator, who helps individuals learn; a leader, who promotes group cohesiveness and direction; a confidant, who can be talked with and trusted; or an expert, who shares valuable insight and information. These are positive roles that create a positive learning climate. However, the teacher may also assume some roles that are destructive to the group climate: the detective, always on the alert for rule violation; the judge, who is always evaluating the worth of individuals; or the powerless victim, who is an easy target for hostility. These roles take the teacher outside the classroom group and put teacher and students in adversarial positions. Some rather neutral roles, such as that of a source of information, a representative of society, or a surrogate parent, might also be assigned to the teacher. These roles may or may not carry power, based on whether or not the students want the information the teacher is dispensing, whether they accept the views of society, and whether they respect their parents or need someone to serve in that capacity.

Teachers will play all of these roles at one time or another. There are times when the teacher must serve as judge, referee, or detective. Teachers certainly are the sources of information and do represent society. Teachers need to make sure, however, that when they must play the role of judge or detective that the role is performed in a fair and just manner. They must not act arbitrarily or abuse the power that goes with the role. Teachers who are viewed as arbitrary or unfair lose credibility with students, and their power is rejected.

Finally, teachers need to remember that the role they perceive as appropriate for a teacher will influence the way they act and the authority and respect given to them by students. Becoming a skilled professional requires that teachers consider the assumptions they make about the role that they must play in the education of a given group of students. Understanding that this role might be destructive to the development

of a positive group climate is a beginning point in creating a successful classroom where incidents of misbehavior are reduced.

UTILIZING GROUP DYNAMICS THROUGH COOPERATIVE LEARNING

When the needs for power, inclusion, belonging, and fun are addressed in the classroom, positive group dynamics can result and learner satisfaction with the class can increase. One of the ways of utilizing cooperative goal structures to accomplish these purposes is through cooperative learning activities. Glasser (1986) states that

changing the structure of the classroom to a more cooperative approach will have the effect of giving students more control and will reduce incidents of inappropriate and apathetic behavior.

An impressive number of studies have found that, when compared to individualistic or competitive approaches, cooperative learning approaches do facilitate the achievement of important educational outcomes. Johnson and Johnson's (1985) review of the research reports that cooperative learning approaches lead to higher achievement, greater interpersonal attraction among students, more positive attitudes toward the subject studied, and a stronger belief that one is liked and supported by other students. These findings appear to be consistent across different grade levels and different achievement levels as well as for the attainment of a variety of educational objectives.

Cooperative Learning Approaches

A number of different approaches to cooperative learning have been developed. They vary in the amount of freedom and autonomy given to students and in their appropriateness for different educational objectives. Some approaches give students considerable freedom in determining not only how a topic is to be studied but also the pace of the lesson. Others even allow youngsters the freedom of deciding when they will be evaluated. All of the approaches emphasize group interdependence. The success of the group depends on the success of all group members, and students are encouraged to help each other rather than compete. The different approaches to cooperative learning require different amounts of teacher planning and preparation. Some of the approaches can be implemented rather easily with relatively minor adaptations to existing materials and content. Other approaches require significant changes in the material and extensive teacher preparation.

Student Teams-Achievement Divisions (Slavin 1980). This approach is one of the easiest to implement in the classroom. Existing materials can be used and are easily adaptable to this approach. In the Student Teams-Achievement Divisions (STAD) approach, students are assigned to learning teams consisting of four or five members. Each team should be composed of a variety of ability levels and be as evenly matched to each other as possible. The objective of each team is to increase the achievement of all team members each week. When each team member makes an improvement, the team is given points. The team that accumulates the most points each week is given some special privilege or prize.

Points are awarded on the basis of the past average of each team member. Therefore, the teacher needs to obtain an average for each class member. This might be done through the use of review papers and quizzes at the beginning of the school year or through student performance on assignments. The averages will be adjusted as the semester unfolds, so it is not necessary to obtain an accurate average for the first assignment. An approximation is appropriate for the first cooperative learning tasks.

Each team member may earn up to 10 points for the team. The points are usually determined by student performance on a 30-item test. For example, a student with a previous average of 15 who scores 20 on the criterion test contributes 5 points to the team total. However, if the student scores 25 or above, 10 points are awarded to the team total. A perfect paper is automatically awarded 10 points regardless of the past average of the student. Therefore, high achievers have an incentive to do their best and to help low achievers to improve. All students, regardless of past achievement and ability level, contribute to the group and obtain some satisfaction if they put forth reasonable effort.

At the beginning of the week each team is given the week's assignment. This assignment is the content to be tested and the material to be used to prepare for the test. The content might be introduced through teacher lecture or class discussion or on an assignment sheet given to all students. Team members then work together to complete the assignment and worksheets provided by the teacher. They study the material together and may even choose to give each other practice quizzes. When the team members believe that they are ready, they ask to take the criterion test. They may not, however, help one another on the test. When they have completed the test, they are scored and the team results posted. The team scoring the highest number of points is given recognition or reward. This might be in the form of recognition in a newsletter, on a bulletin board, or in more concrete reinforcement such as privileges, free time, or some other reward that is desired by class members. Totals may be kept for several weeks and the team that accumulates the highest total given some special reward.

The composition of the teams should be changed from time to time so that different members of the class have the opportunity to work together. However, this should not be done too frequently. Every four to six weeks seems to be a good rate at which to change team membership.

Teams-Games-Tournaments (Slavin 1980). The Teams-Games-Tournaments (TGT) model of cooperative learning is similar to STAD in that heterogeneous teams of individuals study together in preparing to take the criterion test, and the success of the team is linked to the success of all team members. The goal of each team is to accumulate the most points. Existing content and material are easily adapted to the model. The basic differences between TGT and STAD are amount of competition and scoring procedures. Rather than receiving points based on improvement, each individual on the team plays an academic game or tournament with classmates of similar

ability from other teams. Points are given to the team based on how well the team members do in the weekly tournament. The games or tournament activities are content related and may be adaptations of content tests or worksheets.

Students are assigned to five- or six-member teams and are given the same basic assignment as in STAD. At the beginning of the week the teacher explains the assignment and the content to be learned for the week. Team members then assist each other in completing the assignment and studying for the tournament. At the end of the week each team member sits around a table of students with similar ability from two other teams.

The groups of three who compete against each other are ranked according to ability, ranging from a group who are the highest achievers to a group who are the lowest achievers. For the second contest, the winners around each table are moved up to the next highest group, the lowest scoring individual moves down to the next lowest group, and the individual who came in second stays at the table. As a result, each individual is competing against two new opponents each week.

The games are often played using a format similar to a quiz show. Questions are written on cards and placed in the center of the table. Each student chooses a card and tries to answer the question. Each successful answer is given a point. At the conclusion, the points are added up and a team score is determined by how well each individual did in the tournament. The team accumulating the highest total points for the week is the winner of the tournament and is given special recognition or rewards.

TGT requires more teacher planning than does STAD. It is unnecessary for the teacher to have an established average for each student, but some informal assessment of student ability is necessary in order to rank them for the tournaments. Since students move up or down each week based on performance, an informal estimate will be sufficient. Additional time is required for writing tournament questions and supervising the tournaments.

Teachers report that the TGT approach does provide an excitement that is usually missing in the classroom. Even reluctant learners seem to get caught up in the tournaments and become interested in school. Since individual students are competing against two other individuals of similar ability, they believe they have a chance for success and know that their efforts will be rewarded. As in STAD, it is recommended that each team stay together for about a six-week period. The team that accumulates the most points during that time receives some special award or recognition.

Jigsaw (Slavin 1980). The Jigsaw model of cooperative learning is quite different from either STAD or TGT. Jigsaw involves the use of two groups, the "home" group and the "expert" group. Students are placed in heterogeneous teams of approximately six. This initial group is what is called the home group. Unlike STAD and TGT, Jigsaw does not involve competition between teams. Rather, the object is for each member to help other team members do as well as possible on the criterion test. In some forms of Jigsaw, the group grades are given to the team. Each person in the group receives the same grade based on the average of the group members on the test. Other teachers award improvement points to group members as in STAD and provide rewards or reinforcement based on the team's improvement points.

The teacher divides the material to be studied into several different components. For example, a social studies lesson focusing on a specific country might be divided into several subtopics, such as economics, geography, and politics. The material for each component is then combined with study guides, questions, and other support materials. Each member of the home team is assigned to an expert group whose goal is to learn as much as possible about their component. The expert group is composed of all the students from the different home teams assigned to that subtopic. They subsequently return to their home team and teach the others in the group the material they learned.

A potential problem with the Jigsaw approach is absenteeism. The absence of a group member may prevent the flow of information from the expert group to the home team. One possible solution is to assign two individuals to each expert group so that they can work together in learning the material and presenting it to the home team. The Jigsaw approach also requires a considerable amount of teacher preparation and planning. The teacher must decide how many expert groups are needed and must prepare and gather the material for the expert groups. In addition, Jigsaw is most appropriate for content that can easily be divided into several categories. Some content cannot be divided in ways that help students understand the meanings and significance of the material. The teacher must also be available to help the expert groups and to clarify and explain the content for them. It might be necessary to stagger expert group meetings so that the teacher is available when needed. All this often creates organizational and logistical problems.

Learning Together (Johnson et al. 1984). This approach is somewhat similar to Jigsaw. Students are placed in heterogenous groups, and each team is given a project or a task to complete. Within each group, individual students are usually assigned a role or a certain part of the task to complete, for example, recorder, researcher, writer, or artist. Again, there is no competition among teams. The object is for each team to do the best job possible on the task that is assigned. The final project or task is graded, and all members of the team receive the grade given for the task. This approach tends to work best for those tasks that require a number of different skills. In this way, all team members are able to share their strengths with the group and consequently produce a better project or task than would have been possible alone. This approach can also allow considerable freedom for the group members to decide how they will approach the task and what they will actually do for a final project. For example, one high school English teacher allowed teams of individuals to work on a project to share one of Shakespeare's plays with the class. The groups developed enactments and videotapes of a play, rewrites of the play in a contemporary setting, and other creative activities.

Teachers often express concern with group grading. However, Johnson and Johnson (1985) report research indicating that youngsters, after exposure to group grades, favor group grading and believe that it is the fairest approach. Group grading

---

Box 7-3
ARE GROUP GRADES FAIR?

Awarding group grades is one ot the most controversial components of some cooperative learning approaches. Teachers are bothered that students may not see the approach as fair and that it may penalize high achievers while allowing low achievers to get by with little effort.

What is your opinion?

1. **What is your reaction to group grading?**

2. **What specific things might be done to ensure that all individuals in the group are held accountable for doing their best?**

3. **Defenders of group grading point out that all members of athletic teams win or lose depending on the efforts of the total team and, in a sense, share a group grade. Yet they accept the situation as fair. How do you react to this analogy?**

---

can be moderated by awarding grades or points to individuals based on the effort and contribution they make to the group. Students can be allowed to share in this effort by evaluating themselves and the others in their group.

Cooperative learning activities have great promise for helping teachers restructure classrooms so that they become more satisfying places for students. Making classrooms more exciting and capitalizing on group dynamics can help eliminate a number of discipline problems. Dealing with discipline in a cooperative learning classroom is easier for the teacher because the teacher usually has the support of the other members of the group. However, not only do cooperative learning structures help promote more appropriate task-related behavior but they also promote academic achievement. The suggestion to use cooperative learning as a means of preventing discipline problems is based on the premise that the teacher should identify the cause of a problem and try to eliminate that cause rather than merely dealing with the symptom. One of the primary reasons for inappropriate behavior is that schools are not structured to take students' needs into account. Cooperative learning is an approach that does consider the needs of students and does utilize group dynamics in promoting a healthy climate where students feel accepted and worthwhile.

SUMMARY

Because individuals behave differently when they are part of a group, group dynamics is an important consideration for the classroom teacher. For many students, the peer group is a more important source of information and reinforcement than teachers or parents. The wise teacher recognizes the roles that different individuals in the class fulfill and learns how to utilize these roles and the dynamic interpersonal relationship of individuals in a positive way rather than allowing them to interfere with the teaching-learning process. As human beings, students have many social needs that are best met in groups. The needs for acceptance and for belonging may, in fact, be more important for students of today than for previous generations. By recognizing the importance of these needs and structuring the classroom to accommodate them through approaches such as cooperative learning, the teacher can create an environment that is satisfying for students as well as the teacher.

SUGGESTED ACTIVITIES

1. Observe a group of individuals working together. Try to identify the leader and the followers. What behaviors characterize the leader? What techniques does the leader use to influence the group? What seems to happen when more than one person wants to be the leader?

2. In a text dealing with group dynamics, research how to prepare a sociogram. If possible, conduct one with a group of students. State specific actions that a teacher might take to utilize this information to create a more positive classroom.

3. Using your school experience as an information base, identify examples of instigators, class clowns, and scapegoats. Share your experiences with a group of peers and state ways teachers might react to these different roles.

4. Using your experience as a data source, identify teachers who assumed positive and negative roles as their primary behavior. What was your reaction to the teachers? How effective were they as teachers? What types of problems did they have in the classroom?

5. Choose one of the cooperative learning approaches that appeals to you. State why you like that approach and what you might need to do to implement the approach in the classroom.

6. Take one of the cooperative learning approaches and develop a a complete lesson, including all of the materials and procedures that would be necessary for you to implement the approach in a classroom.

BIBLIOGRAPHY

GLASSER, W. 1986. *Control Theory in the Classroom*. New York: Harper & Row.

HOWELL, R. G., and P. L. HOWELL. 1979. Discipline in the Classroom: Solving the Teaching Puzzle. Reston, Va.: Reston.

JOHNSON, D., and R. JOHNSON. 1985. The internal dynamics of cooperative learning groups. In *Learning to Cooperate, Cooperating to Learn,* eds. R. Slavin, S. Sharan, C. Webb, and R. Schmuck. New York: Plenum.

JOHNSON, D., R. JOHNSON, E. HOLUBEC, and P. ROY. 1984. *Circles of Learning: Cooperation in the Classroom*. Alexandria, Va.: Association for Supervision and Curriculum Development.

REDL, F., and W. WATTENBERG. 1959. *Mental Hygiene in Teaching*. New York: Harcourt Brace and World.

SLAVIN, R. 1980. *Using Student Team Learning*. Baltimore: John Hopkins Team Learning Project, Center for Social Organization of the Schools.

Chapter 8

SELECTING A RESPONSE TO INAPPROPRIATE BEHAVIOR

OBJECTIVES

This chapter provides information to help the reader to

1. Identify criteria that should be used when evaluating a classroom discipline plan

2. State basic principles to be considered when choosing a response to discipline problems

3. List the questions to be considered when developing a personal discipline plan

4. Identify the basic components of assertive discipline

5. Define three categories of responses that define alternative responses to misbehavior

INTRODUCTION

The first concern of the teacher is to prevent discipline problems. Everyone makes mistakes occasionally, even teachers. Mistakes and problems are an important part of life, and responding to discipline problems is a normal and important part of being a teacher. However, it is the manner and style that the teacher uses when responding to these mistakes and inappropriate behaviors that is important. These incidents can be important learning experiences or major confrontations that interfere with the relationship between the teacher and the learner and decrease the probability that learning will take place.

There is no shortage of suggestions about what to do when problems occur—and most of the suggestions have been effective for some teachers in responding to misbehavior. However, what works for one teacher in one situation may not work for another teacher in another situation. Unfortunately, no simple solutions to discipline problems exist. A given individual teacher teaching a given group of learners with a unique set of needs will have to be a problem solver and decision maker. Solving problems and making decisions require that the teacher understand alternatives and have some criteria for choosing a specific response. It is the purpose of this chapter to present a range of alternatives to choose from when responding to problems and to provide some criteria for one's choice of response.

THE PURPOSE OF DISCIPLINE

The purpose of discipline is to help students develop self-control so that they may have satisfying and productive lives. The welfare of the student, not that of the parent or the teacher, needs to be kept in the forefront as teachers respond to student misbehavior. Incidents of misbehavior need not be viewed as something that is totally negative, to be avoided at all costs. Rather, they should be considered as opportunities to help a student move toward one of the most important characteristics of a successful life, that of self-control.

Using classroom management and discipline in moving learners toward that goal is the theme of this book. This purpose needs to be kept in mind when considering how to respond to incidents of misbehavior. The basic question should be "How can I respond so that the individual will move toward increased self-control?" This concern should take priority over a desire to keep the classroom quiet or to maintain order. The teacher can respond in ways that may stop a behavior or may cause the classroom to be quiet and orderly but do not help class members move in the direction of increased self-control. In fact, the criterion that should be used in determining the effectiveness of a classroom discipline plan is the extent to which the students are exhibiting increased self-control as the year progresses. If the class is having as many (or more) problems in April as in September, the teacher should seriously question whether or not the approach toward discipline is working.

BOX 8-1   PROMOTING SELF-CONTROL THROUGH RESPONSES TO MISBEHAVIOR

The following are some typical responses to misbehavior. Their potential for facilitating growth in self-control is evaluated.

	ADVANTAGES	DISADVANTAGES
Punishment	Punishment is better than no control at all. It might be an appropriate last resort for serious problems or when a classroom is out of control.	Punishment often leads to a breakdown of communication between the teacher and the learner. When this occurs, the opportunity for growth is blocked. Since the discipline is imposed from outside the learner, the learner often shifts blame for the punishment to the person giving the punishment rather than to the behavior. The potential side effects of resentment and revenge may lead to more serious problems. Finally, punishment does not teach the correct behavior and therefore has little potential for moving the individual toward increased self-control.
Affection/Praise	Many individuals see affection and praise as the exact opposite of punishment and therefore the most desirable approach. It is true that the teacher should care about learners and should provide praise for appropriate behavior. This approach contains the potential for developing a positive relationship between the teacher and learners and it can teach appropriate behavior.	The problem with this approach is that it is still dependent on an outside source to provide the praise and the affection. However, the learner is still dependent on external sources for praise and affection. The youngster may then base behavior on what might be praised by those in groups that encourage destructive behavior. In order for this approach to work, there must be a good relationship between the teacher and the learner. The teacher must be careful that a dependent relationship does not develop, as this would also hinder the movement toward self-control. For praise to be effective, it must be genuine, related to the desired behavior, and given in moderation.

BOX 8-1 (cont.)

	ADVANTAGES	DISADVANTAGES
LOGICAL AND NATURAL CONSEQUENCES	When individuals experience a natural consequence of a behavior, they begin to learn to associate the consequences with the behavior. The choice is left with the youngster to decide whether or not to experience the consequences, thus promoting an acceptance of responsibility for the behavior. Natural consequences allow the teacher to remain out of the situation and in a position to offer assistance when the learner chooses to move in a positive direction. Logical consequences, reactions, or consequences that are logically related to a behavioral problem, such as isolation when someone is disturbing or loss of a privilege when someone misuses it, can also be powerful if used correctly. Allowing a learner time alone to reflect on the problem and clearly pointing out the relationship between the behavior and the consequences can keep the responsibility with the youngster. The approach has potential for helping the student internalize appropriate behavioral standards.	First of all, there are few natural consequences for misbehavior in the classroom that are likely to have the impact of changing behavior. Therefore, the teacher must rely on logical consequences, something that is logically related to the nature of the offense. Many youngsters may see this as a form of punishment and avoid taking responsibility for their behavior. The teacher must not impose consequences as a means of getting revenge. The teacher needs to remain unemotional and convey the message of acceptance of the youngster while not accepting the behavior. This is often difficult to accomplish.
BEHAVIOR BASED ON VALUES AND SELF-CHOSEN PRINCIPLES	This is the goal toward which we should strive. When individuals behave according to self-chosen principles, they have internalized standards of behavior and are exercising a high standard of self-control. Individuals who have reached this stage can adapt to a variety of situations and are not dependent on external pressures. Acting on these principles has the impact of improving self-esteem.	A high degree of maturity is required for individuals to reach this level. In addition, a problem can occur if the student's set of principles is in conflict with that of the teacher. This approach requires the development of commonly held concepts of right and wrong. Reaching this level takes considerable time and effort.

This is not to imply that change may be immediate and dramatic. Those individuals with serious problems are not likely to exhibit a dramatic change in the course of a week or even a month. However, over several months, there should be some evidence that the class, as a whole, is progressing toward more self-control.

BASIC PRINCIPLES OF DISCIPLINE

Several principles should be kept in mind when considering a response to inappropriate behavior. Following these principles can help the teacher ensure that the response is likely to be the most effective in promoting a healthy classroom climate and in creating conditions so that movement toward self-control can occur.

1. The dignity of the learner must be preserved when responding to misbehavior. Methods that humiliate students or cause them to lose their self-respect should not be used. It is interesting to note that a great number of high school learners state that one of the major reasons why they misbehaved is because they believed that the teacher was assaulting their dignity and self-respect. For them, then, misbehavior was a means of getting back at the teacher. Maintaining a respect for the person and helping the learner retain self-respect and a sense of dignity will help create the conditions necessary for learning self-control.

2. Private correction is preferable to public correction. Preserving the dignity of the learner leads to this second principle. Public correction has several potential pitfalls. Not only does it have the potential for public humiliation and a loss of self-respect, but it also provides attention for inappropriate behavior and sets the stage for power struggles between the teacher and the learner. The student may refuse to obey and thereby place the teacher on the spot. Teachers then feel they must respond to this defiance, and a minor behavior problem escalates into a major confrontation. In these situations the teacher may either be at a loss as to how to respond or will respond in a manner that is excessively harsh. Either way, the teacher loses some respect and credibility.

This is not to imply that public correction should never be used. There are times when the teacher must respond in order to stop a behavior that is disrupting a lesson in progress. However, this should be done quickly and unemotionally so that the behavior is stopped with as little intrusion into the lesson as possible. The problem should then be dealt with in depth when the teacher can deal with the student privately.

3. The teacher needs to respond to incidents of misbehavior consistently and fairly. Implicit in this statement is that the teacher needs to respond to incidents of misbehavior. Few problems will disappear if the teacher pretends that they do not exist. Some well-meaning individuals have counseled teachers to ignore misbehavior because this withholding of attention will soon lead to the disappearance of the behavior. This is true *only* if the teacher is the sole source of reinforcement for the learner. However, this is rarely true in the classroom. Other learners may be providing the reinforcement for the behavior. Ignoring the behavior will generally have no impact if the reinforcement is coming from class members and not the teacher.

Responding consistently to misbehavior means that the teacher responds to all incidents of misbehavior and does so each day. If something is against the rule on one day, it is against the rule every day. Those classes characterized by students' constant testing of the rules are usually where the teacher has inconsistently enforced the rules. Consistent reinforcement on a day-to-day basis is the best remedy for this type of problem.

Fairness means that the teacher follows through regardless of who is doing the misbehaving. Teachers have a tendency to overlook the misbehavior of a star learner and be excessively harsh when responding to a learner for whom they have little affection. This uneven treatment leads to resentment. The teacher needs to make sure that if cute little Sarah misbehaves, she will experience consequences just as surely as will Barbara, the perennial problem.

4. The causes need to be the target for the teacher, not just the specific incident of misbehavior. This requires an attitude of inquiry on the part of the teacher. The teacher needs to seek answers to questions concerning why the individual might be behaving in this manner. This is especially true if the behavior problem is one that occurs repeatedly. It may well be that persistent misbehavior signals some deeper, more fundamental problem with the organization and climate of the classroom or some deep personal problems being experienced by the learner. Merely responding to the surface behavior, while it may stop the behavior for a time, will not solve the problem, and it will recur at some later time, perhaps in a more serious form.

It has been the experience of the author that persistent misbehavior is frequently a desperate call for help. The youngster is in serious difficulty and knows no other way to signal that help is needed. Understanding this can help a teacher respond to the student in ways that not only eliminate the problem but also result in great professional and personal rewards.

Being willing to search for the causes of misbehavior requires a professionally and personally secure teacher. The teacher must be willing to consider the possibility that his or her own actions caused the misbehavior. For example, misbehavior might be a sign of learner anxiety and the fear of failure because the lessons are not at the appropriate level of difficulty. Other possible causes might be boredom, a lack of understanding of the importance or relevance of the topic, or poor lesson planning and pacing. In these situations, probing for the causes of the misbehavior might lead the teacher to professional improvement that will prevent future problems. On the other hand, some misbehavior merely reflects youthful exuberance and enthusiasm. If this is the reason for some inappropriate behavior, it should be understood and not treated as a major offense requiring stiff penalties. Occasional, minor infractions may be nothing more than this and should not cause the teacher much concern.

Box 8-2
APPLYING THE BASIC PRINCIPLES

Everyone makes mistakes and everyone has been disciplined. Think about a time when you were disciplined and respond to the following questions.

My experience:

1.   **What was the problem?**

2.   **How did the teacher (or parent) respond to the problem?**

3.   **Which of the principles of discipline were followed?**

4.   **Which of the principles were not followed?**

5.   **What was the outcome? How did you feel or respond?**

6.   **What advice would you give that person that could lead to a more productive response?**

RESPONSES TO MISBEHAVIOR

Choosing an appropriate response to incidents of misbehavior is the next step in effective discipline. Many teachers have difficulty here: They overreact to relatively minor incidents, rely on one or two responses that soon lose their effectiveness, or don't respond at all because of uncertainty about how to respond. It is important that incidents of misbehavior be consistently followed by a response. However, just randomly choosing responses or following an impulse is not likely to achieve the desired results.

Choosing a Response Best for You

Discipline, like so many other aspects of teaching, has no simple solutions or magical formulas that work for all teachers in all situations. Teachers vary in their personality and in their values. What works for one teacher in one environment may not work for another teacher in another environment. The class setting also varies enormously from place to place. Learners bring with them their cultural beliefs and values about the importance of school and appropriate behavior for the classroom. In addition, many have formed expectations based on prior experiences with school. Advanced placement students who have high expectations of success and an academic orientation will respond to teacher correction somewhat differently than will learners with a history of school failure. The following questions and their answers can help teachers choose a response or set of responses that is most likely to be effective.

1. *What are the values and beliefs that I hold concerning the nature of learners and my role as a teacher?* The attitudes and beliefs that you hold toward learners will have an important impact on the way you choose to respond to incidents of misbehavior. The key issue is whether you view learners as basically good or basically bad. If you believe, for example, that learners are not capable or trustworthy, then your response to a discipline problem is likely to be one that is heavy on teacher power and low on learner choice. If, on the other hand, you believe that learners should be given a great deal of freedom because they can be trusted to make appropriate choices, then approaches to discipline are likely to be indirect ones that deemphasize teacher control.

A rather prevalent attitude among many teachers and parents in our society is that individuals should do what is good and right with no expectation of a reward or reinforcer. As a result, few reinforcers are given for what is expected and a great deal of negative attention is directed toward the inappropriate behavior. Individuals who have this attitude are often reluctant to use approaches that emphasize positive reinforcement for expected behavior. To them, providing frequent reinforcers seems somewhat unethical.

Your view of the learning process will also affect your choice of an approach. Teachers who view the learning process as hard work that takes place in a strict, no-nonsense environment will define discipline problems differently and will respond to incidents of misbehavior differently than those who consider learning as a process of activity and exploration that requires freedom and choice.

An understanding of the role of the teacher is yet another area that needs to be considered. If the role of the teacher is defined as one of primarily communicating content and subject matter, and that the social and emotional needs of learners are the concern of others, then little effort will be directed toward helping students deal with these problems or move toward increased self-control.

2. *What is the maturity level of the students I am teaching?* Some responses to misbehavior require more maturity on the part of the learners. It is unrealistic to think that what will work for very young children will also be effective for older children. Some approaches require a considerable amount of abstract reasoning and require that the individual understand the perspective of another. These conditions are not likely to be present in young children and therefore the use of such approaches is not likely to meet with much success.

It is important to realize, however, that age alone is not a reliable indicator of emotional and moral maturity. There are some individuals at the secondary school level who have not yet attained the moral maturity to understand the function of law and accept the notion of social and moral responsibility. These students need to be assisted in their emotional and moral growth if they are to move toward the self-control required of a responsible citizen.

3. *What are the cultural backgrounds and the values of the learners I am teaching?* The influence of culture on the behavior of students is easily overlooked by teachers. Individuals often believe that others view the world as they view it. This causes problems for the teacher who comes from one subculture and has learners from another subculture. Students may have a different view of the role of school and what constitutes appropriate behavior and may interpret teacher responses very differently. For example, some teachers believe that a misbehaving youngster should look them in the eyes when they are delivering a reprimand. However, some subcultures have taught their young that to look an adult in the face is disrespectful. In this case, the student may be attempting to do what is right and is confused by the teacher's anger. Nonverbal behavior is yet another area where different cultures attach different meanings to behavior. Some subcultures do not encourage touching behavior and others do. A teacher who is not used to touching individuals may be viewed as cold and uncaring by students who come from a "contact" subculture.

The teacher who wishes to be successful in developing an effective discipline plan must consider the cultural expectations and norms of the group being taught. This can be accomplished by discussing the culture with members and simply observing the students.

4. *What is the previous school history of the learners in the classroom?* This is an area that must be handled with care and demands a high level of professionalism. Understanding the previous record of success or failure of a student can help the

teacher understand the reasons behind certain behaviors and can be of tremendous value in helping the teacher plan so that problems can be eliminated. However, it is very easy for a teacher to form a set of negative expectations for a student who has a history of discipline problems and failure. The professional teacher needs to learn to use records in an appropriate and professional manner.

If a student has a history of problems, the teacher might be aware that a certain response may trigger negative and hostile reactions. It might be important to make sure that the learner is not put on the spot or embarrassed in front of the class. These responses may trigger a power struggle or a confrontation. More low profile and less threatening responses may be needed for this highly frustrated and fearful learner.

5. *What type of support can I expect from parents?* The support of parents can be extremely important in developing and implementing a discipline plan. The teacher should actively solicit support from parents in a positive manner. In most situations, parents are more than willing to help. However, there are situations where parents are either unable or unwilling to support the school program. This does not mean that the efforts of the teacher are doomed. It just means that the teacher will not be able to depend on those approaches that require parental involvement. It is likely that the school administrator or counselor will need to be kept informed and involved if serious problems arise. Teachers need to remember that they have a responsibility to all learners in their classroom. One individual cannot be allowed to interfere with the learning of others simply because the parent refuses to cooperate. Outside agencies and resources may need to be quickly involved when there is an absence of parental support.

6. *How much time and effort will the response require?* Some responses require more investment of time than do others. Some approaches may require a meeting or a counseling session with the learner. There are situations in the classroom when this time is simply not available. When this happens the teacher may be required to choose, at least temporarily, a less desirable approach in the interest of time. Some approaches, such as behavior modification, may require a considerable amount of out-of-class time to develop the reinforcement plan and considerable in-class time implementing the plan. An elementary teacher with a class of 30 students or a secondary teacher with several different preparations may not have the time to implement a behavior modification plan.

7. *What resources will the response require?* Some approaches to discipline require specific materials or space. For example, behavior modification might require reinforcers that need to be purchased. Other responses might require an isolation area in the classroom or somewhere else in the school. The use of these approaches requires a considerable amount of preplanning and cooperation with others, such as the school principal, to make sure that the time and the space are available to make the plan work.

8. *What support can I expect from the school administration?* The Canters (1976, 2) state that the teacher has a right to expect support from the school administration.

Box 8-3
DEVELOPING YOUR PLAN

In order to begin developing a plan for responding to discipline problems, you need to consider the questions discussed in the test. Take a few minutes to reflect on your answers to the questions and the implications you see for how they will guide your responses.

My plan:

1. What are your values and beliefs about the nature of learning and your role as a teacher? What are the implications that seem to follow from your position?

2. What is your grade level preference? What are the things you would need to consider about students at that level in making decisions about responding to discipline problems?

3. What is your subcultural background? What expectations do you have that might originate with your background? How might these expectations be different for another cultural group?

4. What type of support would you expect from parents? Is it a realistic expectation? How can you obtain more parental support?

5. What is your expectation of support from the school administration? Is that a realistic expectation? What would you do if you were not getting the support you needed?

Teachers do need to accept that they have this right and that the administration needs to be supportive of teacher efforts to develop a positive learning climate. Unfortunately, this is not always the case. Some administrators, like some teachers, are uncertain of appropriate ways of responding to the discipline problems that land in their office.

As a teacher you may have to take an active role in obtaining administrative support. This can be accomplished by meeting with the administrator and explaining your plan and your expectations. This discussion includes the conditions under which a learner will be referred to the administrator and what the administrator will do when a student does come to the office. A common problem of many administrators is the teacher who refers students to the office for trivial problems. Some teachers do not want to deal with any discipline problems, so they quickly send a student to the office. When this happens, the teacher cannot expect the administrator to be totally supportive. Sending a student to the office should be a last resort, tried only when all other efforts have failed.

ASSERTIVE DISCIPLINE

One approach adopted by many teachers in an effort to apply some of the principles just discussed is that of assertive discipline. Assertive discipline, developed and widely disseminated by Lee and Marlene Canter (1976), places the responsibility and the power for controlling the class in the hands of the teacher. The teacher develops the class rules and the range of consequences to be followed. The rules should be kept to a minimum, no more than five or six, and are to be posted in a prominent place in the classroom. In addition, the Canters suggest developing a range of alternatives to be used whenever a rule is violated. The first consequence is to place the student's name on the chalkboard at the first offense. This serves as a warning that the behavior is unacceptable. If the student misbehaves again during the day, a check mark is placed after his or her name. This indicates that the student now must spend 15 minutes in detention or after school. A third offense during the day results in another check indicating that the student must spend 30 minutes in detention or after school. An additional misbehavior results in the student being sent to the office to be dealt with by the school principal or counselor. At the end of each school day all names are erased so that students have a fresh start each day.

The Canters also emphasize giving positive assertions or positive rewards when the class follows the rules. They note that the range of consequences should vary according to the needs of the teacher and the unique situation of the school.

It is important that both the positive and negative consequences chosen are comfortable for the teacher. If the teacher is not comfortable with the consequences, there will be some reluctance to implement them. As a result, teacher responses will become inconsistent and the discipline plan will fail. For example, keeping the student after school is a consequence listed on many plans. However, if the teacher is uncomfortable keeping students after school because of some reason, such as missing a bus or because that is the time when the teacher does a lot of work, then it should not be considered an alternative. The same is true of positive consequences. If the teacher does not feel comfortable giving prizes or parties as rewards for appropriate behavior, other positive consequences should be used instead.

The Canters emphasize that the teacher must constantly remind students that they are choosing either to be rewarded or to experience the consequences. Because the rules and the consequences are clearly identified, students know what will happen if they choose to violate a rule. If they do not want to experience the consequences, then they need to follow the rules.

The Canters point out that one of the barriers to the use of assertive discipline is the leadership style of the teacher. They contend that many teachers use nonassertive management where they allow students to violate their needs as a teacher to teach and the needs of the other students to learn. Other teachers have a hostile style of reacting to students in a negative and arbitrary manner. These teachers often use ridicule and name-calling as a response to problems. The Canters believe that teachers need an assertive style—one where the teacher communicates that rules will be enforced consistently, students will not be allowed to misbehave, and the response to misbehavior is firm, yet calm and businesslike.

The assertive discipline approach seems to work best for inexperienced teachers or those who have not yet developed a successful classroom management style. It provides the basics for gaining control of a classroom and gives the teacher the security of knowing what to do when a problem arises. The approach also requires the involvement of the school principal. Since a trip to the office is always used as a last resort, school principals can more consistently support the teacher because they can be certain that the student has caused serious disruption.

There are, however, some potential difficulties with assertive discipline. On the one hand, the range of consequences might not be appropriate for all students and all offenses. The consequences are not personalized to fit the needs of the student or the nature of the offense. They are more punishments to misbehavior than a natural or logical consequence. In addition, retaining all power in the hands of the teacher and implementing the approach in a rather mechanical manner make it easy for the teacher to ignore what might be causing the behavior in the first place. Finally, when poorly implemented, the approach creates a repressive classroom environment where teachers exercise their leadership through coercion and student needs are overlooked. This negative environment, although it may lessen misbehavior in the classroom, often results in outbreaks of misbehavior such as vandalism and violence outside the classroom.

In summary, although the assertive discipline approach does implement some of the principles suggested, it does not implement others. Once again the major issue should be the extent to which the approach helps students accept responsibility and move toward self-control.

Box 8-4
ASSERTIVE DISCIPLINE

Ms. Young was a firm believer in the assertive discipline approach advocated by the Canters. It seemed to work quite well with her third-grade class, with one exception. One boy still seemed to be unable to follow the rules. Billy would get at least one check after his name every day and spend at least 15 minutes after school. Each night he could be observed sitting in his seat crying. Although Ms. Young felt badly about keeping him after school so frequently, she was convinced that he would eventually get the message that he was the one who was deciding to stay after school, because of his poor behavior, and that he would change.

What is your reaction?
1.   **What do you think about Ms. Young's approach with Billy?**

2.   **Will he eventually change?**

3.   **What might Ms. Young need to do to make the approach work with Billy?**

A RANGE OF ALTERNATIVE RESPONSES

When choosing a response to discipline problems, it is helpful to be aware of alternatives. One way of thinking about alternatives is to order them into categories. Knowledge of these categories can be extremely useful for the teacher in selecting a response that is most appropriate for the situation. A general guideline to follow when selecting a response to misbehavior is that the response should be consistent with the seriousness or the persistence of the misbehavior. If the behavior is severely disruptive or one that threatens the well-being of others, then the response should be a relatively severe response consistent with the nature of the offense. However, if the behavior is the result of youthful enthusiasm, then the response should not be as severe. A first-time occurrence should be treated differently than persistent problems. The range of alternatives, then, should consist of categories that include a range from less severe responses to more severe responses, when dealing with more serious problems. It needs to be noted that severe relates to the seriousness of the response, the amount of time and effort required from the teacher, and the potential impact of the response on the learner. Severity does not mean harshness or the infliction of pain.

The range is also built around a continuum from relatively unobtrusive responses to those that are more obtrusive. When possible, the teacher should try the unobtrusive and less severe measures first. The teacher should attempt to select a response that will have the least disruptive impact on the flow of the lesson. This might mean responding rather unobtrusively at the time and then returning to deal with the problem in more depth when time permits.

The following sections suggest three categories from which the teacher might choose a response: supporting self-control, restructuring the learning environment, and direct teacher intervention. Responses for the less serious behaviors should be drawn from the first two categories. Suggestions for responses to more serious and persistent problems are found under the third category. A teacher need not use every response under each category. Those responses that are most comfortable for the teacher should be selected and tried. In addition, the specific suggestions given under each category are not meant to be comprehensive. A teacher may add promising responses to each category.

Supporting Self-Control

This category includes two basic kinds of responses: positive responses that are intended to support incidents of appropriate behavior and teacher responses that might be directed toward minor offenses. The suggestions in this category allow learners considerable freedom and choice. The intent of the teacher is to communicate in an unobtrusive way that there is a problem. The learner is then given the opportunity to exercise self-control. By allowing the student the freedom to choose to exercise

self-control and then reinforcing this choice, the teacher can help create a positive self-image for the learner and help him or her discover satisfaction in proper behavior. The specific actions grouped under this category should be those that are relatively unobtrusive and require very little direct intervention. In fact, one of the responses of the teacher might be not to intervene at all but to allow the learner to experience the natural consequences of the act.

Restructuring the Learning Environment

When learners are unable to exercise self-control, they will need some assistance. This might be accomplished by altering the learning environment. A relatively simple solution might be to move the seat of the learner or change the composition of the learning group. However, more obtrusive and direct measures such as a teacher-learner conference might be required to begin identifying the causes of the misbehavior and how it can be corrected. If the behavior is a relatively persistent one, the teacher may need to develop a well-thought-out plan of behavior modification. This takes considerably more time and skill but can prove to be very worthwhile in stopping a behavior and putting the student back on the road toward self-control.

Direct Teacher Intervention

The responses in this category should be chosen only if the problem is very serious and after other, less severe and obtrusive measures have been tried. The responses in this category place a great deal of the responsibility in the hands of the teacher. Learner choice and freedom are minimal. In addition, these responses are those that are most likely to have a negative impact on the self-esteem of the individual and therefore provoke resistance. However, there is a time when they must be used. When a teacher chooses one of these responses, it is important that the learner realize it is a consequence of his or her behavior and that it is something he or she earned, not something that the teacher is doing to get revenge. It is important that the link between behavior and consequence remains clear. When possible, the chosen intervention should relate to the nature of the offense. For example, if the offense is one that results in a waste of time, then the learner should be expected to make up the time. If it results in the destruction of property, then restitution needs to be made.

Specific actions that might be grouped under this category include isolation, loss of a privilege, removal from class, or remaining after school. These actions should be implemented with care and as infrequently as possible. If used as a response to minor offenses or used too frequently, they lose their potency.

The majority of the misbehaviors that occur in the classroom can be successfully handled by the suggestions given in these three categories. However, there may be some serious incidents of misbehavior where nothing seems to work. Those problems may require the involvement of individuals other than the classroom teacher: the principal, the school counselor, or even outside agencies.

This chapter has introduced three basic categories of responses to incidents of misbehavior. The following chapters deal with these categories in more depth.

SUMMARY

Teachers often have problems because they lack an understanding of how to respond to incidents of misbehavior. Some teachers tend to overlook problems because they don't know how to respond; others respond in an overly harsh manner because they lack an understanding of more relevant alternatives.

Discipline, like other aspects of teaching and learning, works best when it is personalized. It is extremely unlikely that the same approach will work for all learners and all teachers regardless of the context of their teaching and learning. An important part of this personalization is for teachers to recognize how their own values and beliefs affect their responses. Additionally, the maturity level and the cultural values of those being taught should be considered. Having a clear understanding of the values of the school administration and the support that can be expected from parents are yet other concerns that affect the choices that a teacher might make.

It is important to keep in mind the basic purpose of discipline, that of moving the individual toward increased self-control. Remembering this goal, along with maintaining a respect for students, responding consistently and fairly, and trying to get to the root of the problem rather than merely responding to the surface behavior, can help teachers choose responses that are likely to have success and make their efforts professionally and personally rewarding.

SUGGESTED ACTIVITIES

1. Interview some teachers about their responses to discipline problems. Identify their values and how they seem to perceive their role as teacher. What seems to be their purpose when correcting inappropriate behavior? Group their ideas for responses under the categories provided in this chapter.

2. Observe in several classrooms. See if you can identify the probable goal of the misbehavior and keep notes on the teacher responses to inappropriate behavior. What category of responses seems to occur most frequently? Which teachers seem to get the most positive results from the learners?

3. Interview some learners about their reaction to discipline responses. What do they see as the most common responses that teachers make to inappropriate behavior? Do they perceive these responses to be effective? What do they see as the most effective responses? Why do they think that other learners misbehave?

4. Numerous articles have been written giving recommendations for dealing with discipline problems. Read three articles dealing with discipline. What seems to be the value orientation of the authors? How do they perceive the role of the teacher? What purposes for discipline are implied in their article? Under which category would their recommendations best fit?

BIBLIOGRAPHY

CANTER, L., and M. CANTER. 1976. *Assertive Discipline: A Take Charge Approach for Today's Educator*. Santa Monica, Calif.: Canter and Associates.

DUKE, D. L., and A. M. MECKEL. 1984. *Teacher's Guide to Classroom Management*. New York: Random House.

JONES, V., and L. JONES. 1986. *Comprehensive Classroom Management*. Boston: Allyn & Bacon.

Chapter 9

SUPPORTING SELF-CONTROL

OBJECTIVES

This chapter provides information to help the reader to

1. State the importance of teacher modeling in helping students learn self-control

2. Identify the elements of good communication that can help teachers deal with misbehavior

3. List the steps of the no-lose methods of conflict resolution

4. Explain how the factors to which students attribute their success or failure relate to the development of self-control

5. Describe how logical and natural consequences might be used in the classroom

6. List low profile techniques that can be used when responding to incidents of misbehavior

7. Describe how self-monitoring procedures can be implemented in the classroom

INTRODUCTION

A critical aspect in moving students toward the goal of self-control is teacher response to problems. Some responses can create embarrassment, guilt, anger, and even hostility; and when these emotions occur, learners are not likely to exercise self-control. Instead, they are more likely to resort to even more serious misbehavior. On the other hand, teacher response to misbehavior can lessen the probability of future difficulties. Successful teachers often comment that they have few problems and have difficulty articulating their "secret formula." In reality, they do not have a secret formula but simply respond to incidents in such a manner that serious problems are avoided and minor ones occur infrequently.

When incidents of misbehavior occur in the classroom, the teacher might first consider responding in ways that support the student's efforts to establish self-control. By starting with responses selected from this category, the teacher is communicating respect for the student and confidence in his or her ability to resolve the problem without direct intervention from the teacher. The responses that fall into this category are classified as low profile or unobtrusive responses that do not call undue attention to the misbehavior. These responses keep the responsibility for correcting the problem with learners, providing them with an opportunity to correct the problems. This chapter discusses some of the responses that can be used to support students in their attainment of self-control.

MODELING SELF-CONTROL

In order for students to learn self-control, they must be involved with a responsible adult who demonstrates self-control. Unfortunately, the permissive society in which we live does not seem to provide or value those who do exercise this virtue. Instead, many elements of the culture seem to imply that individuals should be primarily concerned with their own wants and needs and should live for the present rather than the future. Many of our social problems, such as drug and alcohol abuse, can be directly related to the unwillingness or inability of individuals to exercise self-control. The teacher, as a significant other, can fulfill the need for student involvement with a responsible adult who demonstrates self-control. It is not surprising that some teachers who complain of a lack of self-control in students are individuals who have trouble exercising self-control themselves. They are unable to control their emotions, are self-centered, tend to take the path of least resistance, and come to class unprepared.

An uncomfortable beginning step for teachers who wish to solve discipline problems is that of introspection. What messages are being sent by your own behavior? How do you respond when things do not go well? To whom do you attribute problems that occur? Do you take responsibility, or is it always the students, the parents, or the system? Do you admit mistakes? What do you do when you make a mistake in front of the class? Do you see each incident of misbehavior as a challenge to your authority that cannot be tolerated? Are you fearful that others will think you professionally incompetent if they see a student in your class misbehave? When a student does misbehave, what motives guide your response? The answers to these questions may go a long way in revealing why learners may or may not be making progress toward self-control.

Teacher Motives When Responding to Misbehavior

Teacher introspection should consider motives when responding to incidents of misbehavior. Research by Brophy (1985, 199) on teacher introspection has identified seven motives. The following discussion considers each of these motives.

1. *Survival or personal authority.* This motive suggests that the teacher was merely trying to make it through the day or trying to maintain personal authority and power in the classroom. These individuals felt threatened by the class and viewed misbehavior as direct threats to their authority. About 12 percent of the teachers in Brophy's study cited this as a primary motive for responding to misbehavior.

2. *Time on-task or instructional concern.* The motive here was to increase the time the students were working toward the accomplishment of the lesson objective. The teachers' major concern was to get through the lesson and cover the content that needed to be covered. About 24 percent of the teachers responded that this was an important reason for responding to misbehavior.

3. *Group safety or continuity.* The motive of these teachers was to keep the classroom moving in an orderly fashion, not letting anything interfere with the learning and the welfare of the larger group. Individuals could not be allowed to interfere with the smooth operation of the class. About 61 percent of the teachers responded that this was a major reason for responding to problems.

4. *Concerns about the student.* Individuals who chose this as a motive for their response cited that they were concerned about the growth of the individual. Their prime reason for responding was to help students solve problems and develop more positive behaviors. About 46 percent of the teachers cited this as a primary motive.

5. *Future life.* Teachers choosing this as a motive cited a concern about future learning or success of the student. They were concerned that individuals who were not corrected would fail, drop out, or have difficulty with authorities. About 12 percent of the teachers chose this as a reason for their response.

6. *School rules.* Individuals choosing this as a motive simply stated that the reason they responded as they did was because the behavior was a violation of a school rule. Therefore, they had no choice but to respond. About 11 percent of the teachers cited this as a major issue in their response.

7. *Anger or irritation.* Individuals who cited this as a reason for their response basically stated that they disliked the student or were personally angry with him or her. About 11 percent cited this as a basic motive for their response.

Box 9-1
DEALING WITH BILLY

Before she started the school year, Miss Johnson was informed by Billy's previous teacher that he was a problem student. She stated that Billy was the instigator of many disturbances.

During the first week of school, several students seated around Billy are talking loudly and laughing. Miss Johnson decides that she wants to send an early message to Billy and to the class that she will not tolerate disturbances. In addition, she wants to stop the behavior before it spreads. She thinks that Billy is the cause of the disturbance so he is singled out for attention.

"Billy, I do not tolerate that type of behavior in this class. If you want to have another difficult year, then just keep it up. I want you to leave the room and go to the office. I will deal with you later."

"But, Miss Johnson, I wasn't doing anything. I was looking for a pencil so that I could do the assignment."

"I'll not tolerate backtalk from you. Leave the room!"

Billy glares at the teacher and then slowly gathers his belongings and moves toward the door. The rest of the class sits in stunned silence.

What is your response?

1. Was Miss Johnson's response appropriate and fair? Did it demonstrate a concern for the students?

2. Do you think this action will have the desired effect?

3. What would you do instead?

     The researchers discovered that the motives of teachers were related to the type of discipline measure that they used. Those teachers whose motives related to the welfare of the students were more likely to commit to prevention and long-term changes in student behavior. Those who cited school rules, time on-task, or group safety tended to respond to learners in more impersonal ways and to use pressure rather than individual counseling in attempting to change student behavior. Those who had personal motives, such as survival, anger, or personal dislike for the student, viewed behavior problems as direct threats. They seemed to lack successful strategies for dealing with behavior problems and usually responded by moralizing, criticizing, scolding, blaming, and threatening (Brophy 1985, 206).

Helping students learn how to exercise self-control is clearly related to a personal concern about the welfare of students. Students are not easily deceived about the concern that a teacher has for them. The major concerns of the teacher will be identified quickly and his or her motives for disciplining students uncovered. When teacher motives are perceived to be related to their own concern for power and authority, the students will respond negatively. Docking (1987) points out that students often see maliciousness as a way of restoring their self-dignity when confronted by situations where they feel that they are not being treated as persons. Misbehavior is often a symbolic rejection of authority (Docking 1987, 77).

Certain conditions must be met if students are to respond to teacher authority: The teacher must have a good reason for disciplining a student, must be fair in demands, and must have concern for the student as a person. Attempts by the teacher to exercise authority will be rejected unless the students believe that the teacher is exercising authority on suitable grounds and in a suitable manner (Docking 1987, 76). It is imperative that the teacher have motives for responding to discipline problems that give concern for students the highest priority. These are necessary conditions if the teacher is to be successful in helping the student move toward increased self-control.

GAINING COOPERATION THROUGH COMMUNICATION

Student cooperation is necessary in the teacher's efforts to help students continue their growth toward self-control. One of the major roadblocks to obtaining student cooperation is a breakdown in communication. Several researchers have emphasized the importance of communication in obtaining student cooperation (Ginott 1972; Gordon 1974; Harris 1969; Rogers 1969). They emphasize that the language teachers use when interacting with students sends messages that have profound effects on student behavior and self-concept, as does consistent use of certain patterns of communication.

Transactional Analysis (TA) is a framework for looking at how communication patterns between teacher and student create or prevent discipline problems. According to TA theory, there exists several different people or roles inside each of us. Stimuli, in the form of verbal communication from others, call forth these different roles from our past experience. The three basic roles are the "parent," the "child," and the "adult."

The parent role is based on the experiences that individuals have had as helpless children dependent on a controlling parent. The parent role is an imitation of those experiences we have had with our parents and includes the rule-giving, admonishing, and stern, as well as the nurturing, parts of our personality.

The child role is much like that of a very young child. Because the child is immature and young, he or she is freed from behaving in socially acceptable ways. The child role is the uncontrollable, irrational, and childish part of us. Great pleasure is obtained in the testing, exploring, and challenging authority components of our personality. However, a conflict arises when a parent demands that the child behave in socially acceptable ways. These parent demands communicate that the individual is "not OK." Memories of not being OK are permanently etched in our minds. When we feel as if we are being told we are "not OK," the child role comes to the fore, and irrational, often explosive, behavior will result. The child does have a "you're OK" side. This OK side is elicited from memories of carefree times or of being held and nurtured or of exploring and taking risks free from external constraints. Both the positive and negative aspects of the child role have been recorded before the age of five.

The adult role emerges as the individual begins to rationally test the parent role. The basic job of the adult is to update and validate information stored in the parent state and to determine when the child's feelings can be expressed. The basic feeling of the adult state is that "I'm OK."

The premise of TA is that all individuals have a need to feel OK or adequate. When people allow their adult state to develop, they become rational persons who can exercise self-control and use the positive sides of the child and parent roles. However, if there is a great deal of conflict among the three inner roles, individuals misbehave and tend to fall into the more unpleasant and destructive parts of the child and parent roles.

The role of the teacher is to communicate to students by appealing to their adult state or by affirming the positive sides of the parent and child. These two approaches affirm to the student that they are capable and can trust other individuals in their social environment not to "put them down" or make them feel not OK.

One way that teachers can appeal to the adult role is to analyze the questions they ask of students. Those questions that are authoritative, judgmental, controlling, or blaming tend to be from the parent role and are communicating that the other individual is not OK. This usually elicits the child role in the student. Questions that tend to center on the self and convey the attitude that "everyone is picking on me," or "everything wrong always happens to me," are generally from the child state and place the student in an evaluative and controlling role. Questions that indicate that the student is capable of responding in a constructive way and that are not judgmental or controlling but allow the student freedom to respond so that he or she feels worthwhile are questions from the adult role and tend to elicit the adult role in the student.

For example, assume that the teacher has just encountered a couple of students pushing and shoving in the classroom. The following questions illustrate how the teacher is communicating from each of the three roles.

Parent: Alright. Who started this? I want to know right now!

Child: Why is it that I always get the students who can't control themselves?

Adult: What can we do to resolve this problem?

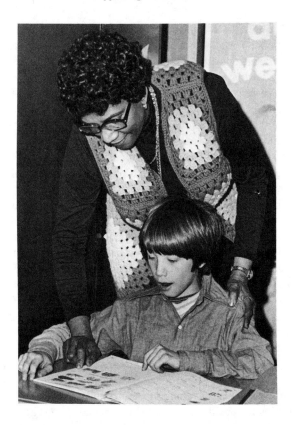

Individuals who continue to see themselves as not OK will act in ways that gain attention from others and continue to reaffirm for themselves that they are not OK. They do this by playing "games." The games that students often play in the classroom are "stupid," "clown," "chip on the shoulder," and "make me" (Ernst 1973). Teachers can best respond to student game playing by identifying the role that the student is playing—Is it the child or the parent? What type of affirmation is the student really seeking?—and then refuse to play the game and respond from the adult role. Affirm for the student his or her own worth as an individual and help the student find a solution to feelings of inadequacy.

In summary, TA does help the teacher understand many instances of misbehavior in the classroom and to develop a communication strategy that will assist the student in exercising self-control and moving more and more into the adult role.

Gordon (1974) has given guidance to teachers in building communication with students. He sees breakdowns in teacher-student communication as the primary cause for most discipline problems. The development of appropriate communication skills is seen as essential in building bridges between the teacher and the student so that the needs of both are understood and met. When this is done, cooperation is the result, and discipline problems do not escalate into major confrontations that block learning and growth toward self-control. The basic communication skills emphasized by

Gordon are collaboration, joint problem solving and decision making, mutual agreements, and nonpower methods to resolve conflicts.

One of the first steps in using Gordon's method is that of identifying problem ownership. Problem ownership is important because the response is different for student-owned problems than for teacher-owned problems. Problem ownership is determined by identifying who experiences the tangible, concrete effects. If the behavior is interfering with the teacher's ability to teach the class or meet his or her needs, then the teacher owns the problem. For example, loud talking or disruptive behavior interferes with the teacher's ability to conduct the class. In this instance the teacher is experiencing the concrete and tangible effects and therefore owns the problem. However, daydreaming or inattentiveness is not interfering with the conduct of the class and the tangible and concrete effects of the behavior are felt by the student. In this case, the student owns the problem.

One of the major breakdowns in communication occurs when teachers respond to student-owned problems. Teachers usually respond by using what Gordon calls the "language of unacceptance" (Gordon 1974, 47). He has grouped the unacceptable messages that teachers send in response to student-owned problems into 12 categories. These 12 types of messages, listed below, block communication and slow down or inhibit the process of problem resolution and learning (48–49):

1. Ordering, commanding, directing
2. Warning, threatening
3. Moralizing, preaching, giving "shoulds" and "oughts"
4. Advising, offering solutions or suggestions
5. Teaching, lecturing, giving logical arguments
6. Judging, criticizing, disagreeing, blaming
7. Name-calling, stereotyping, labeling
8. Interpreting, analyzing, diagnosing
9. Praising, agreeing, giving positive evaluations
10. Reassuring, sympathizing, consoling, supporting
11. Questioning, probing, interrogating, cross-examining
12. Withdrawing, distracting, being sarcastic, humoring, diverting

Gordon states that the first five categories offer solutions to the student's problem. The second three are judgments or put-downs, and the next two are attempts to make the problem go away. Number 11 (the most frequently used) produces defensiveness, and number 12 is an attempt by the teacher to avoid talking about the problem. Remember that these messages set up roadblocks to communication when the student owns the problem. There are times when praising, reassuring, diagnosing, teaching, and advising are appropriate teacher behaviors. However, usually they are not appropriate when a student is experiencing a problem that is interfering with his or her attempts to meet needs. Perhaps an example will illustrate this point: Identify a time when you were having a personal problem and you shared your problem with one of your parents or a friend. How did the person respond and how did you feel? If the person started questioning, teaching, or diagnosing, didn't you become defensive and feel that he or she did not really understand?

Rather than using these 12 roadblocks to communication, Gordon suggests that we begin to use the language of acceptance. One of the key components of this language is "active listening." Active listening involves an interaction with the student where the teacher provides feedback to the student concerning his or her understanding of the message that the student is sending. (This is important because many verbal and nonverbal messages are unclear and easily misinterpreted, and misinterpretation can lead to communication barriers. Minor problems then have a way of turning into major ones.) Feedback can be given by stating the teacher's interpretation in a question form or by simply paraphrasing what the student has said. For example, the teacher might respond to the daydreaming student by stating, "You're bored with this material." The teacher might choose to paraphrase a student message by using a question that begins with the stem "are you saying that ...?"

Active listening has the advantage of opening the door for additional communication about the problems while keeping the responsibility with the student. The goal of active listening is to communicate to the student it is okay to have a problem and that the teacher is willing to listen and help find a solution. The approach seems so simple that many individuals are skeptical of the value of active listening. It is, however, a good beginning for responding to problems that are student owned. Individuals are often amazed at how wrong their interpretation is and how easily a solution can be found once the problem is identified in a nonthreatening manner.

Teacher-owned problems require a different response. They are dealt with through the use of what Gordon calls "I-messages." I-messages communicate what the teacher is feeling and are characterized by the use of "I" rather than "you." There are three parts to an I-message (Gordon 1974, 142–44). The first part involves identifying what is creating the problem in a nonblaming and nonthreatening manner. Examples of this component of I-messages might be "When people talk when I'm talking...," "When I get interrupted when giving instructions...," or "When I can't find the material I left on the table...." The second component identifies the tangible and concrete effect. Examples might be "We have to stop...," "We have to start over...," or "We have to find new material...." In the third component of the I-message, the teacher states his or her feelings. Examples might be "...and I feel very frustrated," "...and that makes us waste time," "...and I get discouraged," or "...and that makes me afraid."

As an example of a complete I-message, here is one that a teacher might use when responding to students not bringing material to class: "When individuals do not bring their material to class, time is wasted as we try to find material for them to use and that is frustrating." Note that the message is not demanding that the students change, it simply identifies the problem and the effect. It is delivered honestly and without anger or blame.

Students, like other individuals, are often so intent on getting their own needs met that they are unaware of the impact of their behavior on others. The I-message provides the student with the reason or the rationale for the displeasure of the teacher.

Many students will respond that they were unaware of the difficulties and offer solutions that are perfectly acceptable. The problem is resolved by open communication and joint problem solving. This communicates a sense of respect and honesty.

Occasionally, students may get defensive when the teacher shares an I-message. Some may feel embarrassed, guilty, surprised, or even become argumentative. This usually signals to the teacher that by confronting the problem, the teacher has caused a problem for the student (Gordon 1974, 145). When this occurs, the teacher should then switch to active listening. This combination of active listening and I-messages can then be used to keep communication open until a resolution can be found.

Box 9-2
GETTING STUDENT COOPERATION

You are teaching a very capable tenth-grade science class. The students are generally well behaved and do outstanding work. A number of the students, however, tend to get to class a couple of minutes after the bell rings. They are not disruptive when they enter, they just wait until the last minute to try to get to class. One day you are observed by your principal. He notes that four students enter the class after the bell and that you do not respond to their tardiness. In your evaluation conference he reminds you that it is a school rule for students to be in class by the time the bell rings and that he considers it a serious problem. He will monitor the problem, and if you are unable to correct it, he will assist you. You are embarrassed and upset about this issue and decide that you need to try Gordon's approach of using I-messages and active listening to try to obtain student cooperation and solve the problem.

How will you respond?

1. **What is the I message that you will use to communicate the problem to the class?**

2. **What will you do if students become angry or defensive?**

3. **What are some possible actions that you might suggest to the class?**

No-Lose Conflict Resolution

At times, both teacher and student are experiencing a problem, one that has a tangible effect on both. For example, a bored student may attempt to relieve boredom by behaving in such a way that the entire class is disrupted. Gordon suggests that rather than engaging the student in a power struggle the teacher employ the "no-lose" method of conflict resolution. He notes that many student behaviors are attempts to cope with teacher power. Most of these then turn into power struggles where someone must win and the other must lose. He suggests that I-messages and active listening be used to identify the problem clearly and then to implement a conflict resolution process that results in a solution acceptable to both parties. The resolution process that he suggests has six basic steps (Gordon 1974, 227–234). They are as follows:

1. *Defining the problem.* One of the most important steps in arriving at any potential solution to a problem is to identify the problem correctly. Many solutions fail because one or both parties in a conflict situation do not understand the problem that needs to be solved. Therefore, the solutions proposed do not address the major issue and do not work. Problem identification is critical if the teacher is to be successful. However, it is important that the teacher not be the only one involved in problem identification. Students must also be involved and must participate in defining the nature of the problem. It is important that students enter into the problem definition stage willingly and believe that their contributions will be heard. They must not feel that they are merely being manipulated by the teacher or that the teacher has a closed mind and is argumentative when the student does make a statement. A beginning step is for the teacher to state his or her problem and not the solution that is desired. Simply using I-messages focused on the problem will get the definition stage off to a positive start.

2. *Generate possible solutions.* This step involves generating several possible solutions to the problem. It is often best to get student input about possible solutions before the teacher offers solutions. Accepting all ideas without evaluation is critical. If the discussion begins to wander, to get away from the generation of solutions, the teacher may need to refocus the discussion by restating that the major purpose is to try to identify different ways the problem can be solved. It is often helpful to write down the solutions that are generated.

3. *Evaluating the solutions.* Once a number of possible solutions have been identified, then each solution can be evaluated. This can be done simply by asking students for their preferences. Those that receive a negative reaction from either students or the teacher should be eliminated. When the teacher eliminates an alternative, it is important for him or her to say why it is not acceptable. The teacher should not hesitate to express opinions and preferences. I-messages can be used to state why a given solution is unacceptable. All individuals who are involved in the problem need to be given the opportunity to express preferences and concerns.

4. *Making the decision.* After the various alternatives have been discussed, an obvious solution will often emerge. If not, those involved need to decide which solution will

be tried. It is important for all individuals involved in the problem situation to agree on a solution. The decision needs to be a consensus rather than a vote.

5. *Determining how to implement the decision.* This step is where many problem-solving efforts fail. It is not enough to identify a solution, but there also must be agreement on how the solution will be implemented. During this stage, the issue of who does what and when must be addressed. Both students and teachers must have a clear understanding of their responsibility. It is usually helpful to write down the implementation plan so that it can be used for a reference if someone does not seem to be following the plan.

6. *Evaluating the success of the solutions.* It is important that some evaluation of the plan be performed. This need not be a highly formalized process but can be done informally to check with all involved parties to get their view of whether things are working. After a short time the teacher should check back with the students and simply ask, "Are we making progress in solving the problem?" "Are you happy with what we have done?" It is important to note that plans do fail. If this happens, the teacher must simply gather the individuals and discuss why the solution failed. It may be necessary to generate another set of solutions and plans for implementing them. Participating in problem solving, making a commitment to a plan, and following through on the plan help students learn responsibility and self-control.

IDENTIFYING WHY PROBLEMS OCCUR AND HOW THEY ARE RESOLVED

A major step in students' moving toward self-control is to help them understand the relationship between their behavior and consequences. Many students with chronic behavior problems lack an understanding of this link, so it is important that they begin to see the connection between their efforts and outcomes or consequences. Glasser (1965) emphasized the importance of helping students understand this relationship. He points out that the teacher should always begin by asking the student to identify what he or she was doing. If the student gives a negative or evasive response, the teacher should repeat the question, "What are you doing?" Repeated efforts by the student should then be followed by the teacher identifying what the student was doing. The student should realize that there was some action on his or her part that led to the confrontation.

The second part of the process is to have the student identify the possible consequences for that action and make a value judgment about the behavior. This is performed by asking the student, "What happens when individuals do that?" "Is that what you want to happen to you?" The responsibility for the behavior and the consequences for the behavior need to remain with the student. When a teacher disciplines students without identifying the behavior that was against the rules, the teacher is allowing students the opportunity to blame the consequences on the teacher rather than on their own actions. Repeated and consistent use of these steps of identifying what a student was doing (not why they were doing it) and what happens when individuals violate those rules helps students begin to realize that consequences are their choice and they can choose to experience or not experience the consequences by changing their actions.

Another step in moving students toward self-control is to help them learn that their own efforts will have a positive result. Attribution theory has provided helpful insight into this process. Attribution theorists assume that individuals naturally search for understanding about why events occur (Stipek 1988, 81). Their perceptions of the causes of events are referred to as causal attributions. Weiner (1984) identified four sets of factors commonly involved in causal attributions.

The first set of factors is related to those causes located within the individual—intelligence, ability, personality, or effort. An individual might attribute failure on an academic task to a lack of ability to perform the task or a lack of effort in not studying. Similarly, individuals might attribute behavior problems to personality characteristics ("I like to talk"; "I'm naturally friendly") or to lack of ability ("I can't understand those problems").

A second set of factors are those causes perceived to be external and beyond the control of the individual. These factors might be related to the environmental situation, the behavior and action of others, task difficulty, or luck. Students are especially creative in offering some of these factors as excuses for their behavior ("I couldn't pay attention because I was distracted by the glare of the light on my paper"; "The person behind me kept asking me questions and it would be rude to ignore him").

A third set of factors involves the perception of the student concerning the controllability of the factors. For example, an individual who attributes failure to a lack of intelligence, personality, environment, or to external factors such as the behavior of others may see these as being beyond his or her control. Other factors, such as effort, are perceived as being controllable. The fourth set of factors is related to intention. This means that the events that happened were intentionally caused either by the student or by others or it was merely an accident or element of chance.

These last two factors, controllability and intentionality, are related to the acceptance of responsibility. Altering individual perceptions of the factors that are under their control and the fact that they can act in a purposeful and intentional manner will produce a change of behavior and help them learn to accept responsibility for their actions.

What this implies for the teacher is that he or she needs to identify those factors to which a given student is attributing failure or poor behavior. Fair enforcement of behavioral standards combined with positive reinforcement for improvements and discussions about what brought about the improvement is needed so that the student begins to believe that his or her efforts will pay off and changes are attributed to controllable rather than uncontrollable factors.

A common problem with some students who experience frequent discipline problems is that they believe they are being singled out for discipline simply because of their past history. They see other students, often high achievers, get away with many of the behaviors for which they are disciplined. As a result, they believe that avoiding difficulty is a result of the environment over which they have no control. Therefore,

they have little reason to try, and they intentionally misbehave in order to get even with the teacher or other students. Student anger is often the emotional outcome when negative events are attributed to external and uncontrollable factors. Teachers who see recurrent anger and frustration in their students should take the time to try and find out the sources. A plan might be developed to help students learn how to bring things under their control.

Another common problem that teachers face in daily classroom life is the student who demonstrates helplessness. These students are often apathetic and do not even try to complete work. They attribute negative events to stable, uncontrollable, internal factors. For example, a student may simply fail even to try to perform a task because he or she perceives that lack of ability or intelligence will prevent success so there is simply no reason to put forth any effort. These perceptions of attributions can be difficult to change. Providing the students with meaningful and important tasks at a level where they can experience success is an important step in helping them overcome feelings of helplessness.

Box 9-3
JUAN'S FAILURE

The school year had gone quite well until after the first grading period. Then one boy in your class, Juan, began to cause minor disturbances. He talked to others when he should have been working, he seldom finished his work, and he was generally apathetic and uncooperative about participating in class activities or discussions. You are puzzled about the change in his behavior. One day you overhear him talking to a friend: "I hate school! I tried real hard this year to do better and my grades were still the same. I guess I'm just too dumb to do well in school."

What is your reaction?

1.   **What are the attribution factors you see at work in this problem?**

2.   **How would you attempt to change Juan's attributions?**

3.   **Would you lower your standards in order to give Juan higher grades so that he would feel better about school?**

Attending to the perceptions of student attributions and working to help students understand the link between their behavior and the consequences, and helping them understand how to take control of their own behavior, are important ingredients in supporting student efforts to establish self-control.

LOGICAL AND NATURAL CONSEQUENCES

Driekurs (1968) emphasized the use of logical and natural consequences when dealing with incidents of misbehavior. It is another step in helping the student understand the link between behavior and consequences and to keep the responsibility for the consequences with the student rather than the teacher. Logical and natural consequences that flow directly from the nature of the misbehavior help the student learn from the experience rather than rationalize that the punishment was the fault of the teacher and unrelated to internal factors that can be controlled.

Driekurs (1968, 75) points out that there is a fine line between natural and logical consequences and punishment. However, he contends that students will quickly understand the difference. Although both punishment and consequences may have results that are undesirable for the offender, the difference lies in natural and logical consequences being directly related to the nature of the offense. For example, a student who forgets to bring proper material to class may be punished by being given more work to complete, being sent to the office, or kept after school. These punishments have little direct bearing on the nature of the offense. In the application of natural and logical consequences, the student may be required to "rent" the required material from the teacher. For example, high school teachers have had success in renting material by exchanging the material for a driver's license or some other valued possession. The student gets the possession returned when the material is returned. The teacher is able to maintain a businesslike manner rather than reacting with anger and creating hostility in the student.

Natural consequences are defined as the natural outcomes of events without the intervention of another (Driekurs, Grunwald, and Pepper 1982, 118). For example, a student who runs in the hall may fall and skin a knee. The injury is a natural consequence of not following a safe practice; the consequence was not planned or arranged by another. Another example of a natural consequence in school might be when a tardy student misses a positive event that occurs at the beginning of the period. Teachers do not threaten, scold, or argue with students. They merely inform them of the potential consequences of their action and then allow students to make the choice. When a student experiences a consequence, the teacher may regret that it happened but should not attempt either to diminish the loss or add additional punishment.

Many of the misbehaviors that occur in school do not have natural consequences that naturally flow from the event. In addition, some consequences are too dangerous and therefore should not be allowed to occur. For example, a student running in the hall may run into an unopened door and experience severe injury. Although the student would probably learn to exercise more self-control the next time, the teacher must do more than warn the student of the possibility of severe injury. This is where logical consequences are applied.

Logical consequences are those events that are guided and arranged by another (Driekurs, Grunwald, and Pepper 1982, 119). However, for them to be effective, they must be discussed and understood by the student. Otherwise, they may be viewed as the arbitrary imposition of punishment by a more powerful adult. Driekurs, Grunwald, and Pepper (120–123) provide the following examples of the use of logical consequences in school settings: Students who cannot walk down the stairs properly must return to the classroom and walk down by themselves; students who turn in sloppy papers will not have their papers graded until they rewrite the papers; class members must repaint classroom walls that they defaced; and students who have difficulty behaving during recess will be required to walk around the yard with the teacher rather than play with their friends.

It is important for the teacher to apply logical consequences in a consistent, matter-of-fact manner. If they are applied inconsistently, students are deprived of the opportunity to understand the link between their behavior and the consequences for those actions. As a result, their growth toward self-control is hindered.

One final comment on the use of logical consequences: They should also apply to the teacher. For example, if the teacher causes the class to be late for recess or dismissal, then the class should be given some additional time as compensation. A teacher who fails to return student papers on time might be required to add points to those papers not returned. The universal application of logical consequences is uncomfortable for many teachers. However, it does provide good modeling behavior for students and can go far in defusing the anger that may occur when a student has to experience an unpleasant consequence.

In summary, an important step in helping students learn self-control is helping them understand the link between behavior and consequences. This can be done by using natural and logical consequences as a response to problems rather than implementing punishments that are arbitrarily chosen. The application of logical consequences to everyone in the classroom, including the teacher, also has the effect of creating a more positive and democratic climate where all individuals are free to learn from their mistakes.

LOW PROFILE RESPONSES TO MINOR PROBLEMS

The majority of misbehavior in the classroom is what might be termed as minor. It is estimated that about 80 percent of the problems are students talking without permission and another 19 percent are misbehaviors related to out-of-seat activity, daydreaming, or generally "goofing off" (Charles 1989, 89). Teacher responses to these relatively minor problems should be of a low profile nature that allows the students an opportunity to self-correct their behavior and practice self-control. Unfortunately, teacher responses to these incidents tend to disrupt the flow of the entire class and focus a great deal of attention on the misbehavior. This is undesirable in that it takes the students off-task, teaches students that the best way to gain attention is through

misbehavior, or puts the student in a position where he or she may be embarrassed and must strike back in order to save face. When this happens, a minor problem soon escalates into a major one.

Therefore, it is important for the teacher to develop a number of low profile responses to minor problems. These low profile techniques are intended to keep the focus of the class on the academic task, preserve the dignity of the student, and send a message that the teacher is aware of the misbehavior and that the offender will be given an opportunity to self-correct before the teacher intervenes. The following are some low profile techniques that teachers can use in responding to minor problems of misbehavior.

Nonverbal Signals

About 90 percent of discipline is body language (Charles 1989, 91). Body language and nonverbal signals, such as posture, facial expressions, gestures, and eye contact, can go far in helping teachers deal with discipline problems. Simply making eye contact with a misbehaving student is often enough to send a message that the teacher is aware of a problem. Combining this with an appropriate facial expression that indicates disapproval will clarify the message. The teacher does need to be careful that the signals are not mixed. Making eye contact with a student and then smiling may result in the student receiving the wrong signal. It is sometimes difficult for teachers to understand this confusion because nonverbal communication is from an unaware sender to a very aware receiver. The teacher may be totally unaware of the nonverbal messages being sent. Students, on the other hand, are constantly looking for these signals and interpreting them. Therefore, teachers need to be conscious of this source of confusion and consciously work to make sure that they are delivering the nonverbal messages that are desired. Videotape recorders are a powerful tool for helping teachers check their nonverbal behavior.

Another part of the nonverbal message is communicated through the posture of the teacher. When responding to a problem, the teacher needs to have a more erect and confident carriage to his or her body. Simply standing up, folding arms across the chest, and moving toward the problem area may communicate to students that they had better return to the task at hand. Another common element of nonverbal responses to discipline problems is the use of gestures. Experienced teachers learn that teaching involves an element of conducting. Just as a musical conductor uses gestures to communicate with the orchestra, the experienced teacher learns to use gestures to communicate with students. Hand signals may indicate the need to quiet down, the need to stop all activity and focus attention on the teacher, or the approval of desired behavior. Head movements are used to designate approval or disapproval of student activity. Gestures are effective communication devices that can be used without interfering with the regular flow of classroom activities.

Proximity Control

Experienced teachers have long known that minor discipline problems disappear when the teacher quietly moves into the area of the classroom where the misbehavior is occurring. This can be done unobtrusively while teaching the class by slowly moving to the area of the disturbance yet continuing to teach. Placing a hand on the misbehaver's chair or desk further enforces the message that the teacher is aware of the problem and is providing the student with an opportunity for self-correction. Most students find it extremely difficult to misbehave when the teacher is standing near them. Teacher movement around the classroom is an important part of management and is useful in both preventing problems and stopping minor behavior problems that may occur.

Using the Student's Name in the Lesson

A typical response to misbehavior is to call the student's name. For example, the teacher may attempt to gain student attention by stating, "John, I want your attention right now!" This is undesirable because it focuses attention on the misbehavior and interrupts the flow of the lesson. A better response is to try to use the student's name in the context of the lesson. Suppose that the teacher was talking with the class on the discovery of the New World and noted that John was engaged in some form of misbehavior. The teacher could respond by saying, "Now if John were a member of the crew, he might have to watch for...." This method quickly gets John's attention and communicates to him that the teacher is aware of the misbehavior while maintaining the focus on the lesson. This is often all that is required to change the behavior from an unacceptable pattern to an acceptable one.

Redirecting Student Activity

Teachers who work with younger students tend to become very adept at redirecting student activity away from undesirable behavior into more acceptable channels. When using this approach, the teacher must be aware of the students in the classroom and respond quickly when it appears that one or more students is beginning to engage in an unacceptable activity. When the teacher notes this pattern is emerging, he or she simply goes to the student and redirects the student to a substitute activity that is acceptable. In some instances this activity might be designed to give the student a quick break and then to get him or her back on the task. An example might be for the teacher to have the student run an errand or perform a housekeeping task that will take only a couple of minutes. When the student returns to the desk, the teacher can then take the opportunity to refocus student attention on the task that needs to be completed.

Another option might be for the student to engage in an alternative activity to accomplish the instructional goal. For example, a student might be having trouble completing a math assignment. The teacher might simply move to the student and state, "John, I would like to see if you could help me by creating these problems on the place value chart."

Box 9-4
DEALING WITH A TALKER

Keith is not really a problem student. He wants to please and is a likable student who does acceptable work. The problem is that he is a constant talker. Whenever students are working independently, he constantly talks to himself or to those around him. It is not loud talking, but it is noticeable. The behavior disturbs you, and you think it bothers those who are seated near him.

What would you do?

1. What might be causing Keith to talk?

2. Do you agree that this is a problem that requires teacher intervention?

3. What would you do to help Keith learn to control his talking?

One word of caution: Redirecting an activity should not be viewed by the students as a reward for inappropriate behavior or as a way to avoid assigned work. Redirecting student activity works best only when the teacher catches an incident in its beginning stages.

These low profile responses are very effective in stopping incidents of misbehavior and providing students with the opportunity to self-correct. This opportunity communicates a sense of respect and trust to the students and is usually responded to very positively by students. Successful teachers handle the majority of their discipline problems using these approaches.

TEACHING STUDENTS TO MONITOR THEIR OWN BEHAVIOR

Some students seem to have difficulty controlling themselves. They do not engage in serious misbehavior, just numerous incidents of minor misbehavior. For these students, an important step toward self-control might be teaching them to monitor their own behavior. Several studies have shown that teaching students to monitor their own behavior is effective in helping them to exercise control (McLaughlin 1976) and has several advantages over other approaches. One advantage is that the student is made more aware of his or her behavior, and the control of the behavior is left with the student rather than with external control by the teacher. Another advantage is that it helps free the teacher to work with the more serious difficulties that might arise in the classroom. This relieves the teacher from constantly playing the role of enforcer.

The teacher can use several methods to help students learn to monitor and control their own behavior. One of the first steps may be to provide students with some verbal questions or thoughts to ask themselves when they are tempted to violate the rules or when they feel that they are about to lose control. One example of this technique might be to provide students with an easy set of directions to follow when they begin to lose control. This can be a simple review of the classroom rules and the consequences that might follow. Students could ask themselves, "Is this what I want to happen?" "Is it worth the trouble it will cause me?" Sometimes it is effective to teach some students how to manipulate their mood when they are getting upset, angry, or anxious. They should be instructed to stop what they are doing for a short time, place their head on the desk, and think of some favorite activities or happy thoughts. When they begin to relax, they can then resume their work.

In addition to these self-verbalization techniques, some students may need to learn to use some physical clues or actions that will help them cope and give them time to think and exercise self-control. For example, students who frequently get upset could be allowed to move to a "time-out" or safe area of the classroom, away from the upsetting environment. They could then close their eyes, clench their fists, and self-verbalize the statements and questions that have been provided. When they feel they have control of the situation, they can return to their desk.

Another method is to have students keep a self-record of incidents and decide on their own reinforcements (Gnagey 1981). The teacher can provide them with some forms or methods for keeping track of both positive and negative behavior incidents.

For example, a student who frequently blurts out answers without first being called on might record the number of times during the day he or she talked without being called on and the number of times he or she followed the rule. This record keeping and a review with the teacher can help the student realize that the behavior is more prevalent and disturbing than he or she had thought. This allows the student the opportunity to decide on his or her own growth targets. Allowing students the opportunity to decide how they will reward themselves when they do improve their behavior is another important step. This also helps to take the responsibility away from the teacher and makes the reinforcement much more effective.

In order to implement self-monitoring in the classroom, it is not enough just to tell students. The most effective technique is for the teacher to demonstrate and model the technique. This might be done on either a whole class or an individual basis. The teacher can identify questions and thoughts to be included in the self-verbalization and then monitor it with the students when the teacher faces a problem situation. The teacher can "think aloud" by asking the questions, providing self-instruction, and changing mood by thinking about something positive. After modeling and demonstrating the approach, the teacher prompts a student when he or she needs to use it and has the student perform the self-verbalization under the guidance of the teacher. After this has been done, the teacher may then have the student whisper the instructions and verbalizations to him- or herself and then perform the task without teacher guidance.

If it appears that students are not able to use this process, the teacher may need to evaluate the procedure, design other more appropriate verbalizations to be used, help them think of reinforcements that they might use, and begin at step one by modeling the process and then gradually moving toward allowing students full monitoring of their behavior.

Self-monitoring techniques have great potential for helping individuals learn self-control and teach them skills that can be used in a variety of life situations. They can be used with a variety of students. Self-monitoring techniques communicate teacher confidence to students that they can behave and exercise self-control.

SUMMARY

The majority of incidents of misbehavior that occur in the classroom are minor. The responses that teachers use can be helpful in teaching students to exercise self-control, or they can have the effect of turning a minor problem into a major one. When responding to these problems, the teacher needs to keep responsibility for correcting the behavior on the student, respect the dignity of the student, and try to handle the problem so that the entire class is not disrupted.

Helping students learn self-control begins with the teacher. Teachers should be models of self-control and models of coping with problems if they are to expect students to acquire these skills. In addition, teachers need to check their motives for responding to problems and make sure that they are directed toward helping the student rather than toward making life easier for the teacher. Teachers, as the classroom leaders, also must take responsibility for ensuring that the classroom climate and the communication patterns are those that facilitate mutual respect and nonpower methods of conflict resolution. Messages of acceptance and no-lose conflict resolution are important components of this communication climate.

Many students do not understand the link between their behavior and the consequences that they experience. Establishing this link is critical if students are to learn self-control. Components of understanding this link are learning to attribute success and failure to their own efforts and to controllable and intentional acts and in experiencing the natural and logical consequences of their actions. Teacher use of low profile and unobtrusive methods for responding to discipline problems allows students opportunity to self-correct their behavior and establishes an environment where self-control is a major focus. These methods are easy to implement and help the teacher maintain an academic focus while still letting students know that unacceptable behavior is not permissible.

Finally, teaching students methods of self-monitoring and coping are important skills that can help individuals throughout their lifetime. They are effective in helping students exercise more self-control and take more positive control of their behavior.

SUGGESTED ACTIVITIES

1. Spend some time observing in a classroom. Tally the types of misbehavior that you observe according to the categories of minor and major incidents of misbehavior. Note how the teacher responds to problems in each category. What percentage of the problems observed were minor and what percentage were major? Did the teacher response differ according to the severity of the problems?

2. Work with two peers in a small group. Each of you should identify a typical classroom problem, such as inattention or talking. One person should play the role of the students, another the teacher, and the third an observer. The teacher should use active listening and I-message in order to clarify the nature of the problem and arrive at a possible solution. The third individual should provide feedback to the person role playing the teacher on the effectiveness and proper use of active listening and I-messages.

3. Interview at least one or two students who are currently having difficulty in school. Ask them to identify what they believe to be the causes of their difficulties. How many of the causes are attributed to internal and how many are attributed to external factors? Do these students perceive a relationship between their behavior and the consequences of their behavior? Design a plan or a list of suggestions that you might use as a teacher to help the students solve their problems.

4. Begin developing a list of specific low profile techniques that might be used when responding to discipline problems. You may start with the ones listed in this chapter. Brainstorm with friends and experienced teachers to get additional items for your list.

5. Develop a plan for self-monitoring that you might use on yourself. For example, perhaps you want to try to decrease your use of unproductive time or change your eating habits. Design a set of self-verbalization instructions or directions that you will follow when faced with the temptation. Develop a method for recording the number of times you overcome the temptation and the number of times you do not. Decide on your own reward when you reach some target. After a couple of weeks, evaluate the effectiveness of the program and consider how you would implement a similar program with a student.

BIBLIOGRAPHY

BROPHY, J. 1985. Teachers' expectations, motives and goals for working with problem students. In *Research on Motivation in Education, Vol. 2: The Classroom Milieu, ed. C.* Ames and R. Ames. New York: Academic Press.

CHARLES, C. 1989. *Building Classroom Discipline: From Models to Practice*, 3rd ed. New York: Longman.

DOCKING, J. W. 1987. *Control and Discipline in Schools: Perspectives and Approaches,* 2nd ed. London: Harper & Row.

DRIEKURS, R. 1968. *Psychology in the Classroom*, 2nd ed. New York: Harper & Row.

———, B. GRUNWALD, and F. PEPPER. 1982. *Maintaining Sanity in the Classroom*, 2nd ed. New York: Harper & Row.

ERNST, K. 1973. *Games Students Play and What to Do About Them.* Millbrae, Calif.: Celestial Arts.

GINOTT, H. G. 1972. *Teacher and Child.* New York: Avon Books.

GLASSER, W. 1965. *Reality Therapy.* New York: Harper & Row.

GNAGEY, W. 1981. *Motivating Classroom Discipline.* New York: Macmillan.

GORDON, T. 1974. *Teacher Effectiveness Training.* New York: David McKay.

HARRIS, T. 1969. *I'm OK—You're OK: A Practical Guide to Transactional Analysis.* New York: Harper & Row.

MCLAUGHLIN, T. 1976. Self-control in the classroom. *Review of Educational Research,* 46, 4, 631–663.

ROGERS, C. 1969. *Freedom to Learn.* Columbus, Ohio.: Chas. E. Merrill.

SAVAGE, T., and D. ARMSTRONG. 1987. *Effective Teaching in Elementary Social Studies.* New York: Macmillan.

STIPEK, D. 1988. *Motivation to Learn: From Theory to Practice.* Englewood Cliffs, N.J.: Prentice Hall.

WEINER, B. 1984. Principles for a theory of student motivation and their application within an attributional framework. In *Research on Motivation in Education, Vol. 1: Student Motivation*, eds. R. Ames and C. Ames. New York: Academic Press.

Chapter 10

RESTRUCTURING THE LEARNING ENVIRONMENT

OBJECTIVES

This chapter provides information to help the reader to

1. Identify ways of altering the environment in order to eliminate discipline problems

2. State the purpose of using time-out areas and time-out rooms as a response to discipline problems

3. Define the principle of reinforcement

4. Distinguish between positive and negative reinforcement

5. State why precise definitions of the behavior to be taught and the behavior to be eliminated are important

6. State the function of punishment and potential problems with the use of punishment

7. List the advantages and the disadvantages of behavior modification approaches

INTRODUCTION

Chapter 4 deals with the influence of the environment on behavior. It is suggested in that chapter that the environment is an important element in the prevention of discipline problems. In a similar vein, altering the environment is an appropriate response when attempts to support student efforts at self-control do not seem to work. A growing body of research documents the important role of the environment on student behavior (Doyle 1986, 399). An important step for teachers experiencing persistent discipline problems is to change the classroom environment for the entire group or for selected individuals. Successful teachers are aware of the importance of changing the environment to improve behavior. One indication of the power of altering the environment is the profound difference that might be experienced when only one or two key students are away from the classroom. Secondary school teachers often see the impact of a changed environment on behavior by noting that students who are poorly behaved in one class or activity are well behaved in others (Doyle 1986, 409).

Altering the learning environment in an attempt to maintain discipline in the classroom is an approach with deep historical roots. Changes in the seating arrangements, changes in the physical arrangement of class activities, and the removal of students are responses to discipline problems familiar to several generations of students.

The specific environment of a classroom—including the physical environment and use of space, the interactions among students, and the interaction between teacher and students—exerts a powerful influence on the behavior of the inhabitants. Some students have developed enough self-control to overcome distractions. However, others have not and therefore need assistance in overcoming the temptations that might be present in the environment. When this occurs, the teacher needs to consider how the environment might be restructured in order to create conditions where self-control can be supported.

Behavior modification is an approach that places primary emphasis on the influence of the environment on behavior. Advocates of this approach contend that behavior is determined by environmental events, those that precede and those that follow it (Gallagher 1980, 3). Behavior modification provides the teacher with some tools for analyzing and solving behavior problems. Basic to this approach is the premise that a primary responsibility of teaching is creating an environment where the desired behavior is possible and is reinforced on a regular basis.

This chapter focuses on some of the ways that teachers might restructure the learning environment so that desired behavior is promoted. In addition, the behavior modification approach to understanding and solving behavior problems is discussed.

MODIFYING THE ENVIRONMENT

When discipline problems are persistent and do not seem to diminish with attempts to support self-control, the teacher should consider how the environment might be modified so that self-control is promoted. Several possibilities might be considered. One is that the seating arrangement of the classroom actually promotes social interaction and off-task behavior. Also, some students might not be able to sit near each other. When moved to another location near other students, the problem often disappears altogether. In other, more extreme cases, it might be necessary to remove the student from the environment until self- control can be regained. This might mean that the student is relegated to a quiet place in the classroom or removed from the classroom.

Rearrangement of Seating

One of the most common ways to alter the learning environment is to change the seating arrangement. Students may need to be moved from areas of temptation. For example, friends sitting near each other may not be able to overcome the urge to talk when they should be working. Other students might find themselves near distracting displays that take their attention from the task at hand. Yet other students might be seated far enough away from the teacher so that they are tempted not to pay attention to the flow of classroom activities. A relatively simple response to persistent minor discipline problems such as these might be simply to move the offender to another area of the classroom. Also, placing students in the action zone might produce the desired effects.

Box 10-1
CLASSROOM SEATING

Maria Shelton believes in allowing students to choose their own seats. She thinks that the freedom to sit near friends or in seats where they feel comfortable will help students develop a positive view toward the class. Her approach does have a few problems. Some students spend quite a bit of time socializing with friends rather than doing their work. She has to remind students of the class rules and spend considerable time monitoring student behavior.

What do you think?

1.   **Do you agree with Maria's reasoning about allowing students to select their own seats?**

2.   **Do you think the misbehavior is serious enough for her to change her approach?**

3.   **What do you think she could do to solve the problems and still allow students to choose their own seats?**

Another situation involves students who sit in a prominent place in the classroom. They might be tempted to seize the stage in an attempt to gain attention, so they may need to be moved to a less prominent space where their attention-getting behavior can more easily be ignored.

If the problem seems to be widespread and involves more than just two or three students, the teacher may need to consider changing the seating arrangement for all of the students in the class. For example, the teacher may need to break up groups of students sitting together in clusters and change the room environment to rows facing in one direction where the opportunities to socialize with others are limited. Areas that are difficult for the teacher to monitor might need to be changed so that the students sitting in those areas know that their behavior can be monitored. Learning centers or optional activity centers may need to be moved or even eliminated until students demonstrate enough self-control to be allowed to use them.

Time-Out Areas

A relatively popular and effective approach used by many teachers is to provide students with a time-out area in the classroom—a desk or a chair in a remote corner. The purpose of the time-out area is to provide students with a place to go until they can gain control and return to work.

The most common use of the time-out area is for misbehaving students. After the student has had an opportunity to quiet down and reflect on the reasons for being there, the teacher then meets with the student to discuss the behavior and decide whether or not he or she is ready to return to the group (Glasser 1977). Since most students do enjoy working in groups, isolation is not a desirable state, and most students will choose to return.

An alternative use of the time-out area is to allow the students to choose on their own to go there. They are encouraged to do this when they feel themselves getting out of control or tempted to violate a classroom rule. The student may then return to the group at any time without any discussion or reprimand from the teacher. Allowing students this privilege can have very positive results. All individuals get frustrated at some time and need a cooling-off period in order to put things back into perspective. Allowing students to do this in the classroom teaches them a valuable skill for coping with anger and frustration. Teachers who use this approach find that the frequency of use of the time-out area tends to decline as the school year progresses. It seems that just the presence of a retreat provides the students with a sense of security and comfort. They know that there is a nonpunitive alternative for them if they do feel out of control.

Removal of the Students from the Classroom

Students who do not respond to minor alterations in the environment or spending time in the time-out area may need to be removed from the classroom. This should be done only when the problem has reached a serious level and if the behavior of the students is seriously hindering the attempts of other students to stay on-task.

Removing students from the classroom serves several purposes. First of all, it communicates that the teacher is serious about enforcing the rules. Second, most students like to be with the group and do not want to be away from friends. Removing them from the classroom deprives them of an audience and of peer support for their actions. Third, the time spent away from the classroom provides both the student and the teacher with a cooling-off period. During this time the teacher may be able to reflect on the problem and decide on an appropriate course of action, thus decreasing the likelihood that he or she will act out of anger and do or say something that will make the problem worse. Finally, removing a student from the classroom also provides the teacher an opportunity to regain control of the rest of the class and work with them so that conditions are more positive for self-control when the misbehaving student is allowed to return.

When students are removed from the classroom, they should be sent to another part of the school where they will be under the observation or supervision of another staff member. Students should never be sent to the hall, the playground, or some other unsupervised area. To do so creates an enormous legal risk for the teacher should the student leave the assigned area and be injured.

Acceptable places to send a student include a designated time-out room set aside by the school for this purpose, to the principal or counselor, or to another classroom. Many secondary schools have established time-out rooms where a teacher is present to supervise. Like the time-out area in the classroom, this is a quiet place where the student may either sit or work on an assignment until the teacher is able to meet with the student and determine if he or she is ready to return to the classroom. Removing students to a time-out room is generally viewed as a serious step and should be done only when the student is having a great deal of difficulty exercising self-control.

Elementary school teachers often find that sending a student to another classroom serves the same purpose as the time-out room. The classroom should be at least a couple of grade levels different from their own. For example, younger students can be sent to a higher class and older students to a lower class. The teacher in the receiving classroom should be a strong teacher and should have already agreed to cooperate in the arrangement. The student can be sent with a specific assignment, and the students in the receiving classroom are instructed not to talk with or bother the student in any way. Once again, the teacher should meet with the student before allowing his or her return to the classroom.

In some schools the preferred place for a student to go is to the counselor or the principal. A teacher should check with the school principal to make sure of the procedure to be used when a student is removed from the classroom. Sending students to the principal for action should be done rarely and only when the behavior has reached a very serious level. An alternative might be for the student to sit quietly in the office until the teacher is able to meet with the student and attempt to solve the problem.

These approaches at modifying the classroom environment have been found to be quite effective in getting the attention of the students and helping them learn how to exercise more self-control. They also have the advantage of allowing both the student and the teacher a cooling-off period and a time to reflect and problem solve. There are times, however, when these measures do not seem to work. If this is the case, the teacher might want to consider altering the learning environment in more systematic ways. This can be done by applying the principles of behavior modification.

Box 10-2
HECTOR'S TEMPER

Hector is generally a likable boy who has had a difficult life. Numerous moves and lost school time have resulted in some severe academic deficiencies. Hector tries hard, but from time to time, he becomes frustrated and loses his temper. When he does this, he becomes very aggressive and disruptive, doing and saying things that he ordinarily would not.

How would you respond?

1. **What could the teacher do to help Hector avoid losing his temper?**

2. **What could be done to help Hector when he first begins to lose his temper?**

3. **How would you respond when he did lose his temper?**

APPLYING BEHAVIOR MODIFICATION

Behavior modification provides the teacher with some powerful tools in understanding and changing student behavior. However, it is an approach that is often misunderstood and misapplied. Many critics see it as mechanistic and cold, a dangerous form of manipulation that bribes individuals to change their behavior by offering them a reward for doing so.

A basic assumption of behavior modification is that all behavior is learned (Gallagher 1980, 3). Behavior is the product of associations the individual makes with desirable or undesirable consequences. For example, a person who receives attention when a particular behavior occurs soon links that behavior with attention. If attention is something that is perceived as desirable, the probability that the behavior will be repeated is increased. Similarly, a young child who touches a hot stove soon associates the hot stove with pain, and the probability that the child will repeat the behavior is decreased. Therefore, a person's behavior at any given time is the product of past reinforcements and the contingencies in the present environment.

Thoughts, feelings, emotions, internal motivation, and expectations for success are all considered irrelevant concerns because the teacher can do nothing to change the internal psychological state of the learner (Stipek 1988, 20). According to behavior modification theory, the specific behavior of an individual results because (1) the person has learned correct associations as a result of past reinforcement history, (2) the person has not learned associations at all, or (3) the person has learned incorrect associations (Madsen and Madsen 1974, 27–28). Since all behavior is learned, teachers who are confronted with students behaving inappropriately can change their behavior by arranging the environment so that the desired behavior achieves consequences that are desirable for the student. This approach is basic to the principle of reinforcement articulated by B. F. Skinner (1971).

The principle of reinforcement states that behavior that achieves desirable consequences has a greater probability of being repeated. As a given behavior achieves desirable outcomes, the behavior is strengthened. On the other hand, behavior that is not followed by desirable consequences is weakened and is less likely to be repeated. Those things in the environment that are desired by individuals are called reinforcers. It is important to note that, by definition, anything that strengthens a behavior or increases the probability of recurrence is a reinforcer.

Reinforcers

There are two basic types of reinforcers, positive and negative. Positive reinforcers are those things that an individual desires. For example, if an individual wants attention, then attention is a positive reinforcer. Negative reinforcers are frequently misunderstood in that they are confused with punishment. Remember that a reinforcer strengthens a behavior or increases the probability that it will be repeated. Punishment does not have this effect. Negative reinforcement is the avoidance of an unpleasant consequence. For example, why do individuals take out the garbage, a rather unpleasant task that has low appeal to most people? They perform this low-interest task in order to avoid something even more unpleasant: the aroma that will fill the house if it is not removed. A teacher might use negative reinforcement by allowing a student who does not enjoy giving an oral report in front of the class the opportunity to do a written report instead.

Unwittingly, teachers often use negative reinforcement in the classroom and end up strengthening undesirable behaviors. An example might be a teacher who sends a student to sit in the hall for misbehaving. The student may be seeking to avoid something that is perceived as even more unpleasant, working on a boring or threatening assignment. Sitting in the hall might be more interesting and less threatening to the student. Therefore, the next time he or she wishes to avoid an unpleasant or threatening assignment, misbehavior is likely to occur. Because negative reinforcement tends to reinforce escape or avoidance behavior, it should be used sparingly. For example, the student who was allowed to miss the oral report assignment was able to avoid an activity rather than learn important skills, such as how to cope with unpleasant circumstances. The major thrust of a reinforcement program in the classroom, therefore, should be on positive reinforcers.

Positive reinforcers are those things that have sufficient value to the student to put forth effort to earn. Several categories of positive reinforcers are available for use by the teacher. These include social reinforcers, symbolic reinforcers, activity reinforcers, and token reinforcers.

Social reinforcers. Social reinforcers are those positive events, such as praise, words of approval, smiles, laughter, or physical contact such as a pat on the back, that occur during social interaction (Gallagher 1980). Social reinforcement is relatively easy to use because it does not take a great deal of effort or involve any cost to the teacher. For social reinforcers to be effective, they must be given consistently and honestly. Teachers who give insincere or undeserved praise learn that its effectiveness as a reinforcer soon disappears. In addition, the teacher should make a conscious effort to apply social reinforcers consistently enough to affect behavior. Occasional praise or comment is likely to have minimal impact on behavior.

Some individuals will try very hard to obtain social reinforcers. However, students who have a long history of failure and problem behavior may not find social approval strong enough to result in a change in behavior. In addition, social reinforcers need to be administered by someone who is a significant other to the student. Individuals who like their teacher may work very hard to obtain social reinforcers from him or her. However, those who are not positive about the teacher may find that the social approval of peers for disobeying the teacher is much more desirable than social reinforcers administered by the teacher.

Symbolic reinforcers. Symbolic reinforcers are such things as stamps, checks, happy faces, gold stars, or a grade given to the student to designate approval. Symbolic reinforcers are often quite useful with young children. A happy face or a gold star is highly prized and will have a direct effect on the behavior of the student.

The most commonly used symbolic reinforcer in the classroom is the grade. However, grades have drawbacks as effective reinforcers. Grades are often not given immediately and are not tied to a specific behavior. Therefore, their value in reinforcing a specific behavior is lost. In addition, young children may not have learned the cultural value of grades and therefore do not place high value on them. Students who have a history of low grades do not believe that a high grade can be earned and therefore will not try. The effectiveness of grades as reinforcers seems to decline during early adolescence and especially among those students who are alienated (Stipek 1988, 24).

Activity reinforcers. Activities that individuals like to do can be used to reinforce behavior. Good examples are attempts to link participation in extracurricular activities with classroom performance. Students are allowed to participate in a high-interest activity only after they have performed well in other areas. Elementary school teachers are using this form of reinforcement when they allow students to erase the chalkboard when they behave in an appropriate manner. Parents are using activity reinforcers when they make a high-interest activity such as viewing a favorite television show contingent on completing homework or performing required chores.

Token reinforcers. Teachers faced with the impracticality of other types of reinforcers might try token reinforcers. Token reinforcers include items such as chips or stamps that can be turned in to the teacher in exchange for an activity or a reinforcer that the student desires. An application of token reinforcement commonly used is in the form of contracts or contingency management systems. In these approaches, the teacher and the student work out an agreement that once the student has obtained a given number of tokens for good behavior, he or she may then engage in some activity or obtain some prize that is desired.

Some Qualifiers in the Use of Behavior Modification

A couple of problems must be considered when applying behavior modification in classroom settings. One relates to the identification of effective reinforcers. Keep in mind that the reinforcer must be something that the student wants. Student and teacher perceptions about what is desirable are sometimes very different. Thus, teachers may think that the environment has been arranged for desirable events to occur while students see them as undesirable events. For example, one teacher with fond remembrances of games played during recess in elementary school attempted to use increased recess time as a reinforcer. However, several students who did not possess much athletic skill viewed the increased time as additional opportunity for humiliation and therefore punishment. Rather than improving their behavior, increased game time led to an increase in the disruptive behavior of these students.

In addition, what is reinforcing for one individual in the classroom might not be reinforcing for another. One might desire attention and enjoy being on center stage, while others might be uncomfortable with the attention and would seek to avoid it. Implementing a behavior modification program for a large number of students in a given class can then pose the significant problem of identifying reinforcers for each student in the classroom. Some reinforcers are effective for many students, but it is unlikely that any one reinforcer will be effective for all. Therefore, behavior modification tends to work best when the teacher can identify specific students who might benefit from behavior modification and identify those reinforcers that would be effective for them.

A second issue relating to the use of reinforcers in the classroom is that the reinforcers generally available to teachers may not be very powerful. Some of the more powerful ones, such as food and money, cannot be used. For example, a teacher simply cannot make eating lunch contingent on good behavior. That would be ethically and legally questionable. Although some teachers do use treats, such as popcorn, as reinforcers, they are not generally as powerful because they are a bonus or an extra that an individual can do without.

Several methods are useful in identifying appropriate reinforcers for a given student. One method is to simply ask students their preferences. Many of them are open and interested in sharing such ideas with their teacher. Talking with students often reveals interests and hobbies that have never surfaced in the classroom. This information can be helpful in choosing activities that might serve as reinforcers as well as helping the teacher relate school activities to personal interests.

Box 10-3
THE CLASSROOM LEADER

Steve is one of the most popular students in the tenth grade. He is a personable, handsome boy with good athletic skills. However, Steve is not academically oriented. He frequently jokes and makes distracting comments when the teacher is teaching. During seat work he talks and seldom gets on-task. Since he is one of the leaders, the rest of the class follows his example. This has made teaching the class extremely difficult.

What would you do?

1.   Do you think behavior modification would work with Steve?

2.   What reinforcers might work with Steve?

3.   How would you apply behavior modification to this problem?

Observing students in a variety of settings is another way to identify reinforcers. The activities that individuals engage in during their free time is frequently a good indication of those activities that the individuals find reinforcing. The teacher can take some of these activities and test them as possible reinforcers.

A key element after choosing reinforcers is to keep data on their effectiveness. The teacher needs to know how often a particular reinforcer is used and the effects of the reinforcer on the subsequent behavior of the student. The reinforcers that the teacher thought would work well may not be as powerful as first thought. Therefore, the teacher might need to engage in additional observation and study in order to identify more powerful reinforcers. In addition, students may grow tired of the same reinforcers and stop responding to them. Therefore, the teacher may need to change the reinforcers periodically.

Specific Behavior to Be Changed

A key element in the application of behavior modification in the classroom is the identification of the specific behavior to be changed. There are two components to this precise definition of the behavior. The first part is to identify precisely the behavior that the teacher wants the student to demonstrate. This is important in that it helps clarify teacher expectations and helps the teacher consider what appropriate behavior is in the classroom. Just performing this step helps teachers become more effective problem solvers. Second, a precise definition of acceptable behavior is important so that the teacher will know what is to be reinforced. Imprecise definitions such as "being a good citizen" are not enough. The teacher needs to define what is meant by "being a good citizen." Does it mean a student staying in his or her seat, raising hands before talking, listening to others while they are talking, asking permission to use materials, arriving in class promptly? The precise definitions of acceptable behaviors and those to be reinforced are key in the success of a behavior modification plan.

Reinforcement Schedules

Once the teacher has identified those events that are reinforcing to the student and has precisely identified those behaviors that are to be reinforced, the next step is to decide when and how to provide the reinforcers. To be effective, the reinforcers need to be employed as soon as possible after the behavior. During the beginning stages of the plan, the behavior should be reinforced every time the behavior is demonstrated. This requirement poses a heavy burden for a teacher who is attempting to manage a classroom of 25 or more students at one time. The teacher may not have time to watch the student and reinforce the behavior every time it occurs.

In such situations, there are a couple of options that the teacher might employ. One involves the use of a teacher aide or helper. This person could be assigned the task of carefully monitoring student behavior during those times when the teacher is otherwise occupied. A token system might work best, with the assistant providing a token every time the student demonstrates the behavior.

If a teaching aide or assistant is not available, the teacher might set aside a specific time when attention will be focused on the behavior of the student. This is especially useful if the teacher can identify specific times during the day or class period when the student is most likely to cause difficulty. For example, if the student seems to demonstrate the inappropriate behavior more during those times when he or she is working independently, then the teacher might set aside that time for several days to focus on the behavior of the student and to reward the times that he or she is following the rules and demonstrating appropriate behavior.

One issue that often arises is whether or not the other students will react negatively if one student is receiving reinforcement and attention and the others are not. The answer is yes, they will, if good behavior is not rewarded and the classroom climate is one where positive reinforcement is scarce. Therefore, for reinforcements to work effectively, the teacher must create a positive classroom atmosphere where positive behavior is rewarded and does have a payoff. Then the more intense attention paid to a specific individual for a short period of time will not be resented. In addition, most students will understand what the teacher is doing and will respect his or her attempts to help a student with a learning problem and to create a more constructive learning environment. Concerns that students will perceive a behavior modification plan as unfair are often mistaken concerns. Most students view the attempts as the sign of a concerned and caring teacher rather than as unfair attempts to favor one student over others.

After the initial program is started and the desired behavior is beginning to occur regularly, reinforcements are given less and less. The best reinforcement schedule now is an intermittent one, where the student does not know when a reinforcer might be given. Once this stage has been reached, the use of behavior modification with a given student becomes relatively simple. The main issue here is to make sure that reinforcers are given occasionally and are not totally eliminated.

Effectiveness of the Plan

The precision of behavior modification in identifying the precise behavior to be changed makes it possible to evaluate the effectiveness of the program with a given student. This is an advantage that behavior modification has over other approaches to dealing with inappropriate behavior.

The first step in evaluating the effectiveness of the program occurs before the teacher starts the intervention. This involves taking baseline data, that is, keeping track of the number of times the appropriate or inappropriate behavior occurs before the reinforcement program is initiated. The teacher should spend several days observing the student and simply tallying the number of times the behavior occurs during a given time interval. It would help if the student could be observed all day or all period. However, this is not always possible. Therefore, the teacher may set aside specific time intervals of from five minutes to an entire class period and observe and record the student's behavior.

The length of time needed to gather the baseline data depends on the severity of the problem and the frequency of occurrence. For some behaviors, two or three days may be all that is needed to get an accurate picture of the frequency of behavioral occurrence. In other situations, the data-gathering period may have to be extended to several days.

Once the data are gathered, the frequency of occurrence can be divided by the number of observations in order to get an average for the occurrence of the behavior. This information will be useful in helping the teacher to decide how to administer the reinforcers and how long it might take to see results. Those behaviors that occur frequently and therefore can be reinforced frequently will show results much more rapidly than those that occur only a few times during an observation or reinforcement interval. For example, if it is identified during a baseline data-gathering period that a student is out of his seat on an average of five times during a given interval, the teacher will need to have a schedule of reinforcement that provides frequent reinforcers for staying in the seat and is likely to see more dramatic changes than a reinforcement program for a behavior that is demonstrated only once or twice during the day.

Evaluating the effectiveness of the intervention program then takes place after the reinforcement program has been in operation for some time. The teacher should discontinue the formal reinforcement program and once again tally the occurrences of the focus behavior. This should be done in much the same manner that the baseline data were gathered. After a few observations, average occurrence of the behavior is determined and compared with the baseline data. This comparison can help the teacher determine the effectiveness of the intervention program. If there has been little or no change in the frequency of occurrence, the teacher may need to consider changing the reinforcers or the reinforcement schedule that was established. If the behavior is changing at an acceptable rate, the teacher should then resume the intervention plan. Remember that if the reinforcements stop altogether, the old patterns are likely to recur.

Elimination of Inappropriate Behavior

An important task for teachers when dealing with inappropriate behavior is to try to eliminate the inappropriate behavior and replace it with desirable behavior. Often, the most difficult component is eliminating the undesirable behavior. An important step in this process is the precise identification of behaviors that the teacher wishes to eliminate. Once again, vague definitions, such as "overly aggressive," "immature," or "hostile," are not enough. The teacher must precisely identify those behaviors that lead to the conclusion that the student is too aggressive, immature, or hostile.

The purpose of this precise identification is to assist the teacher in problem solving so that the frequency of undesirable behaviors can be reduced. One consideration in attempting to reduce the frequency of the behaviors is to reflect on those elements in the environment that might be providing the student with some reinforcement for the behavior. The inappropriate behavior may be a response that the student has learned in order to obtain some desirable outcome.

Withholding reinforcement. According to the principle of reinforcement, behaviors that do not achieve desirable consequences will decrease in their frequency. This principle applies to those behaviors that teachers consider undesirable as well as to those they consider desirable. The inappropriate behavior would not continue unless it was resulting in some payoff for the student. Therefore, the beginning step in weakening a behavior or decreasing its frequency of occurrence is to identify what might be providing reinforcement for the continuing behavior. If these reinforcing events can be identified and removed from the environment, the undesirable behavior will begin to occur less and less frequently.

An example might be helpful in clarifying this point. A teacher was confronted by a student who frequently threw temper tantrums in the classroom. As she searched for possible explanations for the behavior, she arrived at the conclusion that the boy was trying to gain the attention of the rest of the class. This provided two helpful steps in attempting to stop the tantrums. One step was to use attention as a reinforcer and make sure that the boy received attention when he did perform in an acceptable manner. The second step was to try to remove the reinforcer for the inappropriate behavior. She did this by giving a token to each of the children who ignored the temper tantrum. The next time the boy threw a tantrum, she quickly went around the room and provided tokens to those students who continued working. She gave them the token and said, "Thanks for ignoring Johnny." In this way she changed the environment by removing the reinforcer for the temper tantrum: student attention. After two or three more tantrums, Johnny realized that his behavior was not gaining him anything he desired: Students were ignoring him and he was not receiving any tokens. In a short while, the temper tantrums ceased.

This illustration brings up an important point that is often lost in classroom applications of behavior modification. The teacher is not the only person who may be providing reinforcement in the classroom. An entire classroom of individuals, and in some cases individuals outside the classroom, might be providing reinforcers for a particular behavior. In fact, some of these individuals, powerful peers or parents, are able to provide more powerful reinforcers than the teacher. Therefore, a teacher's withholding reinforcers may have little impact on behavior. For this reason, the advice of well-meaning individuals to "ignore a behavior and it will soon cease" often is ineffective. It is not the approval or reinforcement of the teacher that the student desires, but reinforcement from some other source. The teacher must identify that other source and seek to eliminate it.

Administering punishment. A second way that behavior is weakened is through the use of punishment. Punishment is defined as something that is undesirable, painful, or discomforting that results from a misbehavior. Because it is an undesirable outcome of behavior, punishment weakens or decreases the probability that a behavior will recur. Punishment can be quite effective for stopping an unwanted behavior. However, behavior modification theorists are reluctant to advocate the use of punishment because it may have several undesirable side effects.

Punishment may actually reinforce undesirable behavior rather than decrease it. This may occur because the perceptions of the teacher may be different from those of the learner. The teacher may think that sending a student out of the room is punishment while the student views escaping a boring lesson as a reinforcement. A student who receives little attention at home would see any type of attention, even punishment, as preferable to being ignored.

Another potential problem is that while punishment may stop inappropriate behaviors, it does not teach appropriate ones. Unless appropriate behaviors are taught, other undesirable behaviors are likely to take the place of the behavior that was punished. Therefore, in order to be effective, punishment needs to be combined with positive reinforcement of appropriate behaviors.

Box 10-4
KEEPING SUSAN UNDER CONTROL

Susan seems to be in perpetual motion. She is unable to stay in her seat and do her own work and is constantly bothering others. She always has to get a book, sharpen her pencil, or get a drink. The teacher has tried taking away privileges, putting her name on the board, and keeping her after school. Nothing seems to work.

Apply behavior modification to this problem:

1. **What would be the first thing you would do in applying behavior modification to this problem?**

2. **What behaviors would you pinpoint to change?**

3. **What type of reinforcers would you try? Why?**

4. **How would you go about implementing your plan?**

A third potential drawback in the use of punishment is that it may produce long-lasting fears and anxieties that can interfere with performance. This is especially true if students believe that the punishment inflicted is unfair or malicious. They blame the teacher for the punishment and associate the punishment with the teacher rather than with the inappropriate behavior. An overreliance on punishment in the classroom can result in a negative orientation that is harmful to teacher-learner communication and to the teaching and learning process.

Other criticisms of the use of punishment center on the assertion that the use of punishment serves as a model for aggressive behavior and that it teaches students that the infliction of pain is an acceptable means of settling interpersonal problems. Although this assertion is not universally held, it is a valid concern that must be taken seriously by teachers. Teachers are significant others in the lives of many students and do serve as role models. Consequently, they must be concerned about what is modeled as appropriate behavior.

In summary, the use of punishment is effective for stopping a behavior and is appropriately used when the behavior is dangerous or when very few appropriate behaviors seem to exist for the teacher to reinforce. It is only a beginning point to gain control until appropriate behavior can be developed and reinforced (Gallagher 1980, 43).

Advantages of Behavior Modification Approaches

Behavior modification approaches provide a teacher with a systematic plan for attacking a particular discipline problem. A consistent theory underlying behavior modification provides some basic principles that can be applied to solving a specific problem.

Behavior modification seems to be especially useful for working with students who do not initially respond well to less intrusive means of control. For this reason, behavior modification approaches have been used extensively in special education classes. The smaller number of students also helps to create conditions that facilitate implementation of behavior modification approaches. Behavioral approaches are also popular because they place primary responsibility and authority with the teacher for dealing with discipline problems. Some teachers like the approach because it does place them in control; some administrators tend to favor the approach because it makes it easier to hold the teacher accountable. A basic tenet of the approach is that all of behavior is learned, and if the appropriate reinforcers are found and applied systematically, the teacher can replace inappropriate behavior patterns with appropriate ones.

An emphasis on the influence of the environment on learners' behavior also places the focus on elements that the teacher can control. Variables over which the teacher has little control, such as home life or the present internal emotional state of the learner, are not considered to be relevant factors. The clear focus on observable and measurable behaviors does not allow teachers to excuse inappropriate behavior. This serves as an antidote to the professed helplessness of some teachers to control the behavior of the students in their classroom.

Disadvantages of Behavior Modification Approaches

One of the most important disadvantages of behavior modification is that the emphasis on external controls may interfere with the development of self-control. Some studies (Kohlberg 1970; Selman 1980) seem to indicate that a primary emphasis on external rewards inhibits individual development of higher levels of moral development. There is also some evidence that an overreliance on extrinsic rewards may interfere with the attainment of important educational objectives. Several studies indicate that rewards have a negative impact on the willingness of students to attempt difficult or challenging tasks (Stipek 1988). Other studies indicate that the use of extrinsic rewards may also have a negative effect on student motivation (Doyle 1986, 423). Students who are already interested in a task become less interested when external rewards are provided to them for engaging in the task.

Another major disadvantage of behavior modification approaches is that effects may be short term. Rewards may be effective in eliciting the desired behavior only under conditions where the rewards are present (Stipek 1988). The behavioral change may not transfer to situations outside the classroom or to other classrooms where the rewards are not present. Since accepting challenges and attempting difficult tasks are important educational outcomes, an overreliance on extrinsic rewards should be avoided.

Another major concern is that the emphasis on observable student behavior may keep the teacher from identifying how the problem behavior might be prevented in the first place. Many of the problems can be traced to poor teaching methods, poor interpersonal skills, or inappropriate exercise of teacher power. The inappropriate behavior might be student attempts to cope with boredom, anxiety, or anger. Unless these conditions are addressed, there is little chance that behavior modification will have the desired effects. The attention to modification of learner behavior might be misplaced. Rather than attempting to modify the behavior of the students, the attempt should be to modify the behavior of the teacher.

SUMMARY

Altering the learning environment is an appropriate response to discipline problems that occur in the classroom and can create conditions so that the students can begin to exercise self-control. First steps in altering the environment might involve such simple measures as moving a student's seat or providing a time-out area within the classroom. More serious behavior can be dealt with by removing the misbehaving student from the classroom. This communicates to all students that the teacher is serious about enforcing the rules, and it allows the teacher an opportunity to cool down and do some problem solving before talking with the offending student. It also allows the teacher an opportunity to regain control of the rest of the class.

A more systematic method for altering the environment of the classroom is the use of behavior modification, a technique based on the principle of reinforcement. This principle maintains that behaviors eliciting desirable consequences are likely to recur. Therefore, the teacher needs to alter the environment so that the desired behaviors are reinforced and the undesired ones are not. This requires a precise definition of the behaviors to be developed and an identification of the environmental events that are reinforcing to a particular student.

Behavior modification is a powerful approach to changing behavior and can be very effective. However, it does require considerable effort and time on the part of the teacher. The sheer numbers of students in a typical classroom may make it difficult for the teacher to implement a successful behavior modification plan in the classroom. An overreliance on extrinsic reinforcers may actually hinder students' moral development and growth toward self-control. In addition, extrinsic reinforcers may cause students to be overly cautious and avoid more complex learning activities. Behavior modification should be applied judiciously to the behavior of students in the room. Finally, the use of behavior modification might be inappropriate in dealing with a behavioral problem that is a symptom of something more basic in the classroom environment. Teachers may need to consider how their actions and/or the quality of their instruction are contributing to the problem.

SUGGESTED ACTIVITIES

1. Observe in a classroom and note elements of the environment that might be distracting to students and could lead to problems. Observe to see if those elements do distract students in the classroom and pose a potential solution to the problem.

2. Conduct a survey of nearby schools and classrooms. How many of the schools have a time-out room, and how many teachers use a time-out area in their classroom? Identify the procedures used for sending students to the time-out area and what they must do before being allowed to return. Ask teachers to comment on the effectiveness of the system.

3. Conduct a discussion with your peers on your reactions to behavior modification. Discuss such issues as your views about the use of behavior modification and the issue of whether or not it is bribery. Have individuals share any experiences they may have had with the approach.

4. Conduct an experiment with behavior modification. Identify a behavior of a friend, spouse, or child that you would like to increase. Define the behavior in precise terms, gather baseline data, implement a program of reinforcements, and evaluate the program after about two weeks to see if the behavior did increase. Write up your experiment and identify why you think the program was or was not effective.

5. Observe in a classroom where behavior modification is in use. Identify the specific behaviors that the teacher is attempting to change and the reinforcements that are being used. Write an analysis of your observations, noting what appear to be the strengths and weaknesses of the approach.

BIBLIOGRAPHY

DOYLE, W. 1986. Classroom organization and management. In *Handbook of Research on Teaching*, 3rd ed., ed. M. Wittrock. New York: Macmillan.

GALLAGHER, J. 1980. *Changing Behavior: How and Why*. Morristown, N.J.: Silver Burdett.

GLASSER, W. 1977. 10 steps to good discipline. *Today's Education*, 66, 60–63.

KOHLBERG, L. 1970. Stage and sequence: The cognitive-developmental approach to socialization. In *Handbook of Socialization Theory and Research*, ed. D. Goslin. Chicago: Rand McNally.

MADSEN, C. H., JR., and C. K. MADSEN. 1974. *Teaching/Discipline: A Positive Approach for Educational Development*. Boston: Allyn & Bacon.

SELMAN, R. 1980. *The Growth of Interpersonal Understanding: Developmental and Clinical Analyses*. New York: Academic Press.

SKINNER, B. F. 1971. *The Technology of Teaching*. New York: Appleton/Century/Crofts.

STIPEK, D. 1988. *Motivation to Learn: From Theory to Practice*. Englewood Cliffs, N.J.: Prentice Hall.

Chapter 11

DEALING WITH PERSISTENT MISBEHAVIOR

OBJECTIVES

This chapter provides information to help the reader to

1. Define the four common mistaken goals of misbehaving students

2. State how teachers can identify the mistaken goals

3. Describe actions that should be taken once the mistaken goals have been identified

4. List Glasser's steps toward effective discipline

5. Define each of the three types of classroom meetings

6. List alternative consequences that can be applied to classroom problems

INTRODUCTION

Direct and firm teacher action may be required when other methods of dealing with misbehavior do not work. Although the majority of the problems are minor and can be handled by low profile methods that support self-control, some students persistently misbehave. These problems are the ones that cause teacher anxiety and burnout. Behavior modification techniques might be a long-range solution, but the teacher often does not have the time to implement the method and wait for results. The misbehavior must be stopped, and stopped immediately. More intrusive actions that require teacher assertiveness are called for.

Several potential problems are associated with direct teacher intervention. The intervention may result in power struggles between the teacher and the student. These tests of will can easily frustrate the goal of helping the student to move toward self-control and can actually lead to a worsening of the problem. In addition, excessive teacher intervention can remove responsibility from the student for solving the problem. For these reasons, direct teacher intervention and demonstrations of teacher authority and power need to be exercised carefully and with good judgment. They should be used only after other approaches have failed to achieve desirable results.

Several individuals have suggested methods that the teacher can use in directly confronting student misbehavior. The remainder of this chapter reviews some of those approaches.

TEACHER ASSERTIVENESS

During the latter part of the 1970s, assertiveness training programs gained considerable popularity. These programs were designed to help individuals express their wants and feelings and to be more assertive in standing up for their own rights and needs. One of the major contemporary issues facing teachers is a sense of powerlessness and a need to be assertive. There is a long list of reasons why these feelings of powerlessness exist. Parents are more likely to challenge teacher authority, the status of teachers has dropped, lawsuits have increased, the role of the teacher has become less well defined, and well-meaning critics of education have charged that the schools are oppressive. These factors caused confusion among the teaching ranks, and many were fearful of reprimanding students and demanding appropriate behavior in the classroom. The assertiveness training movement communicated to teachers that it is acceptable to demand that students behave appropriately and that teachers should not feel guilty for doing so. One of the basic reasons that the assertive discipline approach (Canter and Canter 1976) became so popular was that it applied some of the principles of the assertiveness movement to the classroom and affirmend to teachers that it was all right for them to be assertive.

Teachers do have a right, and a professional obligation, to act when students are behaving in ways that interfere with the rights of others or that are self-destructive. They have an obligation to maintain a learning environment where it is possible for students to feel safe and to learn. Student behavior that threatens these conditions must be stopped, and stopped quickly. Stopping the behavior and communicating clear messages about teacher expectations are the beginning step in creating an environment where students achieve success and move toward self-control.

The Canters (1976) call this type of teacher response to misbehavior the "assertive response style," a style that involves clear and firm communication to the students about behavioral expectations and the resulting consequences if they are not followed. The assertive teacher is one who is willing to consistently follow words with actions.

It is possible for the assertive teaching style to be misused. Teachers can get so enthusiastic about the use of their power that they forget the needs of the students. When taken to this extreme, the use of teacher assertions can become a destructive force. Teachers can, however, be assertive without being overly oppressive.

Because the use of an assertive teaching style involves the use of teacher power, it may create power struggles between the teacher and the student and result in anger and hostility. Glasser (1965) makes an interesting point when dealing with this issue. He points out that adults must be willing to endure the anger that sometimes results when students are held to the responsible course of action and that holding a student to the responsible course will never permanently alienate the student. Parents and teachers are familiar with this behavior. Youngsters who are angry threaten to withhold their love and affection unless they are allowed to get their own way. Parents who give in to this threat are not doing their children any favors. Dealing with problems in a firm manner and holding the students accountable will teach them that they can be responsible, with improved relationships as a result.

IDENTIFYING MISTAKEN GOALS

Understanding the goals of students is the important first step in dealing with persistent misbehavior. Dreikurs states that every action of a student has a purpose (Dreikurs, Grunwald, and Pepper 1982, 13). Therefore, even incidents of misbehavior have some reason behind them. Changing the behavior and moving the student toward self-control require that the teacher first understand the reason behind the action. Dreikurs points out that actions that might be termed misbehaviors are the result of mistaken notions that students have about themselves and how to achieve significance and status. Therefore, misbehavior can be seen as the result of a student having lost the belief that acceptance and significance can be achieved through acceptable means. Although the student is probably not aware of them, there are four mistaken goals that the student might be trying to achieve: attention, power, revenge, and a display of inadequacy in order to be left alone.

Defining Mistaken Goals

Attention-seeking. Attention-seeking is a common goal for most people. Individuals want to be noticed and accepted. They want to feel that they are significant enough to capture the attention of others in the group. Many individuals learn how to accommodate this goal by performing in ways that are socially acceptable. For example, many students learn that they will gain the attention and affection of significant others by doing well in school. However, students who are frustrated in their attempts to do well in school or who do not receive attention regardless of their efforts, often learn that they can gain attention through misbehavior. Teachers unwittingly reinforce the behavior. They think that they are punishing or humiliating a student when, in fact, they are providing the student with what is desired, attention. Attention-seeking students prefer humiliation and punishment to being ignored.

Power-seeking. We all have a need to feel that we have some power. We need to have some control over what happens to us and believe that we can manipulate the environment. Once again, individuals who have been frustrated in gaining power through acceptable means may discover that their only way of feeling powerful, and therefore significant, is through socially unacceptable means—in other words, misbehavior. Through their inappropriate behavior, students are trying to prove that they are the boss and that the teacher is powerless to force them to behave.

Efforts to control the student usually lead to a power struggle. The student will demonstrate defiance and disobedience through arguing, crying, acting stubborn, or throwing a temper tantrum in order to prove his or her power. These reactions only cause more frustration for the teacher and present a challenge that few teachers seem able to resist. They want to teach the student that the teacher is the boss. However, teachers can rarely win a power struggle with the student. Even engaging the student in a power struggle confirms the student's mistaken notion that the way to feel significant is to misbehave and force the teacher to deal with his or her power. Once a power struggle takes place, the probability is that the relationship between the student and the teacher will deteriorate and that even more serious problems will occur.

Revenge. The anger and the frustration that usually follow power struggles lead to revenge. When students feel hurt and angry or believe that people have been unfair to them, they try to get even. Their reasoning is that they have been hurt and therefore they have the right to hurt others. These students are convinced that no one likes them or believes they are significant. Therefore, their behavior is not their fault, but it is

Box 11-1
LOUIS'S DEFIANCE

Pat Taylor thinks that the class would be a good class if it were not for Louis. Louis is a teacher's worst nightmare. He constantly challenges and tests the authority of Pat. When an assignment is given, he is likely to blurt out, "Who cares about this stuff?" If he is corrected by Pat, he usually responds with, "You can't make me." His defiant attitude and constant disruption seem to create a constant war of nerves in the class.

What do you think?

1.   What mistaken goals might Louis be pursuing?

2.   How would you try to meet his needs and change his goals?

3.   What consequences would you apply when Louis does challenge the teacher?

caused by the way others treat them. Because the student bent on revenge does hurt other people and does cause hostility, the retaliation of others in response to their behavior is taken as proof that they were right in the first place. No one likes them, and they have a right to strike out.

The revenge-seeking student is one of the most difficult problems for the teacher. Teachers who are unaware of this goal may fall into the trap of trying to get even with the student and therefore continue to provide justification to the student for his or her continued acts of revenge.

Display of inadequacy. Some students who are unable to achieve a sense of significance through acceptable means may become so discouraged that they simply give up for fear that they will again be proven insignificant. As a defense mechanism to avoid even trying a task, these students will hide behind a display of inadequacy. They will go to great lengths to discourage the teacher from attempting to help them. Like the revengeful student, this student has serious problems and causes a great deal of frustration among teachers. Unfortunately, it is easier to ignore and give up on students displaying inadequacy than those seeking revenge. Consequently, they do not receive the help they need. This confirms what they thought all along: they are insignificant and inadequate.

Identifying Mistaken Goals

Teachers who are unaware of the goal that a student is trying to achieve may behave in ways that reinforce the student's attempts to feel significant and powerful through inappropriate behavior. Therefore, the first step in taking corrective action is to identify the goal of the student.

Dreikurs (Dreikurs, Grunwald, and Pepper 1982, 25) identifies two basic ways that the teacher can identify the student's goal. The most reliable indicator is the teacher's immediate reaction to the behavior. If a teacher wants to yell at or nag a student, the goal is usually attention. If the first reaction of the teacher is that the student is challenging or testing teacher authority, then the goal is usually power. A first reaction of feeling hurt or defeated often indicates that the goal of the student was to get revenge. Feeling frustrated to the point of throwing up your hands and leaving the child alone is usually an indication that the student is seeking to be left alone through a display of inadequacy. In all of these situations, the first reaction of the teacher is the wrong one.

A second indication of the student's goal is through the student's response to correction. If the student stops a behavior when reprimanded but then starts again after a short time, attention is the probable goal. If the student becomes defiant when reprimanded and continues to misbehave, the goal is probably that of power. A student who becomes abusive and angry when reprimanded and who complains that he or she is being picked on and unjustly accused is often seeking revenge. A student who is passive and does nothing when reprimanded is usually demonstrating a sense of inadequacy and simply wants to be left alone.

Responding to Students Seeking Mistaken Goals

Merely identifying the behavior is not enough. The teacher needs to have a plan of action that will help the student move away from these mistaken notions and toward self-control. As stated above, it is usually the wrong response to act according to first impulse because that usually provides reinforcement for the inappropriate behavior.

Dreikurs recommends that a first step in dealing with a student who is misbehaving is to disclose the goal to the student and to observe the reaction. The disclosure needs to be done in a matter-of-fact, nonthreatening manner and never as an accusation. Therefore, the disclosure is best not done when the teacher is angry. Disclosing the goal has the effect of opening up communication between the teacher and the student. In addition, most students are unaware of the goals that they may be pursuing through their misbehavior, and disclosing their mistaken goals helps them understand their behavior and be more purposeful in becoming more productive.

The process of disclosing the goal to the student is best done by using simple questioning techniques. The teacher should begin by asking the student if he or she is interested in knowing the reason for his or her behavior. If the student replies in the affirmative, then the teacher continues with a follow-up question. If the student says no, the teacher can simply respond by saying, "I would like to tell you what I think" and then continue with the follow-up question.

The follow-up questions usually start with the stem "Could it be that?..." For example, follow-up questions intended to reveal a goal of attention-getting might be phrased, "Could it be that you would like me to pay you more attention?" or "Could it be that you want me to come and help you more?" Questions intended to reveal the goal of power could be phrased, "Could it be that you want to show me that I cannot make you behave?" or "Could it be that you want to be the boss?" Revenge goals could be revealed through "Could it be that you want to hurt me or others?" or "Could it be that you want to try to get even?" Inadequacy might be addressed through the question, "Could it be that you want to be left alone because you are afraid to fail?" or "Could it be that you want to be left alone because you can't be the winner?"

Dreikurs (Dreikurs, Grunwald, and Pepper 1982, 28) indicates that the teacher can often tell when the goal has been correctly identified by the student's reaction to the question. Although the student may answer "no," a recognition reflex such as a grin, embarrassed laughter, or body language indicating some discomfort usually confirms that the teacher has been correct in the diagnosis of the goal.

The teacher can also make several other responses when students are misbehaving. These vary according to the goal that the students are attempting to fulfill. One basic principle that should be followed when responding to incidents of misbehavior is not to follow the first impulse. Rather, the teacher should do something that is very different and unexpected.

Responding to attention-seeking. A first attempt at dealing with attention-seeking behavior is refusing to give attention to inappropriate behavior and then giving attention to students when they are behaving. Ignoring the behavior once will not result in the desired change. The student has had years of gaining attention through misbehavior and one time will not be enough to result in a change. However, teacher persistence will pay off, and the incidents of inappropriate behavior will begin to diminish.

In some situations ignoring the behavior is not possible. Instead, other actions might be valuable. One action would be to have a personal conference with the student. During this conference the teacher should discuss the situation with the student in a calm, but firm, manner. The teacher should identify the goal for the student and suggest they work out a plan. In working out the plan the teacher might ask the student how many times attention is desired during the period or the day. Each time that the student misbehaves in an effort to gain attention the teacher can merely state, "John, that's one." "John, that's two." This procedure shows the student the number of times he or she is actually seeking attention in unproductive ways.

The number of incidents is often surprising to the student and he or she will choose to make changes. However, if the incidents continue, the student may be seeking power and the teacher may need to move to other responses. The use of logical consequences, such as having the student make up the time that is spent disrupting the class, may be productive.

Box 11-2
THE CLASS CLOWN

It is your first year of teaching and you are extremely nervous about being able to handle discipline problems. The first couple of weeks have gone quite well and you are just beginning to relax. Then, unexpectedly, Bill decides to perform his clown act. He starts making funny faces and noises during the reading lesson. The whole class begins giggling and looking at him. It is obvious that he is enjoying the attention. You sense that you are losing the class and that their attention is no longer on the lesson. You look at Bill and ask, "Bill, would you please hold the noise until after class?" You are surprised when he responds with a clear, "No."

What will you do?

1.　**What do you think the goal or goals are that Bill is pursuing?**

2.　**How will you respond?**

3.　**What might be done to prevent the problem?**

Responding to power-seeking. Many teachers find it very difficult to avoid a power struggle with the student. The culture of education is steeped with an autocratic tradition that the teacher is to be obeyed and his or her authority may not be challenged. Students, however, do not share this tradition. Those who are power hungry take great delight in drawing teachers into power struggles.

Teachers must realize that drawing a line and challenging a student to defy teacher authority is asking for trouble. It is much easier simply to refuse to engage in a power struggle. Often, an unexpected sympathetic or friendly reaction to a student who is trying to gain power is enough to stop the behavior. For example, the teacher might respond with statements such as, "I'm sorry that you feel so alone and powerless" or "I know you are feeling angry but if you continue you will force me to...." Another response is simply to admit that the student cannot be forced to behave. Admitting that the teacher has limited power and refusing to rise to the challenge often takes all of the fun out of attempting to engage the teacher in a power struggle. The teacher does not demand that the student stop or change but simply states, "You are right, I cannot make you behave. However, if you want to continue this misbehavior you need to do it elsewhere." Removing the student from the situation, and thus from the audience, is often enough to stop the behavior.

Box 11-3
HILDA'S DESTRUCTIVE BEHAVIOR

Hilda comes from a large family. There is some evidence to suggest that she has been an abused child. She rarely disrupts class but destroys the property of others when she is not watched closely. One day she got hold of a set of new pencils that one boy had brought to school and proceeded to break each of them into small pieces. On another occasion she defaced one of the bulletin boards that displayed student work. On the playground and after school she frequently hits and hurts younger students.

What would you do?

1. **What might be Hilda's reason for these behaviors?**

2. **What consequences would you have for her destructive acts?**

3. **How might you prevent the problem?**

Responding to revenge-seeking. Students who are attempting to achieve revenge are students with serious problems. They are hurting inside and are just looking for an excuse to explode. A major step in dealing with such a student is to change the relationship between the student and the teacher and, if possible, work on the relationship between the student and the rest of the class.

One of the important ingredients in changing the teacher-student relationship is to treat the student with respect. This is very difficult to do when a student is often treating the teacher in an abusive manner that may cause emotional discomfort. However, the teacher is the professional and has an ethical obligation to take charge of the situation. The teacher should never pursue the same mistaken goal by trying to get revenge on a misbehaving student. This justifies the behavior of the student and communicates that revenge is acceptable.

The teacher should treat incidents focused on getting revenge in a matter-of-fact manner. Even though the teacher might be upset, it is important to communicate to the student that you have self-control and will not retaliate. Removing the student from the situation in a quiet and nonthreatening manner provides the student with an opportunity to cool down. The teacher can discuss the situation with the student by identifying the goal the student was pursuing and then asking the student to apologize or make restitution. The teacher might offer to help the student anytime he or she is feeling angry and resentful. The security of a confident and assertive teacher provided to students produces a calming effect on them, removing much of the anger that is seething inside. They begin to realize that not everyone is against them and that they do have some worth.

Discussion with the entire class may also be needed. The purpose of these class discussions should not be to place blame but rather to help the class understand how their treatment affects others. Role-playing situations may be especially helpful in stimulating a discussion about feelings, anger, and revenge. This understanding can then be applied in creating an environment where individuals are accepting of each other and where the need for power struggles and revenge is eliminated.

Most students who are seeking revenge feel very much alone and on the outside. The teacher may need to help them gain group acceptance. This might be done by talking with the student and helping the student understand the impact of his or her behavior on others. The students might simply be deficient in social skills and not understand the relationship between their behavior and the reactions of others. The teacher needs to model and teach some appropriate social skills. Helping the student gain acceptance can also be accomplished by finding something he or she can do well and focusing on that ability or skill. Many disruptive students have been completely changed by a teacher who was interested enough in them to discover their talents and to consider them worthwhile. Once the teacher accepts the student, the class soon follows.

Responding to displays of inadequacy. Students who display inadequacy are students who are extremely discouraged and have given up. Overcoming this discouragement is a major task for the teacher. Once again the student who is displaying inadequacy is a student with serious problems and must not be ignored.

A beginning step in overcoming displays of inadequacy is never to give up on the student. Communicating to the student a sense of optimism and celebrating every success, no matter how minor, are important ingredients. This also means that the teacher must be careful not to place the student in high-risk situations. When activities and tasks are presented to this student, they need to be broken down into small steps so that the student does not feel overwhelmed.

Placing students in cooperative learning groups where they are working with others and where their failures are not given the spotlight is also a useful approach in overcoming the discouragement that students displaying inadequacy feel. Helping such a student, like helping the student seeking revenge, is a time-consuming process, and immediate results should not be expected.

Box 11-4
FRUSTRATING FRANK

Frank is not an especially troublesome student. In fact, he is extremely passive and apathetic. He doesn't do any work, and at the end of the class turns in a blank piece of paper. Getting low grades does not seem to disturb him. He just sits by himself and doodles the day away. When the teacher tries to assist him, he just shrugs his shoulders or states, "I don't know" or "I don't care."

What would you do?
1.   **What would you identify as Frank's problem?**

2.   **What would you do to try to get him to do some work?**

GLASSER'S STEPS TOWARD EFFECTIVE DISCIPLINE

Another successful approach to serious and persistent discipline problems is that outlined by Glasser. Glasser's approach has its roots in his 1965 book, *Reality Therapy*. His later works have built on and extended this model into schools.

The basic principles around which Glasser has built his response to discipline problems are powerful yet simple. First of all, he believes that all behavior is a matter of choice. Individuals choose to behave the way they do. Good behavior is the result of good choices and bad behavior is the result of bad choices. Many individuals attempt to justify their choices by focusing on the past and events in their past. In essence, they are looking for excuses for their behavior. However, Glasser points out that we live in the present and must face the reality of the consequences of our behavior (Glasser 1965, 68). A student may have had a less than desirable home life but, although regrettable, it still does not excuse him or her from behaving responsibly. Because behavior is a matter of choice and individuals have rational minds and are able to choose, they can understand acceptable behavior and can choose to behave appropriately.

Individuals should also learn that their behavior produces consequences, and should they choose to behave inappropriately, they will face the consequences of that behavior. Glasser (1969) states that a teacher should not attempt to manipulate circumstances so that a student does not experience the reasonable consequences of behavior.

It is not enough for students to face the reality of their behavior; they must also learn how to fulfill their needs in satisfactory and productive ways (Glasser 1965, 7). One of the reasons that individuals behave in unproductive ways is that they have not learned how to fulfill their needs in responsible ways. This failure leads to low self-esteem and self-worth. These feelings produce a failure identity, which then leads individuals to behave in irresponsible ways that do not help them fulfill their needs. Glasser believes that the school and teachers have an important role to play in helping students to learn social responsibility and to develop a success identity (Glasser 1969, 29).

A prerequisite for success in using the Glasser approach is for the teacher to be warm, personal, and willing to be involved. Glasser notes that many students have not learned how to be responsible because they have not been involved with responsible and caring adults (Glasser 1965, 19). Therefore, the first step in the implementation of the Glasser approach is for the teacher to establish a warm and caring interpersonal environment. If this dimension is missing, the approach becomes a mechanical exercise with little chance of success.

Once this environment is in place, the basic principles of reality therapy can be applied. The process of implementing reality therapy is best done through an individual conference with the student. This conference should be conducted in private, in a businesslike environment free from anger and hostility. For this reason Glasser suggests that a first reaction to a discipline problem is to remove the student from the group. This might involve sending the student to the time-out corner in the classroom or out of the classroom to the office or time-out room. After the student and the teacher have had an opportunity to cool down and think about the behavior, then the conference can be conducted.

Implementing the Steps

The following steps are suggested as an effective way of implementing the basic concepts of reality therapy.

Ask student to describe behavior. This step in the process has the student describe what he or she was doing. This behavior identification should be done immediately and should precede sending the student to a time-out area. The purpose of this step is to help the student understand the relationship between his or her behavior and the consequences. The student must understand that it is his or her present behavior that led to the problem. The intention is to get the student to accept the responsibility for the behavior. Only when a student accepts responsibility for a behavior can the process of change begin to occur. This step can be implemented by asking the student the simple question, "What are you doing?"

Many students will seek to avoid responsibility by trying to avoid the question. A common response is "Nothing." When this happens, the teacher should simply repeat the question. Another avoidance technique is to identify another behavior. For example, a student might state, "I'm sitting in my seat." When this happens, the teacher simply follows this up with, "What else are you doing?" If the student refuses to identify the inappropriate behavior after about three attempts, then the teacher should identify the behavior for the student. This should be done directly and with little display of emotion.

Accept no excuses for misbehavior. Another attempt to avoid responsibility for the behavior is to try to identify an excuse for the behavior. The student may respond to the question of what he is doing by trying to shift the blame to another. For example, a student might respond, "Well, Mary was talking to me." When this occurs the teacher can either ignore the answer and ask again, "What were you doing?" or accept the answer by stating, "I understand, but what were you doing?" It is important that the teacher keep the focus on the inappropriate behavior and not allow excuses to shift the responsibility to another.

When responding to a problem behavior, the teacher should never ask, "Why are you behaving that way?" The why question opens the door for excuses and invites the student to place the responsibility for the behavior on something other than his or her own choice.

Have student make value judgment about behavior. Having the student make a value judgment about the behavior is an attempt to get the student to recognize how the behavior is interfering with his or her ability to satisfy needs. The student is ultimately the only one who can change behavior and the student must identify the behavior as undesirable and counterproductive. Glasser suggests that teachers can help students in this by asking them, "How is this behavior helping you?" or "How is the behavior helping others?" The latter question is often used to help students realize that they must demonstrate responsibility by fulfilling their needs in ways that do not interfere with the ability of others to fulfill theirs.

Most students will quickly acknowledge that misbehavior is not helping them. When students state that misbehavior is helping them, the teacher may need to state how the behavior is interfering with the needs of others in the classroom. Once again, this statement needs to be delivered in a firm and businesslike manner, not as an angry accusation.

Have student identify consequences. A teacher who has focused on the establishment of rules and has outlined some consequences for violators will have established the necessary conditions for this step. There are two reasons for this step in the process. The first is to make sure that students understand the direct link between inappropriate behavior and consequences. They need to see that it is their behavior that is leading to the consequences and not a vindictive or angry teacher bent on punishment. An understanding of the link makes it possible for students to comprehend that their behavior is a matter of choice and the consequences that are experienced are also a matter of choice. After the student has identified the consequences, the teacher should then ask, "Is that what you want to happen?" If a student refuses to identify the consequences or purports not to know what happens when individuals misbehave, the teacher might suggest two or three suitable alternatives.

Develop a plan with student for changing the behavior. The purpose of this step is to help students establish a plan that will help them fulfill needs in a productive way and to begin to eliminate their unproductive behavior. This step can be implemented simply by asking the student, "What kind of plan could you work out so that this will not happen again?" If a student is reluctant to answer, the teacher might simply state, "You think about it and I will return in a few minutes and discuss it." Teachers should not accept superficial answers that are not specific. It is helpful to pursue the development of a plan by asking students why they think this will work and what should be done if it does not. Once again the purpose is to keep responsibility with the student. Therefore, the teacher must resist the temptation to force a plan on the student. The student must make a commitment to the plan, and this commitment may be only a superficial one if the student believes he or she has no choice but to follow a plan determined by the teacher. The teacher does need to offer support by providing some suggestions and asking how he or she can help.

The plans that are made should be very simple and short term. It is unproductive to have students spell out a complicated plan that covers an entire semester. They will not be able to complete the plan and therefore will not learn responsibility. Initial plans for students who are chronic behavior problems might cover one period or one day. The intent is for the student to be successful in completing the plan. The teacher might need to remind the student of the plan from time to time and might also need to evaluate the success of the plan with the student. If the student violates the plan, then the teacher and the student have another conference and develop a new plan. It may well be that several plans will need to be developed before the student realizes that the teacher means business and a plan is developed that is successful.

Invoke reasonable consequences. The development of a plan does not preclude the administration of reasonable consequences. A student who has violated a rule and misbehaved needs to realize that reasonable consequences do follow. The consequences for misbehavior should be undesirable or unpleasant to the student but should never be punishing or harmful. However, it is of equal importance that desirable and pleasant events also follow when students do behave. This helps them learn that they can experience desirable and pleasant events or undesirable and unpleasant events by their choice of behavior. This gives them a sense of power and control over what happens to them and leads to increased self-control.

Be persistent. An important point in making the process work is for the teacher to be persistent. Persistence communicates that the teacher is serious and has confidence that the student can be responsible and can choose to behave in appropriate ways. A fact that many teachers overlook when dealing with ongoing incidents of misbehavior is that they are often the indication of a serious problem. This problem has taken some time to develop and will probably take some time to remedy. There are no magic bullets that will quickly and permanently change a student's behavior. In fact, the

---

Box 11-5
BUT IS IT EFFECTIVE?

You are a new teacher who agrees with the Glasser approach. During your first observation and conference with your school principal, you tell her how you respond to misbehavior. The principal says, "Well, I guess that is okay. However, it seems like a waste of time to me. These students only understand punishment. If I were you, I would just come down hard on them with severe punishments anytime they get out of line."

What would you do?

1. **How do you react to the principal's statement?**

2. **Do you think there is any validity in her concern that your method takes too much time?**

3. **What would you say to the principal so that you could respond to problems in a way that is comfortable to you, yet would not result in your being considered unreceptive to suggestions?**

---

student may test the teacher's commitment, and the behavior may get worse before it gets better. Teacher persistence is an absolute must if changes are to be made.

Notify parents. For those few students who seem to be unable to follow a plan and who are constantly disrupting the class, a conference with the parents may be necessary. Prior to the conference the teacher should keep records of the incidents of misbehavior in order to document the seriousness of the situation. When conferring with the parents, identify the problem and ask for their input or advice. The teacher needs to communicate very clearly that it is because of a concern for the student and his or her well-being that they are meeting. Defensive parents who feel that the teacher is blaming them for their child's problem will be of very little help in achieving a long-term solution.

In those few instances where parents seem unwilling to assist, the teacher must remember that it is acceptable to be assertive and to stand up for his or her rights. Parents can be informed in a firm manner that the behavior must be changed or more drastic measures will follow. It might be necessary to involve the school principal in the conference so that appropriate alternatives can be explained to the parents. Glasser points out that teachers should not have to put up with someone who is constantly disrupting the class and interfering with the ability of others to learn. If the parents are unable or unwilling to help, then they should be referred to a counseling agency that can help them.

Classroom Meetings

Another component of Glasser's approach to discipline in the classroom involves classroom meetings. Classroom meetings are a means of getting students involved in decision making about their own education. They are intended to help the students develop a sense of relevance for school and a sense of responsibility for what happens in the school. Glasser's basic thesis is that when students are involved, believe that teachers are concerned about them as individuals, and are allowed to discover the relevance of education, most discipline problems will be prevented.

Classroom meetings involve arranging the class in a circle so that the environment is conducive for wide participation. The teacher introduces the topic and gets the meeting underway. The role of the teacher then becomes one of a discussion leader. The meetings should be kept relatively brief, approximately 10 to 30 minutes, where students are allowed to present their feelings and ideas without fear of retaliation. The purpose is for the students to share their concerns and to become involved in making decisions. By doing this they develop a sense of ownership for what happens in the school and learn how to be responsible.

Glasser defines three types of meetings that might be held: social-problem-solving meetings, educational-diagnostic meetings, and open-ended meetings (Glasser 1969, 143).

Social-problem-solving meetings are those that focus on the problems that students have in living together in the school environment. Discussions during these meetings might focus on a discipline problem. The teacher should call the classroom meeting, identify the problem, and then allow students the opportunity to discuss why the problem seems to be occurring and to suggest solutions. The intent is to obtain a commitment from the class for a plan that might solve the problem. The major outline of the meeting could follow the basic steps of reality therapy used with individual students: identifying the behavior causing the problem, making a value judgment, identifying reasonable consequences, and developing a plan.

Educational-diagnostic meetings are those that are directly related to what the students are studying and learning in school. During these meetings, students may ask questions about the relevance of what they are studying or the reason for studying certain topics in a given way. The teacher may use these meetings to diagnose student

---

Box 11-6
AN UNHEALTHY INTERPERSONAL CLIMATE

One of the major problems in your classroom are cliques. Students have formed into groups, and some students have been left out entirely. The suggestions and contributions of these rejected students are ignored and they frequently are the butt of pranks. A couple of the rejected students have just quietly quit responding or participating. A couple of the others have started to retaliate. You are afraid that the problem may escalate into a major confrontation.

What would you do?

1. **Do you think a classroom meeting would work? Why or why not?**

2. **Write out the focus and a plan for a classroom meeting on this issue.**

3. **What would you do to try to keep the meeting from becoming a major confrontation between the students?**

---

motivation and understanding as well as the impact of different teaching approaches on the students.

Open-ended meetings are the type that Glasser thinks should be used most frequently. These are meetings where the teacher might provide the focus by asking thought-provoking questions related to the lives of the students or to the curriculum. The intent of the meeting is to allow students considerable freedom in searching for personal meaning and in thinking about problems and issues. The basic difference between this type of meeting and the others is that the teacher is not looking for specific answers or solutions but is allowing students an opportunity to express their thoughts and feelings.

In summary, Glasser has provided some specific suggestions for working with students who demonstrate inappropriate behavior. His basic point is that students need to learn that behavior is a matter of choice and that they can choose to behave

appropriately. Individuals need to learn that behavior has consequences and they must face the reality of those consequences. Those who choose to behave in appropriate ways receive desirable consequences; those who behave in inappropriate ways face undesirable consequences. When students are involved with a teacher who cares about them and who is persistent in working on solutions, students begin to learn that they can act responsibly. This sense of responsibility leads to improved self-esteem and better choices.

IDENTIFYING ALTERNATIVE CONSEQUENCES

Both Dreikurs and Glasser mention the importance of applying logical and reasonable consequences. A major problem for new or inexperienced teachers is in identifying reasonable or logical consequences. What is needed is for teachers to develop a set of consequences that can be applied to classroom situations. It is important for a teacher to realize that no set of consequences will work for all teachers all of the time. The consequences developed need to be ones that are comfortable for the teacher. Otherwise, they will be reluctant to use them and become inconsistent in their responses to misbehavior. In addition, consequences that are effective for one group of learners might not be effective for another group. The teacher needs to become familiar with the class and to use his or her own creativity in designing consequences.

A beginning point might be to brainstorm a list of consequences that might be implemented when students misbehave. It is then helpful to develop a hierarchy that begins with simple and relatively unobtrusive measures and moves to more intrusive and appropriate ones for serious and repeated misbehavior. The teacher can then begin moving through the range of alternative consequences as the situation demands. New consequences suggested by the students or by other teachers can be added to the list as the year progresses.

This simple list of consequences has the effect of providing the teacher with a great deal of security in knowing how to respond when a problem occurs. Inexperienced teachers who try to think of something on the spot often draw a blank and respond in counterproductive ways. Numerous suggestions for responses to discipline problems have been mentioned in previous chapters. Those can be used to form the basis of the hierarchy of consequences. Other responses can also be added to the hierarchy. A few responses are discussed in the remainder of this chapter.

Clarity and Firmness in a Verbal Response

Verbal responses are a typical teacher reaction to student misbehavior. However, many of the verbal responses that teachers make are ineffective. They tend to put the student on the spot, draw attention to the misbehavior, and set the stage for a power struggle. Therefore, verbal responses should be used with caution. At times, a verbal response is appropriate and necessary. When this occurs, teachers should consider several points as they deliver a verbal message.

First of all, the teacher should deliver the message in a businesslike manner. Verbal abuse of the student, sarcasm, shouting, or displays of anger should be avoided. They only cause resentment and set the stage for retaliation. Kounin (1977), in an

impressive research study on teacher responses to misbehavior, identified two variables that were effective in delivering a verbal message: clarity and firmness.

Clarity involves identifying who is misbehaving, what that person is doing, and what he or she should be doing. A verbal message involving clarity might be as follows, "John, stop your talking and begin working on your math problems." This message indicates that John is the target, his talking is inappropriate, and he had better get back on-task.

Firmness means using a tone of voice and body language to indicate that the teacher means business. As the teacher is delivering the message, he or she should make eye contact with the student, move toward the student, and maintain an erect posture. These are all signs to the student that the teacher is serious. Mixing the verbal and the nonverbal messages, for example, telling a student to stop something while smiling, communicates insincerity. The student is not sure that the teacher really means it and is likely to continue the behavior until the message is sent in a more forceful manner.

Loss of Privileges

The loss of privileges can be an especially effective consequence. However, it will work only if students have some privileges to lose, and if they are privileges that students desire. Unfortunately, many secondary school students are given few privileges and therefore have nothing to lose. A wise teacher will begin at the first of the year to identify some privileges that are desired by the students. For example, some secondary school teachers have discovered that students like to listen to music while they are engaged in seat work. This is a privilege that can be withheld as a consequence of misbehavior. Others might include being allowed free time or being the first in line for lunch. Some schools consider extracurricular activities a privilege and participation depends on appropriate behavior.

There are abundant activities that elementary school teachers can use for privileges. Most elementary school students enjoy serving as teacher helpers and monitors. Loss of the classroom job for a short time is often effective. Choice of a recess activity or being made the captain of a team or custodian of the playground equipment are other highly valued privileges that can be awarded for good behavior or withheld for misbehavior.

Time After School or Detention

Staying after school has a long history as a consequence for inappropriate behavior. It can be an effective consequence if it is a logical consequence for behaviors that waste class time. Considerations such as the legal issue of providing transportation to get the student home must be addressed before implementing an after-school penalty. Some secondary schools have implemented Saturday detention hall where students must spend time as a consequence for misbehavior.

This type of consequence should be used very carefully and only as a last resort. Keeping a student after school is often the easy way out for a teacher and is used

indiscriminately to punish a student and to get even. For example, a third-grade teacher had after-school as a normal consequence if a student misbehaved more than once a day. One third-grade student had developed a reputation for being "bad." The teacher was watching for the boy to misbehave and he was constantly exceeding the limit and was kept after school. Night after night he sat alone in the classroom. It was obvious that the consequence was not having the desired effect of helping the student learn self-control. Obviously the after-school punishment was doing nothing to solve his problem or to help him learn self-control. Such an insensitive use of punishment will soon create an angry and bitter young boy. Excessive use of after-school or detention time often causes anger and resentment and may result in more serious and anonymous violations such as vandalism.

When using after-school or detention as a consequence, the teacher should make sure that the student understands why he or she is spending the time. It should logically fit the offense, and it should not be excessive. The teacher should take the opportunity to confer with the student and to work out a plan that will help the student avoid the consequences in the future and to move toward self-control.

Cost-Payoff Analysis

Another step that can be taken is to have students who are experiencing behavior problems conduct a "cost-payoff analysis" (Jones and Jones 1986, 328). A cost-payoff analysis is having students identify the short- and long-term pay-offs or benefits of their inappropriate behavior and the short- and long-term costs of their behavior. The purpose of this analysis is to outline systematically the benefits and detriments of a given behavior. It forces students to think more deeply about the consequences and makes it more likely that they can make a more informed value judgment about the behavior. Systematically outlining the costs and the payoffs can then help students make better choices about their behavior and alternatives for fulfilling their needs.

After performing the analysis, the teacher and student can discuss the payoffs and the costs and add those that might have been omitted. Once this is done, the student can then be asked to decide if the payoffs outweigh the costs. A teacher should not force the student to make this decision. It is only when the student honestly decides that the costs are too great that a real commitment to improvement can be obtained. If the student makes this commitment, a plan can be developed to help overcome the problem and help the student obtain the payoffs in a productive and acceptable manner.

Involving Others

A few students seem to be so difficult that nothing seems to work. Teachers who have tried several alternatives and have met with little or no success should not hesitate to involve others. Teachers are not psychologists or psychiatrists and cannot be expected to solve all problems. Some problems are just too serious for the teacher, and seeking outside assistance is not a sign of failure. It is the professional thing to do.

Allowing a student to continue on a path of self-destruction is not professional or compassionate. The student may need help, and need it quickly. Not seeking help under the mistaken notion that it is a personal failure for the teacher can lead to tragedy. The teacher must always consider the welfare of the student over professional ego. When a student is out of control or exhibiting serious problems, the teacher should quickly seek the assistance of school counselors, psychologists, and principals. These individuals can assist the teacher and, if necessary, the parents in understanding the problem and in seeking assistance for solving it.

SUMMARY

Persistent misbehavior causes teachers the most concern. At times, students do not respond to less intrusive measures. When this occurs in the classroom, the teacher must realize that it is permissible to be assertive and to expect that a student will obey. Teachers should not think that they have no rights, nor should misbehaving students interfere with their right to teach and the right of others to learn.

Several steps can be taken in response to these more serious incidents. Dreikurs and associates have provided teachers with helpful ways of identifying the goals that students might be pursuing so that teachers do not inadvertently fall into the trap of continuing to reinforce students' behavior. Once these goals have been identified, teachers can then take some action. Dreikurs suggests that revealing the goal to the student, not responding to the first impulse but doing something unexpected, and implementing logical consequences are productive ways of changing the behavior and the goals that the student is pursuing.

Glasser has made a sound contribution to the work with problem students through reality therapy. He has suggested a specific approach to students that is best done in a private conference. This approach involves identifying what the student was doing, making a value judgment about the behavior, identifying reasonable consequences, making a plan, and implementing reasonable consequences. Teachers need to be warm and supportive individuals who model self-control for the student and who are persistent in their efforts.

An important step for teachers who expect to work toward self-control in the classroom is the development of a hierarchy of consequences. This hierarchy should begin with relatively simple and unobtrusive responses and move progressively to more intrusive and serious ones. The development of this hierarchy can provide teachers with a plan of action and a sense of security when facing serious discipline problems.

SUGGESTED ACTIVITIES

1.   Interview several teachers about assertiveness. Do they agree that teachers generally have not been assertive enough? How can teachers demonstrate assertiveness without alienating students and parents? Do principals support teacher assertiveness?

2. Observe in a classroom and see if you can classify student behavior as attention-getting, power, revenge, or withdrawal.

3. Identify a potential discipline problem that concerns you. Apply Dreikurs' natural and logical consequences and Glasser's steps to the problem. Write out how you would respond and what you would say at each step.

4. Identify situations and develop a plan for conducting each type of classroom meeting.

5. Work with a small group of individuals to prepare a list of alternative consequences that might be used in responding to discipline problems.

BIBLIOGRAPHY

CANTER, L., and M. CANTER. 1976. *Assertive Discipline: A Take Charge Approach for Today's Educator*. Santa Monica, Calif.: Canter and Associates.

CHARLES, C. 1989. *Building Classroom Discipline: From Models to Practice*, 2nd ed. New York: Longman.

DREIKURS, R., B. GRUNWALD, and F. PEPPER. 1982. *Maintaining Sanity in the Classroom: Classroom Management Techniques*, 3rd ed. New York: Harper & Row.

FROYEN, L. 1988. *Classroom Management: Empowering Teacher-Leaders*. Columbus, Ohio: Chas. E. Merrill.

GLASSER, W. 1965. *Reality Therapy: A New Approach to Psychiatry*. New York: Harper & Row.

————. 1969. *Schools Without Failure*. New York: Harper & Row.

JONES, V., and L. JONES. 1986. *Comprehensive Classroom Management: Creating Positive Learning Environments*, 2nd ed. Boston: Allyn & Bacon.

KOUNIN, J. 1977. *Discipline and Group Management in Classrooms*. New York: Holt, Rinehart and Winston.

Chapter 12

DEALING WITH SERIOUS BEHAVIOR PROBLEMS

OBJECTIVES

This chapter provides information to help the reader to

1. Identify causes of attendance problems

2. Describe measures that can help prevent cheating

3. List steps that can be taken to deal with theft

4. State the seriousness of vandalism for schools

5. State measures to be taken when confronting violence between students

6. Identify causes of violence against teachers

7. Identify actions to be taken when confronting drug and alcohol abuse

8. List the steps to be followed in preparing for and conducting a parent conference

INTRODUCTION

The majority of discipline problems that occur in the classroom are relatively minor. However, the few serious discipline problems that do occur are the ones that cause teachers many sleepless nights. Offenders seem almost immune to efforts to help them change their behavior and move toward a productive life. Teachers frequently feel that they are engaged in a constant struggle with these students, as each day brings another confrontation. One student in the classroom with serious behavioral difficulties can change the climate of the entire class and turn a satisfying experience for the teacher into an exceedingly frustrating one.

The fact that these problems are serious and persistent indicates that easy solutions are not likely. Teacher persistence over a period of weeks and months may be needed before any improvement is noticed. In addition, frequent lapses of behavior are the norm. Just when the teacher believes that progress is being made, the student will once again demonstrate the old behavioral pattern. The frustrations that accompany efforts to work with students who have serious behavior difficulties often cause the teacher to give up. However, such behavioral disorders are often students' way of signaling for help. They desperately want someone to notice them and their problem, yet they do not know how to ask for or receive help. The teacher who gives up is only confirming to students that no one cares or will help.

Serious problems in the classroom may be the result of problems that exist outside the classroom. Many problems have their roots in larger societal concerns. Crime, drugs, and antisocial behavior in society will lead to the occurrence of these problems in school. This does not mean that the teacher is powerless to act. It only means that the problems will be more difficult to solve and that the involvement of the entire school and even the community might be required in order to make significant progress.

This chapter provides suggestions for dealing with those problems that interfere with developing and maintaining a positive classroom environment: persistent attendance problems, cheating, stealing, vandalism, violence, and substance abuse. The chapter concludes with a section on working with parents and other professionals in helping students with serious problems.

ATTENDANCE PROBLEMS

Serious attendance problems that cause teachers concern are of two types—those students who are frequently tardy to class and those who are frequently absent. Frequent tardies are often the more serious for a teacher. Just when the teacher has the class started, the tardy student arrives to disrupt the flow of the lesson and create a disturbance. It is much easier to overlook students who are frequently absent because they are simply not causing any disturbance. Frequent, unexcused absences are often bothersome because they are interpreted by the teacher as a statement of disinterest and low regard for the teacher and the subject. Therefore, teachers often take unexcused absences as a personal affront.

Attendance problems are a major concern throughout the United States. Some

inner-city schools report daily absence rates of over 50 percent, and school administrators list attendance as the most serious discipline problem (Duke and Meckel 1984, 47). The disruption in the learning process caused by frequent absences and tardiness is a major factor in low achievement.

Identifying Causes of Attendance Problems

The first step in correcting any problem is to spend time diagnosing the problem and identifying the causes. A variety of explanations account for the persistent attendance problems teachers and schools are experiencing. Time used in diagnosing these problems is well spent by helping the teacher and school officials eliminate unproductive approaches. For example, one study reported that approximately 8 percent of secondary school students stated that they stayed away from school at least one day a month because they were afraid to go to school. Lack of attendance due to fear must be dealt with very differently than lack of attendance due to apathy.

One of the major causes of attendance problems in schools is lack of student success and fear of failure. Just imagine being required to attend a job or a school where you believed you had no chance of success. After a short time frustration and bitterness would take hold. For some students, this frustration takes the form of aggression; for others, it results in avoidance behaviors. Even the fear of being caught and punished for truancy is minor compared to the humiliation and fear that accompany persistent failure.

Another cause of attendance problems is apathy. Apathetic students see neither the importance nor the relevance of school. They do not enjoy school and do not believe that the school is interested in them or their success. They see the school as a cold and uncaring bureaucracy. The curriculum is not viewed as especially relevant, and teachers are individuals who are out to get students rather than help them. School rules are arbitrary and insensitive to the feelings of students. Many of the teachers may

---

Box 12-1
TARDY TROUBLE

Wilma is an insolent girl in her sophomore year who obviously dislikes school. When she is in class, she is a disruptive influence. One of her worst problems is her excessive number of tardies. She usually comes in about five minutes late, slams the door, and noisily makes her way to her seat. Today, as she enters, you decide you are going to put a stop to her tardiness.

> *"Wilma, why are you tardy?"*
> *"I had to go to the bathroom. You didn't want me to go in here did you?"*
> *"Wilma, I don't appreciate your attitude."*
> *"Yeah, well I don't appreciate yours either, so I guess we're even."*

You sense that the class is watching this encounter to see who is going to win. You don't want to let Wilma get away with this disrespect, but you are not quite certain what to do.

What would you do?

1.   **How might you have handled the tardiness differently?**

2.   **What might prevent the problem from occurring?**

3.   **Now that there is a confrontation, how might you respond?**

---

be frustrated and unenthusiastic as they simply go about doing a job. School is simply not a pleasant place to be. Therefore, attendance problems may simply be a form of passive resistance to school and school policy. Administrators and teachers need to remember that more school rules and stiffer penalties are not the answer. Students must accept the rules and believe that it is in their best interest to support them.

Teachers who experience numerous tardies or cuts need to perform some self-evaluation. It may well be that they waste time getting the class started and make little effort to help students understand the importance of what they are studying.

Finally, fear of violence is another major cause of attendance problems. Unfortunately, schools are places where violence does occur, not safe havens separate from the outside world. Changing patterns of attendance may require considerable effort to make the school a safe place. The issue of violence is dealt with later in this chapter.

Approaches to Solving Attendance Problems

The seriousness of attendance problems and the resulting loss of academic progress demand creative approaches to the issue. The search for solutions should start with the teacher and move to the school and then to the community.

The teacher. The beginning point for solving attendance problems is with the teacher. Possibly, the teacher's attitude and behavior contribute significantly to the problems. This is especially true of teachers who are experiencing burnout. Burnout may result in a lack of enthusiasm and excitement for teaching. Some teachers have lost confidence in their ability to teach a given group of learners. Others have simply fallen into bad habits that tend to prompt tardiness and poor attendance.

The following questions might be helpful for a teacher who is concerned about how to solve persistent attendance problems:

1. How do you feel about teaching?
2. Do you look forward to going to school?
3. Are you interested in the subjects you are teaching?
4. Do you believe that the students in your classes are capable of learning?
5. How do you try to relate what you are teaching to student interests and concerns?
6. Do you start class on time?
7. Do you begin your classes with something that is interesting?
8. How do you try to maximize student success in your classroom?
9. Is your classroom a pleasant place to be?
10. How do you and your students have fun in your classroom?

Teachers may discover that they no longer enjoy teaching and are not capable of teaching students in their classroom. Professional help and counseling may be required to help them evaluate their career and decide whether or not to continue teaching. Professional development activities such as visiting other teachers in similar schools and attending meaningful workshops might help to develop a new enthusiasm. In some cases, a transfer to another school or taking a leave from teaching might be required.

Students. Conferring with students who are chronically absent or tardy, and doing so in a way that allows students to identify the factors contributing to the problems, can be fruitful in identifying and removing causes.

Teachers should not simply excuse persistent attendance problems. Instead, they should be consistent in following through with consequences when students violate attendance rules. The use of logical consequences, such as making up lost time or missing out on fun or highly desired activities, is also helpful in letting students know that the teacher is serious about attendance and will follow through. When firm and consistent behavior is coupled with prevention, great strides can be made to diminish the frequency of attendance problems.

CHEATING

Cheating is of universal concern. Not only is the issue an ethical one, but cheating also denigrates the importance of school tasks and interferes with valid assessments of student progress. Handling the problem of cheating can be especially difficult because it is so widespread in society. Teachers find it difficult to extol the virtues of honesty when the practices of business people and public officials regularly skirt the law.

Identifying Causes of Cheating

One of the basic causes for cheating on school tasks is fear of failure. This is especially the case with "high-stakes" tests and assignments, those that carry a heavy weight in determining student success or failure. The emphasis on high-stakes tests to determine whether or not a student passes to the next grade or graduates has led to an increase in their use and probably to an increase in cheating behavior.

Another cause of cheating is that students do not perceive the relevance of learning tasks. The value and importance of the learning tasks are not communicated to them. Because they see the tasks as unnecessary hurdles with little or no personal relevance, they spend inadequate time preparing for them and therefore are insecure when faced with a crucial task. In addition, because the task is perceived as having little value, any means of getting by it is justified.

Finally, cheating would drop dramatically if students really believed that an honest display of their knowledge and skill would be beneficial to them. If they felt that teachers would use the information to help them learn and achieve, then they would be less likely to provide inaccurate information to the teacher. Unfortunately, most students see school tests as the means by which the teacher gives grades and labels students rather than as a means of diagnosing learning difficulties in order to help students achieve success.

Approaches to Solving Cheating Problems

Students can be very creative in their efforts to cheat, and teachers who attempt to solve the problem by playing detective are usually frustrated. In fact, the detective efforts of teachers often serve as challenges to students to find some way of outsmarting them. Therefore, prevention is the real key to solving cheating problems.

An important aspect of prevention is for the teacher to administer fair tests and assignments. Tests that contain trick questions or that are not perceived by students to be accurate measures of important objectives communicate that the teacher is more concerned with spreading students out on a grading curve than actually assessing their knowledge and growth. The first step for teachers who seem to be plagued with cheating is to check the tests and assignments. Are they valid and worthwhile?

Another important component is to convince students that it is in their own best interest not to cheat. Teachers need to demonstrate visibly to students that they use test results for the benefit of students. This means that tests need to be more diagnostic and the results need to be communicated to students and used to increase student skill and mastery. Teachers can demonstrate the value of accurate information by meeting with students to discuss the results of their tests and planning additional experiences that will help them master the material. When students believe that tests and assignments are useful to them, the temptation to cheat will be eliminated.

The importance of any one test or assignment should be diminished. When the stakes are high and success is dependent on one or two major tasks, cheating becomes a means of self-preservation. More frequent testing and more frequent assignments help lessen the importance of the assignment or test and reduce the number of cheating incidents.

When students are caught cheating on a test, a private conference with the teacher is an appropriate response. Public accusations and ridicule only invite denial, defensiveness, and retaliation. In private and without anger, share with the student the information and ask the student to explain and identify possible consequences. While consequences should be implemented, they should not overshadow the use of the conference as a way to diagnose and eliminate the causes of cheating. Possibly the teacher will need to teach students appropriate study skills so that they come to learn that success is possible without cheating.

STEALING

Persistent loss of personal and school property leads to a serious deterioration of student and teacher morale and the creation of a climate that is not conducive to good learning or behavior. This is one of the most serious problems that teachers face. It is often difficult to handle because those who steal may be difficult to catch.

Identifying Causes of Stealing

Some students may resort to stealing because of jealousy. They believe that it is unfair that one student has objects that they covet. Other students may steal objects simply to get revenge on another student or the teacher. They feel unjustly treated by that individual, so they decide to take a prized possession in an effort to hurt him or her. Other students steal because they have low self-esteem and are trying to get attention. Students in this last category are often easy to identify because they usually make sure they get caught.

Approaches to Solving Stealing Problems

One of the first steps in solving stealing problems is to remove the temptation for stealing. When students bring prized possessions to the classroom, the teacher can volunteer to keep them in a safe place and then return them at the end of the day or the period. Teacher belongings, such as money, should be kept in a safe place (a locked desk drawer or cabinet) where students do not have access. When teachers leave the room, they should lock the door to prevent entry.

When there is a high incidence of stealing, class discussions dealing with value issues and respect for personal property can be helpful. Students can share their feelings and frustrations and suggest ways of solving the problem. This will be especially helpful if students believe that their best interests are threatened by stealing behavior. Use of peer influence and peer pressure to refrain from stealing is one of the most powerful approaches.

Individuals who are caught stealing need to be counseled in a private and nonthreatening manner. Natural consequences are appropriate measures to use with these students. They can be required to return the stolen material or to make restitution. They can then be denied access to desired objects or activities until they demonstrate responsibility. As with cheating, it is important to identify the causes for stealing and to deal with the causes rather than the symptoms.

VANDALISM

The cost of vandalism for school districts in the United States every year is enormous. In addition to the costs to repair the damage caused by vandals, vandalism can be very disruptive to the educational process. The destruction of equipment and materials makes it very difficult to provide a quality education for all students.

The problem of vandalism is often one that needs to be treated at a school or even a community level. Teachers, however, do have some responsibilities in helping prevent vandalism and in cooperating with authorities when vandalism does occur.

Identifying Causes of Vandalism

Vandalism is almost always an expression of anger and antagonism. Some of this anger and antagonism might be against society in general, and the school is an easy target. However, many acts of vandalism are expressions of anger and frustration directed at the school. This happens when the school is viewed as a threat rather than as a positive force. For example, the author participated in a community study of an inner-city school where participants discovered that the people in the community viewed the school as a threat second only to the police department. Where this climate exists, vandalism is certainly to be expected.

Approaches to Solving Vandalism Problems

Like so many problems, there are no simple or easy answers. The efforts of all teachers and staff are required if serious incidents of vandalism are to be prevented. An individual teacher can seldom prevent these acts. Perhaps the single most important preventive action that can be taken by a school is to build school pride. Students who are treated with respect and dignity and who feel that the school is working with them rather than against them will not vandalize.

Another effective schoolwide measure is to try to reduce "neutral turf." Neutral turf are those areas of the school, such as halls, rest rooms, and playgrounds, where there is no sense of clear ownership. These areas are not seen as the responsibility of any one person or group of individuals and are where a great deal of vandalism occurs. Neutral turf can be reduced by assigning responsibility for these areas to specific individuals or groups. For example, classes or teachers can be assigned the responsibility of taking care of the halls and the rest rooms in close proximity to their classroom. Students can be allowed to decorate the halls so that they have a pride of ownership as well as a responsibility to keep their area clean and free of graffiti. School administrators need to be highly visible and accept the responsibility for monitoring difficult neutral turf areas.

Classroom meetings to discuss incidents of vandalism and their consequences are useful in helping teachers identify the causes of vandalism and in dealing with student anger and hostility. They should be allowed to express their feelings openly without fear of retribution. Action then needs to be taken so that students believe that their feelings are respected and that they do have some outlet for their anger other than vandalism.

Students who are guilty of vandalism are best treated using natural consequences. They should be required to clean up any mess and to make restitution for any damage. Some parents try to relieve their son or daughter from responsibility by paying for damages. If possible, the students responsible should be held accountable and should make the restitution or repair the damage themselves.

Serious problems of vandalism that occur when the school is not in session might require the assistance of the local community. Community surveys to discover the attitude of the community toward the school can be helpful. Efforts can then be made to develop positive community attitudes. The community needs to believe that the school is important and that everyone has a stake in maintaining it. Community meetings between school officials and community representatives where the problem of vandalism is discussed and support from the community is solicited can be extremely helpful in solving serious vandalism problems.

VIOLENCE AGAINST OTHER STUDENTS

Violence against other students is an issue that causes considerable concern. Most new and inexperienced teachers worry about student fights and their ability to respond quickly before someone is injured. Violence against other students is a serious problem that is disruptive to the educational environment.

Identifying Causes of Violence Against Students

The causes of violent behavior in schoolchildren have been the subject of much debate. Students are regularly exposed to violence in their community as well as on television. Fighting and aggression are frequently portrayed as an appropriate and even masculine response when an individual's self-respect is assaulted. Unfortunately, the only method of conflict resolution that many students observe is fighting and aggres-

---

Box 12-2
THE AGGRESSIVE STUDENT

Tony is a rather large fifth grader. He is a poor student and has been retained twice. He has a quick temper, and if he feels he is being ridiculed or if he gets frustrated, he explodes. Today, as you walk into the room after recess, something has angered Tony and he is hitting one of the other boys. The other boy is defending himself and is hitting back.

What would you do?

1.   **What is your first step in confronting the incident?**

2.   **What would you do if you have a concern for your own safety?**

3.   **What consequences should follow this fight?**

---

sion. This helps explain why fights between students often break out over trivial issues such as name calling. Students see this as a direct challenge and assault to their dignity and therefore must respond with the society-sanctioned response, fighting. We are living in a violent society and that violence will certainly affect the school.

Acts of violence and bullying behavior are also attempts to gain power. Power-hungry students unable to fulfill this need through constructive behavior often resort to physical aggression in an attempt to prove their power. Teachers working with students who frequently engage in acts of violence against other students might note that those students involved are usually the ones who are having difficulty succeeding in other aspects of school life.

Revenge is yet another reason for acts of violence against other students. Those students who feel lonely, left out, and rejected by other students may resort to violent acts in an attempt to hurt others. They may not even strike back at those who are causing the pain, but may choose easy and convenient targets, such as weaker and more defenseless students.

Approaches to Solving Problems of Violence Against Students

When confronted by acts of violence between students, teachers should first stop the act before someone is injured. Second, they should treat the causes so that the probability of future acts is decreased. The first consideration, stopping the action before injury occurs, requires quick and firm action. If the fighting is out of control, help from other teachers or administrators should be requested immediately. A teacher should not try to step between students when there is a great probability that the teacher will be injured. However, the presence of a teacher who approaches individuals with a firm manner and who demands a stop to the fighting will usually be successful. Most students are also afraid of injury and are relieved to have an excuse to stop without losing status in the eyes of peers.

Once the fighting has stopped, it is usually wise to separate the students and allow them a cooling-off period. After sitting and considering their actions as well as possible consequences, they can then be counseled individually. When approaching students who have been engaged in acts of violence, the teacher should have a serious, businesslike manner. Approaching students in a threatening or angry manner increases their hostility and provokes defensive reactions that will get in the way of long-term resolution. In addition, teachers need to be careful about quickly assessing blame for the incident. It takes two people to fight, and there is usually blame on both sides.

Because of the seriousness of violence against students, school administrators should be informed and involved in the decision about the consequences of the act. Fighting and aggression are serious acts and should not be tolerated in school. Therefore, the consequences should be serious ones. Many schools have adopted the policy of automatic suspension for any student involved in an act of violence. Other, less serious consequences may be assigning the students to an isolation area or imposing loss of privileges. When privileges are withheld, they should be those that are logically related to the behavior, for example, not allowing the students to participate in those activities where fighting is possible.

Treating the causes of violence is difficult and time consuming. There are no easy approaches that will quickly and immediately remove student anger and hostility. Those individuals who feel powerless need to be provided with some avenues for feeling important and powerful. Those who are lonely and left out need to be given some status so that the need for revenge is removed. Finally, conflict resolution and coping skills can be taught to provide students with other, more socially appropriate ways to deal with anger and fear. Indeed, for some students with a history of violence, special counseling and help from school counselors and psychologists might be required.

VIOLENCE AGAINST TEACHERS

It was a dark and cloudy evening in late November. Mrs. Jones was making her way through the parking lot at the conclusion of another school day. She was thinking of all the things she had to get done that evening. She had to stop by the store, fix dinner, arrange for a neighbor to let in the washing machine repair man tomorrow, grade papers, and prepare materials for the followingday.Suddenly her thoughts were disturbed by a sudden noise behind her. As she turned, she was suddenly struck by something and knocked to the ground. Her books, papers, and purse went flying. She felt something, probably a foot, strike her in the ribs. Several other blows struck her in the back. The wind was knocked out of her and she could feel the pain from her skinned knees and hands. There was an intense pain in her side and in her right shoulder. She heard a voice shout, "Hey, teacher, we get detention, you get lumps. You'd better back off or we'll show you who is really tough!" As she tried to raise her head, all she saw were the backs of several boys disappearing around the corner of the building.

Acts of violence against teachers have grown to alarming proportions in recent years. One study reported that 5,200 secondary school teachers were physically attacked in a one-month period (West 1984). Teachers who worry about their own safety are not in a position to deliver the best possible instruction or to interact with students in positive and constructive ways. It is important, however, for teachers to recognize that violence against them is a possibility and to learn preventive measures to protect themselves.

Identifying Causes of Violence Against Teachers

One explanation of violence against teachers is that it is the final outcome of power struggles between students and teachers. Students become frustrated in their attempts to cope with teacher power, so they ultimately decide to seek revenge on the teacher. The student might feel as if he or she is backed into a corner and the only way to maintain the respect of peers is to strike out at the teacher. Another reason is that teachers, as representatives of authority, are accessible targets. Students who have hostility toward adult society in general, but find it difficult and dangerous to vent that hostility toward other symbols of authority such as the police or their own parents, focus on the teacher. These are deeply troubled students who are bent on revenge. The teacher may not be the sole cause of the anger but is simply a convenient target.

Approaches to Solving Problems of Violence Against Teachers

Violence against teachers, like violence against students, is a serious problem that cannot be ignored. When it occurs, school authorities need to be involved immediately. Regardless of the reasons for the act, violence cannot be excused or tolerated. Therefore, serious consequences are necessary for offenders. Many schools have a policy that results in the automatic suspension of any student who commits an act of violence against a teacher.

Teachers can use several steps to prevent acts of violence. One of the first steps is to exercise common sense in their daily activities. For example, teachers need to make sure that they don't present themselves as easy targets for students who are seeking revenge. Precautions such as not being alone in the classroom with doors unlocked late in the evening or not entering a volatile situation alone when students are angry and likely to react with aggression are important considerations.

Teachers who establish good communication with class members are often able to identify those students who have deep-seated anger and hostility. They must then communicate to these students that they care about them and are interested in helping them find ways of dealing with their anger and hostility. Counseling and therapy or class meetings where students are allowed to express their feelings and frustrations are possible solutions.

Perhaps the best way to prevent acts of violence against teachers is for teachers to convince students that they are on their side and are willing to work on their behalf. Students will rarely harm someone they believe is trying to help them. This means that teachers need to establish a warm, caring relationship with students. Teachers who threaten students with ultimatums carrying serious consequences or who use physical force when disciplining are inviting retaliation and violence.

Teachers who find themselves in conflict situations with students must remember that they are the trained professional in the group and that they need to take charge and find a resolution that does not result in violence. Those who worry about saving face or demonstrating their power are not creating conditions that will allow for a successful resolution. Modeling is an important technique for teaching students how to cope with anger without violence.

DRUG AND ALCOHOL ABUSE

Drug and alcohol abuse in the schools has received national attention as a societal problem of great proportions. In fact, many school officials report that it is one of the most serious problems they face. The negative influence of drugs on learning and on the classroom climate is well documented. Drugs in the school can be the origin of behavior problems, violence, and theft. The problem is not confined to any one type of school or to any particular grade level. Students are experimenting with drugs and alcohol at earlier ages, and suburban as well as inner-city schools are affected. Those individuals who think that they can avoid the problem by choosing to teach in only the "best" neighborhoods are being unrealistic.

Dealing with alcohol and drug abuse in the schools is further complicated by society's tendency to assign to schools the responsibility for solving complex social problems. Alcohol and drug abuse is a problem for all of society, and measures taken by schools will have limited success.

Identifying Causes of Drug and Alcohol Abuse

The causes for drug and alcohol abuse are numerous. Some individuals begin abusing drugs as a result of peer influence to be a part of the in group. Others take drugs as a coping mechanism for difficult life situations. Still others get involved as a symbol of rebellion. Those who tend to be more mature and who are prematurely attempting to be "adult" are also likely to engage in alcohol and drug abuse.

School factors that might contribute to drug and alcohol abuse are lack of trust, boredom, and feelings of insignificance. Students who do not trust school officials or who do not believe that they can trust what school officials tell them are likely to reject appeals to "just say no" and to experiment because usage is a rejection of school and

---

Box 12-3
SUBSTANCE ABUSE

Cindy is a rather insecure ninth-grade student. You have noted that she wants very much to be a part of the in group. However, she has trouble gaining the acceptance of others. You have Cindy in your fifth period English class that meets after lunch. Today when Cindy enters the room she is acting strangely. She is talking very loudly and lacks coordination. Her conversation is incoherent and jumbled. Other students are watching her and giggling. The pupils of her eyes are dilated and you suspect she is under the influence of drugs.

What would you do?

1. **What would be the first steps you would take?**

2. **What, if anything, would you do to try to get Cindy some help?**

3. **What might you do to deal with the issue of drugs with the whole class so that they would not see the problem as an amusing one?**

---

school authority. Those bored with school may experiment because it involves excitement and risk taking. Students who do not feel worthwhile or accepted by teachers may use drugs as a means of coping with rejection and a low self-concept.

Approaches to Solving Problems of Drug and Alcohol Abuse

A beginning point for moving toward a solution for drug and alcohol abuse is to adopt a "zero tolerance" policy. Drugs are destructive to the educational environment and cannot be tolerated. This means that teachers should not avoid dealing with a drug abuse problem. Avoiding the problem is not helpful to the student. The student is facing serious difficulty and needs help. To look the other way may result in tragedy. However, overcoming the problem is not easy. Dealing with such serious social problems is time consuming and difficult. Students who are under the influence of alcohol or drugs need to be removed from the classroom environment immediately.

If the teacher feels threatened, the assistance of other school personnel might be required.

When counseling students who may have a problem, it is important not to label the student or to fix blame. There are usually many reasons for the abuse, and fixing blame only creates defensiveness. When students learn that a teacher can be approached with a problem without fear of being put down, an important first step has been taken. School counselors and administrators may need to be brought in so that the student can be referred to individuals or agencies with the expertise to help. Since teachers are not drug counselors or trained therapists, they should not attempt to solve problems for which they are not equipped. To try to do so may only delay help that has a higher probability of success.

Prevention is the key for solving problems of abuse. These prevention measures involve the teaching of responsible decision making as a regular part of the curriculum, the development of a positive school environment, the teaching of coping skills for dealing with peer pressure, and the development of fun activities that are alternatives to drugs.

One of the most important measures in finding a solution is to involve the entire community. When the school and the community work together, significant progress can be made. Schools can assume the leadership role in bringing the community together to discuss the problems and to search for alternative solutions. The school might find it very useful to sponsor information sessions and workshops to help parents and community leaders understand the nature of the problem and agencies that can offer assistance. Schools that have been willing to become involved in such efforts discover that the increased contact with the community leads to school improvement extending far beyond the resolution of drug and alcohol abuse.

WORKING WITH PARENTS

A common element in solving serious discipline problems is the involvement of parents. Parents need to be involved and informed when their son or daughter is having difficulty. Schools and teachers lose a great deal of credibility with parents when they allow problems to continue without informing parents and seeking their assistance.

Unfortunately, many teachers are reluctant to involve parents. They are often afraid that the parents will be uncooperative and hostile. While it is true that some parents who had an undistinguished career as students may be initially defensive and hostile, teachers need to remember that parents do want their children to be successful in school. Some parents may act as if they do not care, but it is usually because they feel defeated and powerless. Accepting the assumption that parents do want the best for their children helps the teacher approach parent contacts in a more positive manner.

A common point of contact with parents is the parent-teacher conference. Successful parent-teacher conferences do not just happen; they require considerable planning and thought. Parents are understandably nervous and apprehensive. This is especially true if the conference concerns a problem because parents often view a behavior problem as a reflection on themselves as parents. They may be humiliated

---

Box 12-4
PLANNING A PARENT CONFERENCE

Robert is a seventh-grade student of average ability. He is somewhat lazy and does not work unless really pushed. His parents, however, have ambitions for him to excel in school and go to a prestigious university. At the end of the grading period you give him a "D." The next morning you have a call from his mother. Robert's parents are concerned about the grade and are convinced that the problem is a personality conflict between the two of you. They want to have Robert transferred to another class.

What would you do?

1. **Suppose you arrange a parent conference? What would you do to plan for the conference?**

2. **How would you react to the charge that the problem is a personality conflict?**

3. **What would you do to make sure that the conference stays positive and focuses on the problem rather than becoming a hostile confrontation?**

---

and defensive. These feelings of fear and defensiveness must be overcome if the conference is to be successful. It is the responsibility of the teacher to take the initiative and create the conditions for a successful conference.

Preparing for the Conference

Prior to the conference, gathering relevant and important data is one of the most important steps. If the conference involves a serious behavior problem, the teacher should keep objective, nonjudgmental anecdotal records on the occurrence of the problem. These records can be quick notes that identify the time of the incident, describe the student behavior, and indicate any actions that were taken. Samples of student work are also very important pieces of data that can be shared with the parent.

A teacher should also review the student records and note the parent's name, the marital status of the parent, and the presence of other siblings in the household. Parents will be impressed that the teacher has enough interest in them to know the names and ages of other children in the household. Health problems should also be noted and may hold a key to understanding the problem the student is experiencing. Finally, the teacher should state the objective of the conference and the major points to be covered.

Setting the Stage for the Conference

The success of a conference might be determined by creating a pleasant and positive climate. Creating this climate begins by meeting the parent in the school office. Parents should not be expected to wander around the school building looking for the teacher or the site of the conference. Greeting the parent in a friendly and relaxed manner and showing common courtesy can also help to lessen parental anxiety and fear. The conference should be conducted in a comfortable place, and the parent might be offered a cup of coffee or a soft drink, and, if possible, cookies or snacks. Eating helps relieve tension and communicates to the parent that the teacher is considerate and is appreciative of his or her coming. In addition, the teacher should not be behind a desk but should be seated next to a parent at a table. This indicates to parents that they are respected and accepted as equals.

Conducting the Conference

Throughout the conference keep the focus on the student. Communicate that the concern is for the teacher and the parent to work together to help the student attain success. The purpose of the conference should not be to place blame or to demonstrate power but to solve a problem and help the student. Beginning the conference by indicating positive things about the student can serve to relieve some of the tension. Encourage the parent to talk and participate in the conference. When dealing with a behavior problem it is useful to state, "We are having a problem. I know you are interested in the success of your child and I would appreciate your advice and assistance in dealing with the problem. Do you have any thoughts on what might be causing the problem?" This often acts as a door opener and lets the parent know immediately that his or her input is important. After the parent has had an opportunity to talk, the teacher might then guide the parent through the student's file and share the anecdotal records and copies of the work.

Clear communication is an important component of any parent conference. The teacher must make sure that the comments of the parent are understood and that the parent understands the points made by the teacher. Teachers should avoid educational terms or jargon not understood by the average parent. For example, one parent approached the author with the question, "What's Bloom's taxonomy?" A teacher had referred to the taxonomy several times during the conference and had never bothered to define it.

Active listening is a good communication skill that is profitably used in parental conferences. Accepting the points of view of the parent without arguing is a very valuable aspect of the conference. The thrust of the conference is to solve problems and not win an argument.

The teacher must also make sure that the conference is conducted in a professional manner. The conference should stay focused on educational matters, cover important matters, and come quickly to the point. Teachers should not avoid frankness and should state the issues in a direct yet supportive manner. It is important for the teacher to present a possible plan of action for solving the problem but also to be open to modification and suggestions from the parent. Many parents with difficult children feel defeated and are appreciative of solid, workable suggestions for the parent and teacher to work together. The teacher then becomes an ally rather than a threat. However, a parent should never leave the conference with the feeling that the only purpose of the conference was for the teacher to "preach" to them about the behavior of the child and what should be done. Although the conference should be as concise and brief as possible, plenty of time should be set aside for the conference so that it does not appear that the conference is rushed. Parents should not get the impression that the teacher does not have time to listen to their concerns or discuss the progress of their children.

Often parents leave a conference overwhelmed or confused about the purpose of the conference or their responsibilities as parents. In order to avoid this confusion, conclude the conference with a summary of the main points and the agreed-upon plan of action. The parent should then be asked if there is any confusion or misunderstanding about the summary and the plan of action. End the conference on a hopeful note with a positive statement about the student and an expectation that the problem will be solved.

Postconference Follow-up

As soon as the conference has concluded, the teacher should write a short and objective summary of the conference. This summary should include any important information that was brought out in the conference, the main points made during the conference, and the plans for action that were established. It must then be dated and placed in the student's file for reference during additional conferences or if other individuals, such as the school administrator or counselor, are consulted at a later date.

The teacher then must follow through and make sure that the actions decided on in the conference are implemented quickly. After an acceptable time interval, the teacher should contact the parent to check on the progress of the plan at home as well as to report progress at school. This is easily done through a brief phone call. This follow-up ensures the parent that the teacher is a serious professional interested in making progress. In addition, if progress has been made, this phone call serves as a reinforcer for the parent and helps develop a positive attitude.

In conclusion, parent conferences can make a valuable contribution to enhancing the image of the school as a place where people care and where assistance is provided. They can help strengthen the contact between home and school that is so essential for quality education. Teachers must learn not to fear conferences but, rather, how to plan for and conduct them in a positive and professional manner.

SOME FINAL THOUGHTS

As we conclude this book, a few final comments seem to be in order. It is likely that an individual preparing to be a teacher will be overwhelmed and discouraged by the number of things that go into making a good teacher. One of those overwhelming areas is classroom management and discipline. There are no easy answers, and teachers need to develop their own personal style and method for dealing with problems. That is what is so exciting and challenging about being a teacher.

Yes, discipline problems can be difficult and can cause sleepless nights. There are times when little progress is evident and teacher efforts seem to be just wasted energy. But, then, that difficult student exercises some self-control and demonstrates progress. Those students who were once hostile now become supporters of the teacher. A student who seemed to be on the path to a life of difficulty now shows the promise of a successful life. In fact, many experienced teachers find that the most difficult students are the ones they remember fondly and are the ones who return to thank them for their efforts. These are the rewards of teaching! I hope that this book has provided you with the foundation for experiencing those rewards.

SUMMARY

Difficult discipline problems are the ones that cause teachers a great deal of concern. Because they are serious, there are no easy answers. Solving these problems requires considerable time and effort. However, teachers should understand that serious and persistent behavior problems are often a student's way of signaling for help. Therefore, when dealing with students who have serious problems, it is not enough to treat the symptoms. The causes also need to be addressed. Unless they are, the problems will only continue to escalate.

Treating serious discipline problems requires teachers who are firm, yet fair; consistent, yet caring; and tough, yet tender. They place highest priority on helping the student and are persistent in their efforts to solve problems. An important ingredient in their efforts is the involvement of parents. Dealing with parents in professional and positive ways is essential in developing a partnership between parents and teacher, who work as allies.

Although the difficult cases are the most troublesome, they also can be the most rewarding. Helping students learn to exercise self-control and to move toward a happy and fulfilled life is the real essence of teaching.

SUGGESTED ACTIVITIES

1. Reflect on the various problems described in this chapter. Which are of most concern to you? Why are they of concern? Identify a plan of action that you could take to obtain the necessary knowledge and skill to become more comfortable with this type of problem.

2. Interview teachers at several different grade levels. Identify which of the serious problems discussed in this chapter are most prevalent in the schools where they teach and how they respond to these problems. Are there any patterns in the types of serious problems that seem to occur at different grade levels?

3. Identify several articles or books that deal with alcohol and drug abuse in the schools. Read the material and develop a list of behavioral characteristics that can be used to identify individuals who are involved in substance abuse. In addition, describe any programs that have been found to be effective in preventing abuse.

4. Using the material in this chapter, as well as other material on parent involvement, develop a checklist that would be helpful for planning and conducting parent conferences. Divide into triads, choose one of the problems discussed in this chapter as a focus, and role-play a parent/teacher conference to discuss the problem. One individual will play the teacher, the second the parent, and the third an observer who will provide feedback to the person playing the teacher. Rotate the role playing so that all individuals have an opportunity to play the teacher.

5. Now that you have completed the book, write out your philosophy and views of classroom management and discipline. Use this as the basis for developing your own personal approach. Include in this approach a range of consequences that you would feel comfortable using when responding to discipline problems.

BIBLIOGRAPHY

CANGELOSI, J. 1988. *Classroom Management Strategies: Gaining and Maintaining Students' Cooperation.* New York: Longman.

CURWIN, R., and A. MENDLER. 1988. *Discipline with Dignity*. Alexandria, Va.: Association for Supervision and Curriculum Development.

DUKE, D., and A. MECKEL. 1984. *Teacher's Guide to Classroom Management*. New York: Random House.

FROYEN, L. 1988. *Classroom Management: Empowering Teacher-Leaders*. Columbus, Ohio: Chas. E. Merrill.

WEST, E. 1984. Are American schools working? Disturbing cost and quality trends. *American Education* (May), 16.

INDEX

A

Academic learning time, 78
Accountability, maintaining, 104
Action zone, 61-62
Active listening, 150
  at parent-teacher conferences, 222-23
  and problem identification, 152
Activity boundaries, identifying, 66
Activity reinforcers, 173
Allocated time, 74-76
Ambiance, classroom, 66-69
  background music, 68-69
  behavioral setting, 67-68
  influence on teacher/student behavior, 66
  softening the environment, 68
Anger, students', 144, 155
Assertive discipline, 135-37
  difficulties with, 136
Assertiveness, teachers, 185-86
Attendance problems, 4, 207-11
  approaches to solving, 210-11
  identifying causes of, 208-10
Attention, gaining students', 102-3
Attention-seeking, 187
  responding to, 190

B

Background music, classroom, 68-69
Behavioral setting, 10, 67-68
Behavior identification, 195-96
Behavior modification, 166, 170, 171-81
  administering punishment, 178-80
  advantages of approach, 180
  disadvantages of approach, 181
  and effectiveness of plan, 176-77
  eliminating inappropriate behavior, 177-80
  qualifiers in use of, 173-75
  reinforcement schedules, 175-76
  reinforcers, 171-73
  specific behavior to be changed, 175
  withholding reinforcement, 178
Boredom, and misbehavior, 40
Burnout, teachers, 3-4

C

Cheating, 211-12
  approaches to solving problem, 211-12
  identifying causes of, 211
Circular seating arrangement, 63
Clarity:
  of directions, 84-85
  of rules, 28
  teachers', 96-97
Class clown, 115, 191
Class period/school day:
  routines for beginning, 79-80
  routines for ending, 82
Classroom activities, 83-84
Classroom ambiance, See Ambiance, classroom
Classroom density, 69-70

Classroom meetings, and persistent misbehavior, 199-201
Classroom routines, *See* Routines
Classroom rules, *See* Rules
Classroom space/school facilities, routines for using, 8
Cluster seating arrangement, 63
Coercive power, 24-25
Competence, and physical environment, 59
Competition:
  and acceptance, 111
  and high-density classrooms, 70
  and motivation, 51
Competitive goal structures, 112
Conflict resolution, 152-53
Connected discourse, 100
Consequences of misbehavior, 156-57
  alternative consequences, 201-4
  invoking reasonable consequences, 197
  student's identification of, 196-97
Consistency, teachers, 30
Cooperation, gaining through communication, 146-53
Cooperative goal structures, 113-14
Cooperative learning, 117-22
  activities, 121-22
  and group dynamics, 117-22
  Jigsaw model, 119-20
  learning together, 120-22
  Student Teams-Achievement Divisions (STAD), 117-18
  Teams-Games-Tournaments (TGT), 118-19
Cost-payoff analysis, 203
Creative repetition, 100
Crowded classrooms, and withdrawal behavior, 69
Curriculum, and discipline problems, 6

D

Dangles, 101-2
Decorations, classroom, 66
Democratic approach, to establishing rules, 26-27
Density, classroom, 69-70
Detention, 202-3
Dimension, of lesson management, 96-102
Dimension, physical environment, 60-70
  classroom ambiance, 66-69
  classroom density, 69-70

spatial dimension, 60-66
Directions, clarity of, 84-85
Direct teacher intervention, 139
Discipline:
  assertive discipline, 135-37
  definition of, 2
  economic losses associated with lack of, 4
  goal of, 7-9
  and motivation, 34-55
  principles of, 128-30
  purpose of, 13, 125-28
  seriousness of problem, 3
  time/effort required for response, 133
Discipline problems, *See* Misbehavior
Discrepant events, capturing attention with, 48
Displays of inadequacy, 188
  responding to, 193
Drug and alcohol abuse, 218-20
  approaches to solving problem, 219-20
  identifying causes of problem, 218-19

E

Educational-diagnostic meetings, 199-200
Emergencies, routines for, 82-83
Enforcement, rules, 30
Engaged time, 77-78
Expert power, 20
External locus of control, 52
Eye contact, with misbehaving students, 158-59

F

Fear of failure, and motivation, 51
Flip-flops, 102
Followers, 115-16
  class clown, 115
  instigators, 115
  scapegoat, 116
Fragmentation, 99

G

Goal structures, 112-14
  competitive goal structures, 112
  cooperative goal structures, 113-14
  individualistic goal structures, 112

Grades, as reinforcers, 173
Group dynamics, 11, 108-23
  and cooperative learning, 117-22
  followers, 115-16
  individual needs and group influence,
    110-14
  leaders, 114
  teacher roles, 116-17
  utilizing through cooperative learning,
    117-22
Group focus, 102-5
  maintaining alertness/accountability, 104
  misbehavior, responding to, 105
  participation/involvement, gaining,
    104-5
  satiation, avoiding, 103
  student attention, gaining, 102-3
  variety, 103

H

Helplessness, students' feelings of, 155
High-density classrooms, privacy and, 70
High-traffic areas, movement in, 65

I

Identification motive, 45, 47-49
I-messages, 150-51
  and problem identification, 152
Individualistic goal structures, 112
Instigators, 115
Intellectual growth/stimulation, and physical
  environment, 59
Internal locus of control, 52
Involvement, gaining, 104-5

J

Jigsaw approach, to cooperative learning,
  119-20
Job satisfaction, teachers, 3

L

Language of acceptance, 149
Leaders, groups, 114
Leadership and authority, 9, 15-33
  leadership styles, 19-25
  teacher values/beliefs, 16-18

Learning environment:
  restructuring, 12, 139, 165-83
  seating arrangement, 167-68
  See also Physical environment
Legitimate power, 23
Lesson management, 11, 92-107
  connected discourse, 100
  creative repetition, 100
  dangles/truncations, 101-2
  dimensions of, 96-102
  flip-flops, 102
  fragmentation, 99
  group focus, 102-5
  and immediacy, 94
  lesson momentum, 99-100
  lesson smoothness, 100-102
  objectives/goals, 95-96
  overdwelling, 99-100
  overlapping, 98-99
  teacher clarity, 96-97
  thrusts, 100-101
  "withitness," 97-98
Lighting, classroom, 68
Listening, See Active listening
Locus of control, and motivation, 52
Logical consequences, 156
Loss of privileges, 202

M

Management and discipline domain, 9-13
Materials, managing, 82
Mazes, and directions, 97
Minor problems, low-profile responses to,
  157-61
Misbehavior:
  accepting no excuses for, 196
  alternative responses to, 137-39
  and attendance, 4
  causes of, 6-7, 129
  consistency and, 129
  and curriculum, 6
  developing plan with student for
    changing,   197
  logical/natural consequences, 156-57
  responding to, 105, 131-35
  restructuring the learning environment,
    139, 165-83
  students' value judgment about, 196
  supporting self-control, 138-39, 142-64
  teacher motives when responding to,
    144-46

Misbehavior (con't)
See also Persistent misbehavior; Serious
misbehavior
Mistaken goals:
attention-seeking, 187
displays of inadequacy, 188
identifying, 186-94
power-seeking, 187
responding to students seeking, 189-94
revenge, 187-88
Models/charts/displays, of directions, 89
Momentum, of lessons, 99-100
Monitoring:
rules, 30
student work, 86-89
providing assistance, 88-89
teacher movement, 87-88
Motivation, 10, 34-55
and competition, 51
and discipline, 34-55
and fear of failure, 51
learner needs/interest, 37-48
and locus of control, 52
motivation factors, 37-38
and need for achievement, 51
and need fulfillment, 39
perceptions of effort, 49-50
and probability of success, 50-53
Music, in classroom, 68-69

N

Natural consequences, 156-57
Need for achievement, and motivation, 51
Need fulfillment, and motivation, 39
Needs/interests of learners, 37-48
accommodating, 45-48
identifying, 37-39
physiological needs, 39-40
psychological needs, 41-44
social needs, 44-45
Negative reinforcers, 171-72
No-lose conflict resolution, 152-53
Nonverbal signals, 158-59

O

Open-ended meetings, 200
Opportunity cost, 37
Overdwelling, 99-100
Overlapping, 98-99

P

Pacing decisions, 83-84
Parents:
notification of, 198-99
support of, 133
Parent-teacher conferences, 220-23
conducting, 223-24
postconference follow-up, 223
preparing for, 221-22
setting stage for, 222
Participation, gaining, 104-5
Perceptions of effort, 49-50
Persistence, of teacher, 197-98
Persistent misbehavior, 12, 185-205
classroom meetings, 199-201
Glasser's approach to discipline, 194-99
mistaken goals, identifying, 186-94
teacher assertiveness, 185-86
See also Misbehavior
Personal identity, and physical environment,
58-59
Physical environment, 10-11, 56-71, 166
design of space, symbolic impact, 57-58
dimensions, 60-70
planning goals, 58-60
softening, 68
See also Learning environment
Physiological needs, 39-40
comfort of learners, 40
need for sensory stimulation, 40
Positive reinforcers, 172-73
Postconference follow-up, 223
Posture, as nonverbal message, 159
Power-seeking, 187
responding to, 191
Practice, rules, 28
Privacy needs, and physical environment,
60
Private correction, versus public correction,
128
Probability of success:
increasing, 52-53
and motivation, 50-53
Problem ownership, 149
Proximity control, 62-63, 159
Psychological needs, 41-44
security, 41
self-esteem needs, 42
success experiences, 44
Punishment, administering, 25, 178-80
Puzzling situations, capturing attention
with, 48

R

Reality therapy, 194-99
  implementation, 195-99
Referent power, 21
Reinforcers, 171-73
  and elimination of inappropriate
    behavior, 177-80
  types of, 171
Responsibility sharing, 30-31
Revenge-seeking, 187-88
  responding to, 192-93
Reward power, 23-24
Routines, 79-83
  areas needing, 79-83
  development of, 83
  for emergencies, 82-83
  predictable/recurring events, identifying,
    79
  teaching, 83
Rows, arrangement of, 63
Rules:
  clarification, 28
  establishment of, 25-30
  monitoring, 30
  practice, 28
  specification, 27-28

S

Scapegoat, 116
School administration, support from, 133-35
Seating arrangements:
  modifying, 63-65, 167-68
  students' desks, 63-65
  and student self-control, 65
  teacher's desk, 65-66
  types of, 63
Security:
  and physical environment, 59
  as psychological need, 41
Self-control, 7-9
  assisting students to develop, 9
  definition of, 7
  modeling, 143-46
  promoting through responses to
    misbehavior, 126-27
  responses promoting, 12
  and seating arrangements, 65
  See also Supporting self-control
Self-esteem, 42, 62
Self-monitoring, by students, 161-62

Semicircular seating arrangement, 63
Sensory stimulation, need for, 40, 47
Serious misbehavior, 12-13, 207-26
  attendance problems, 207-11
  cheating, 211-12
  drug and alcohol abuse, 218-20
  stealing, 212-13
  vandalism, 213-14
  violence against students, 214-16
  violence against teachers, 216-18
  working with parents to solve, 220-23
Signal system, 89
Social needs, 44-45
  caring, 44-45
  love/affection, 44, 47
  need to belong, 44
Social power, 19-25
Social-problem-solving meetings, 199
Social reinforcers, 172
Spatial dimension, 60-66
  action zone, 61-62
  activity boundaries, 66
  student desk arrangement, 63-65
  teacher proximity, 62-63
Specification, of rules, 27-28
Stealing, 212-13
  approaches to solving problem, 212-13
  identifying causes of, 212
Stress, teachers, 3-4
Student activity, redirecting, 160-61
Students:
  behavior modification, 171-81
  cultural backgrounds/values, 132
  dignity of, 128
  maturity level, 132
  redirecting activity of, 160-61
  removal from classroom, 168-70
  school history, 132-33
  self-monitoring, 161-62
  withdrawal behavior, 69
Student's name, used in lesson, 159
Student Teams-Achievement Divisions
    (STAD), 117-18
Student work:
  managing, 81-82
  monitoring, 86-89
Supporting self-control, 138-39, 142-64
  gaining cooperation through
    communication, 146-53
  identifying why problems occur, 153-56
  logical/natural consequences, 156-57
  minor problems, responses to, 157-61

Supporting self-control (con't)
  modeling, 143-46
  no-lose conflict resolution, 152-53
  student self-monitoring, 161-62
Symbolic reinforcers, 172-73

T

Tardiness, *See* Attendance problems
Task difficulty, perceptions of, 49-50
Teacher-owned problems, 150
Teachers:
  assertive, 185-86
  beliefs about student abilities, 17
  burnout, 3-4
  clarity of lessons, 96-97
  consistency, 30
  desk placement, 65
  eye contact, 158-59
  intimidation by power of learners, 17
    job satisfaction, 3
  leadership and authority, 9, 15-33
  movement in classroom, 87-88
  posture, 159
  proximity, 62-63, 159
  roles, 116-17
  stress, 3-4
  values/beliefs, 16-18, 131-32
Teaching aide/assistant, 175-76
Teams-Games-Tournaments (TGT), 118-19
Thrusts, 100-101
Time after school, 202-3
Time management, 11, 72-91
  academic learning time, 78
  allocated time, 74-75
  classroom activities, 83-84

classroom routines, 79-83
clear directions, providing, 84-85
student work, monitoring, 86-89
time spent on lesson objectives, 76-78
transitions, 85-86
Time-out areas, 168
Token reinforcers, 173
Token system, monitoring student behavior
  and, 175-76
Transactional Analysis (TA), 146-49
Transitions, 85-86
  minimizing wasted time during, 85
Truncations, 101

V

Values/beliefs, teachers, 16-18, 131-32
Vandalism, 213-14
  approaches to solving problem, 213-14
  cost of, 4
  identifying causes of, 213
Verbal response, clarity/firmness in, 201-2
Violence against students, 214-16
  approaches to solving problem, 216
  identifying causes of, 214-15
Violence against teachers, 216-18
  approaches to solving problem, 217-18
  identifying causes of, 217
Violence in schools, statistics, 4

W

Withdrawal behavior, 69
Withholding reinforcement, 178
"Withitness" concept, 97-98

indiscriminately to punish a student and to get even. For example, a third-grade teacher had after-school as a normal consequence if a student misbehaved more than once a day. One third-grade student had developed a reputation for being "bad." The teacher was watching for the boy to misbehave and he was constantly exceeding the limit and was kept after school. Night after night he sat alone in the classroom. It was obvious that the consequence was not having the desired effect of helping the student learn self-control. Obviously the after-school punishment was doing nothing to solve his problem or to help him learn self-control. Such an insensitive use of punishment will soon create an angry and bitter young boy. Excessive use of after-school or detention time often causes anger and resentment and may result in more serious and anonymous violations such as vandalism.

When using after-school or detention as a consequence, the teacher should make sure that the student understands why he or she is spending the time. It should logically fit the offense, and it should not be excessive. The teacher should take the opportunity to confer with the student and to work out a plan that will help the student avoid the consequences in the future and to move toward self-control.

Cost-Payoff Analysis

Another step that can be taken is to have students who are experiencing behavior problems conduct a "cost-payoff analysis" (Jones and Jones 1986, 328). A cost-payoff analysis is having students identify the short- and long-term pay-offs or benefits of their inappropriate behavior and the short- and long-term costs of their behavior. The purpose of this analysis is to outline systematically the benefits and detriments of a given behavior. It forces students to think more deeply about the consequences and makes it more likely that they can make a more informed value judgment about the behavior. Systematically outlining the costs and the payoffs can then help students make better choices about their behavior and alternatives for fulfilling their needs.

After performing the analysis, the teacher and student can discuss the payoffs and the costs and add those that might have been omitted. Once this is done, the student can then be asked to decide if the payoffs outweigh the costs. A teacher should not force the student to make this decision. It is only when the student honestly decides that the costs are too great that a real commitment to improvement can be obtained. If the student makes this commitment, a plan can be developed to help overcome the problem and help the student obtain the payoffs in a productive and acceptable manner.

Involving Others

A few students seem to be so difficult that nothing seems to work. Teachers who have tried several alternatives and have met with little or no success should not hesitate to involve others. Teachers are not psychologists or psychiatrists and cannot be expected to solve all problems. Some problems are just too serious for the teacher, and seeking outside assistance is not a sign of failure. It is the professional thing to do.

Allowing a student to continue on a path of self-destruction is not professional or compassionate. The student may need help, and need it quickly. Not seeking help under the mistaken notion that it is a personal failure for the teacher can lead to tragedy. The teacher must always consider the welfare of the student over professional ego. When a student is out of control or exhibiting serious problems, the teacher should quickly seek the assistance of school counselors, psychologists, and principals. These individuals can assist the teacher and, if necessary, the parents in understanding the problem and in seeking assistance for solving it.

SUMMARY

Persistent misbehavior causes teachers the most concern. At times, students do not respond to less intrusive measures. When this occurs in the classroom, the teacher must realize that it is permissible to be assertive and to expect that a student will obey. Teachers should not think that they have no rights, nor should misbehaving students interfere with their right to teach and the right of others to learn.

Several steps can be taken in response to these more serious incidents. Dreikurs and associates have provided teachers with helpful ways of identifying the goals that students might be pursuing so that teachers do not inadvertently fall into the trap of continuing to reinforce students' behavior. Once these goals have been identified, teachers can then take some action. Dreikurs suggests that revealing the goal to the student, not responding to the first impulse but doing something unexpected, and implementing logical consequences are productive ways of changing the behavior and the goals that the student is pursuing.

Glasser has made a sound contribution to the work with problem students through reality therapy. He has suggested a specific approach to students that is best done in a private conference. This approach involves identifying what the student was doing, making a value judgment about the behavior, identifying reasonable consequences, making a plan, and implementing reasonable consequences. Teachers need to be warm and supportive individuals who model self-control for the student and who are persistent in their efforts.

An important step for teachers who expect to work toward self-control in the classroom is the development of a hierarchy of consequences. This hierarchy should begin with relatively simple and unobtrusive responses and move progressively to more intrusive and serious ones. The development of this hierarchy can provide teachers with a plan of action and a sense of security when facing serious discipline problems.

SUGGESTED ACTIVITIES

1.   Interview several teachers about assertiveness. Do they agree that teachers generally have not been assertive enough? How can teachers demonstrate assertiveness without alienating students and parents? Do principals support teacher assertiveness?

2. Observe in a classroom and see if you can classify student behavior as attention-getting, power, revenge, or withdrawal.

3. Identify a potential discipline problem that concerns you. Apply Dreikurs' natural and logical consequences and Glasser's steps to the problem. Write out how you would respond and what you would say at each step.

4. Identify situations and develop a plan for conducting each type of classroom meeting.

5. Work with a small group of individuals to prepare a list of alternative consequences that might be used in responding to discipline problems.

BIBLIOGRAPHY

CANTER, L., and M. CANTER. 1976. *Assertive Discipline: A Take Charge Approach for Today's Educator.* Santa Monica, Calif.: Canter and Associates.

CHARLES, C. 1989. *Building Classroom Discipline: From Models to Practice,* 2nd ed. New York: Longman.

DREIKURS, R., B. GRUNWALD, and F. PEPPER. 1982. *Maintaining Sanity in the Classroom: Classroom Management Techniques,* 3rd ed. New York: Harper & Row.

FROYEN, L. 1988. *Classroom Management: Empowering Teacher-Leaders.* Columbus, Ohio: Chas. E. Merrill.

GLASSER, W. 1965. *Reality Therapy: A New Approach to Psychiatry.* New York: Harper & Row.

————. 1969. *Schools Without Failure.* New York: Harper & Row.

JONES, V., and L. JONES. 1986. *Comprehensive Classroom Management: Creating Positive Learning Environments,* 2nd ed. Boston: Allyn & Bacon.

KOUNIN, J. 1977. *Discipline and Group Management in Classrooms.* New York: Holt, Rinehart and Winston.

Chapter 12

DEALING WITH SERIOUS BEHAVIOR PROBLEMS

OBJECTIVES

This chapter provides information to help the reader to

1. Identify causes of attendance problems

2. Describe measures that can help prevent cheating

3. List steps that can be taken to deal with theft

4. State the seriousness of vandalism for schools

5. State measures to be taken when confronting violence between students

6. Identify causes of violence against teachers

7. Identify actions to be taken when confronting drug and alcohol abuse

8. List the steps to be followed in preparing for and conducting a parent conference